Scarborough
in the Great War

Scarborough in the Great War

Your Towns & Cities in the Great War

Stephen Wynn

Pen & Sword
MILITARY

First published in Great Britain in 2018 by
PEN & SWORD MILITARY
An imprint of
Pen & Sword Books Ltd
47 Church Street
Barnsley
South Yorkshire S70 2AS

Copyright © Stephen Wynn, 2018

ISBN 978 1 47382 861 2

The right of Stephen Wynn to be identified as Author of this work has been asserted by him in accordance with the Copyright, Designs and Patents Act 1988.

A CIP catalogue record for this book is available from the British Library.

All rights reserved. No part of this book may be reproduced or transmitted in any form or by any means, electronic or mechanical including photocopying, recording or by any information storage and retrieval system, without permission from the Publisher in writing.

Printed and bound in England
By CPI Group (UK) Ltd, Croydon, CR0 4YY

Typeset in Times NR MT by SRJ Info Jnana System Pvt Ltd.

Pen & Sword Books Limited incorporates the imprints of
Atlas, Archaeology, Aviation, Discovery, Family History, Fiction, History, Maritime, Military, Military Classics, Politics, Select, Transport, True Crime, Air World, Frontline Publishing, Leo Cooper, Remember When, Seaforth Publishing, The Praetorian Press, Wharncliffe Local History, Wharncliffe Transport, Wharncliffe True Crime and White Owl.

For a complete list of Pen & Sword titles please contact
PEN & SWORD BOOKS LIMITED
47 Church Street, Barnsley, South Yorkshire, S70 2AS, England
E-mail: enquiries@pen-and-sword.co.uk
Website: www.pen-and-sword.co.uk

Contents

Sources		*vi*
Acknowledgements		*vii*
About the Author		*viii*
Chapter 1	A Brief History of Scarborough	1
Chapter 2	1914 – Starting Out	4
Chapter 3	1915 – Deepening Conflict	35
Chapter 4	1916 – The Realisation	71
Chapter 5	1917 – Seeing it Through	92
Chapter 6	1918 – The Final Blow	118
Chapter 7	VAD Nurses from Scarborough	136
Chapter 8	Those who Died after the Armistice	173
Chapter 9	Scarborough War Memorial – Oliver's Mount	180
Chapter 10	Aftermath	195
Chapter 11	Some who Returned	202
Index		000

Sources

www.scarboroughsmaritimeheritage.org.uk
www.cwgc.org
Wikipedia
www.ancestry.co.uk
www.britishnewspaperarchive.co.uk
www.wrecksite.eu
www.1914-1918.invisionzone.com
www.winchestercollegeatwar.com

Acknowledgements

My thanks to Roger Hildreth for providing the War Diary entry for the 5th Battalion, Yorkshire Regiment, for 26 April 1915. Very much appreciated.

About the Author

Stephen is a retired police officer having served with Essex Police as a constable for thirty years between 1983 and 2013. He is married to Tanya and has two sons, Luke and Ross, and a daughter, Aimee. His sons served five tours of Afghanistan between 2008 and 2013 and both were injured. This led to the publication of his first book, *Two Sons in a Warzone – Afghanistan: The True Story of a Father's Conflict*, published in October 2010.

Both Stephen's grandfathers served in and survived the First World War, one with the Royal Irish Rifles, the other in the Mercantile Marine, whilst his father was a member of the Royal Army Ordnance Corps during the Second World War.

Stephen collaborated with Ken Porter on a book published in August 2012, *German PoW Camp 266 – Langdon Hills*. It spent six weeks as the number one best-selling book in Waterstones, Basildon in 2013. They have also collaborated on other books in this local history series.

Stephen has also co-written three crime thrillers, published between 2010 and 2012, which centre round a fictional detective named Terry Danvers.

Scarborough in the Great War is one of numerous books which Stephen has written for Pen and Sword on aspects of the Great War, including several in the Towns and Cities of The Great War series which commemorate the sacrifices made by young men up and down the country. He has also written *Against All Odds: Walter Tull, the Black Lieutenant* about a professional football player, who became the first black officer to lead white soldiers into battle in the First World War.

CHAPTER 1

A Brief History of Scarborough

Scarborough today is both a borough and a town within the county of North Yorkshire which covers a large stretch of coastline down the eastern side of Yorkshire, one of its nearest neighbours being the North Sea.

Two of the similarities the town of Scarborough has today with that of a hundred years ago, are its fishing industry and its attraction as one of the major holiday destinations on the Yorkshire coast. Its harbour, home to the town's fishing fleet, is overlooked by the eleventh-century ruins of Scarborough Castle which is also one of its most prominent features.

There is evidence to suggest both Stone and Bronze Age settlements existed in what is now Scarborough, and during the fourth century, it was also the location of a Roman signal station, albeit for a brief period. In the following centuries, Scarborough, which is believed to have been founded around 966 AD, had both Saxon and Viking influences.

King Henry II granted Scarborough its first charter in 1155 which allowed the town to have a market. As can be seen by its early history, the trauma and fighting of the First World War was nothing new for Scarborians.

In 1312 Scarborough Castle was home to Piers Gaveston, the 1st Earl of Cornwall. Although a favourite of both King Edward I and his son, Edward II, his conduct and behaviour were not always appreciated by members of the nobility, which ultimately resulted in his exile on three separate occasions. So bad was the last occasion of his exile that it was decided that should he ever return, he was to be treated as a common outlaw. Despite this threat hanging over his head he returned to Scarborough Castle, which led to its siege in 1312, by the barons Percy, Warenne, Clifford and Pembroke. Gaveston was eventually captured and taken to Warwick Castle where he was executed. He was only 28 years of age. Rumours, although never confirmed, suggested that Gaveston and King Edward II were lovers.

Only six years later in 1318 the town was sacked and burnt to the ground by the marauding Scots under the command of Sir James Douglas, one of Scotland's chief commanders during the First War of Scottish Independence.

During the English Civil War, between 1642 and 1651, Scarborough Castle was the scene of many a battle between Royalists and Parliamentarians; this continuous stream of fighting left much of the town in ruins.

By the 1660s, Scarborough had become popular as a spa location because of the discovery by Elizabeth Farrow in 1626 of a natural spring which she believed to have health-giving properties. This was later written about by a Doctor Wittie and subsequently attracted numerous visitors to the town who were keen to experience at first hand the therapeutic qualities of the town's water. Scarborough became a much sought after holiday destination, especially for wealthier people and city dwellers.

With the arrival of the railway in Scarborough in 1845 there was a massive increase in the number of visitors arriving for leisure and recreation, who were able to stay at such locations as the Crown Hotel, which opened the same year on Tuesday, 10 June and which overlooks the picturesque South Bay. This was Scarborough's first purpose-built hotel, although it would be a staggering twenty-two years before it was actually completed.

The town remained a popular destination, both for the wealthy holidaymaker or the more frugal day tripper, all the way through to the outbreak of the First World War.

Scarborough's Grand Hotel.

CHAPTER 2

1914 – Starting Out

By the end of 1914 the town of Scarborough was well and truly on the map, not only had twenty-two of its young men been killed in the war, but its place in history was guaranteed by the events of Wednesday 16 December of that year, when it was bombarded by two battle cruisers of the Imperial German Navy. It was an event which would be remembered by those who had lived through that day, long after the war was over.

Those young men who died during the first five months of the war were:

Albert Featherstone **Bennett**
Daniel **Bratt**
Absolom **Cave**
Dudley Luis de Tavora **Fernandes**
F. **Hawxwell**
Douglas **Horton**
Percy **Ireland**
Charles John **Jones**
Robert **Jowsey**
James Elijah **Mann**
John **Mansfield**
George James **Medd**
Arthur William **Meller**
Joseph E. **Monkman**
John Richard **Pegg**
T.W. **Reed**
William **Reynolds**

George Henry **Saturley**
W. **Smith**
W. **Thompson**
Harry **Wilson**
John Lionel **Wordsworth**

The first man from the town to die during the war just a matter of weeks old was Second Lieutenant Arthur William **Mellor** of the 1st Battalion, East Yorkshire Regiment. He was 31 years of age when he was killed in action on 20 September 1914, with the war just weeks old. He has no known grave, but his name is commemorated on the impressive Memorial to the Missing, in La Ferté-sous-Jouarre, a small town which is about 40 miles east of Paris, in the Seine-et-Marne region of France.

The Memorial to the Missing commemorates the names of 3,740 British officers and soldiers whose bodies were never found, after they had fallen during the Battles of Mons, Le Cateau, the Marne and the Aisne, between August and October 1914.

The exotically named Second Lieutenant Dudley Luis de Tavora **Fernandes**, of the 2nd Battalion, Bedfordshire Regiment, was killed by a German artillery shell on 22 October 1914. He had joined the Bedfordshire Regiment, which at the time was stationed in Pretoria, South Africa, after having passed out from the Royal Military College at Sandhurst on 13 September 1913. Having returned from South Africa with his battalion, he was sent to France, arriving on 6 October 1914, only to be killed seventeen days later, his young life extinguished at the age of 21. He does not have a grave, but his name is commemorated on the Menin Gate Memorial, in Ypres, Belgium.

The 1901 Census showed him as a 7-year-old boy living with his younger sister, Marjorie and their grandfather, Thomas Fernandes, a retired wine merchant, at 25 Grosvenor Crescent, Scarborough. The National Probate Calendar, Index of Wills and Administrations, which covered the date when Dudley was killed, showed his home address as being 'Coomrith', Bodorgan Road, Bournemouth.

Captain John Lionel **Wordsworth**, who was born on 21 April 1882, in Manningham, Yorkshire, was 32 years of age and serving in the 5th (Royal Irish) Lancers when he was killed in action on 4 November 1914. He was killed by a German shell which exploded close to his position near Ypres. The circumstances of his death dictate that he has no known grave, but his name is commemorated on the Menin Gate Memorial.

The 1911 Census records that John, who was only 18 years of age at the time, was already a lieutenant in the army, having been gazetted as a second lieutenant on 23 May 1906. He was further promoted to the rank of lieutenant two years later on 16 May 1908 and was a boarder at 11 Wenlock Terrace, York.

His brother, Captain W.H. Wordsworth, lived at 'The Glen', Scalby, Scarborough.

Wednesday, 16 December 1914 was a cold, foggy day in Scarborough, as the mist drifted slowly in from the North Sea, not untypical for the time of year. Despite the freshness of the early morning air some people were bathing, some still nice and warm in their beds; others were eating breakfast, or on their way to work, totally oblivious what was about to befall them.

Out at sea, two ships from the Imperial German Navy's battle cruiser squadron, the SMS *Derfflinger* and the SMS *Von der Tann*, were preparing to carry out their audacious attack on the town and its inhabitants. Somehow they had managed to travel undetected across the North Sea and quietly position themselves in preparation to carry out their wanton carnage.

The war was about to become very real as the roar of the battleships' massive guns burst into life as they commenced their surprise and indiscriminate bombardment. By the time it was all over, eighteen of the townspeople were dead, all of them civilians and over half of them women and children, with many more injured. Numerous buildings were either damaged or destroyed, including the Scarborough lighthouse, churches, private houses, shops, hotels, including The Grand, boarding houses, a hospital, public offices and buildings, such as Kingscliffe Camp, one of the locations throughout the town where soldiers were billeted. Scarborough Castle and the Sea Bath Infirmary were also hit.

The Scarborough lighthouse on Vincent's Pier was hit twice during the bombardment; once half way up the main tower and

One of Scarborough's homes damaged by the German bombardment.

Damaged buildings.

once in the harbourmaster's quarters. The overall damage was deemed to have made the structure unsafe and within a matter of days it was pulled down. It was not rebuilt until 1931.

As a prequel to this attack, the German submarine SM *U-17,* under the command of Oberleutnant zur See Johannes Feldkirchner, had been sent to the area of the North Sea immediately off the coastline of Scarborough and Hartlepool to check the state of British coastal defences. Feldkirchner reported back that he had seen little in the way of any defensive batteries, that there had been no mines laid by the British within twelve miles of their coastline, and that a steady stream of merchant shipping was prevalent in the area. Add to these facts that Britain's naval presence in the same area was nowhere near the level that it should have been. Some had been redeployed, others were undergoing urgent repairs, and one, HMS *Audacious*, had been sunk after striking a German mine.

Germany knew full well that her navy was a lot smaller in size and capability than the Royal Navy, especially in the early stages of the war. With this in mind the German authorities wanted to avoid a major sea battle with the British fleet at all costs. Royal Navy vessels were carrying out regular patrols of home waters in an effort to deter, detect and prevent any German shipping from reaching the British mainland. Germany, on the other hand, had a policy of keeping their fleet in the safety of their home ports, only venturing out when they chose to do so.

Scarborough wasn't the first British coastal town to be attacked in this way. Great Yarmouth had been the location of a similar attack on 3 November 1914. One of the reasons Germany carried out these attacks was to try and get Britain to break up her Grand Fleet, thus providing the opportunity to pick off these separated ships and increase the power and strength of her own High Seas Fleet.

As with the attack on Great Yarmouth, the intention was to make good their escape across the North Sea, so having finished with the attack on the North East coast of England, SMS *Kolberg* was engaged in mine laying duties, the hope being that any British ships that gave chase would be damaged or destroyed by the mines.

During the attack on Scarborough and the nearby towns of Hartlepool and Whitby, the German ships fired over 1,000 shells, which damaged over 300 properties and killed a reported 137 people, injuring another 592, most of whom were civilians. Of those killed eighteen of them were from Scarborough, as were 228 of those injured.

Remarkably the British authorities had known of Germany's intention to set sail her battle cruiser squadron from their home bases, because they possessed copies of the code books that Germany used to communicate with her ships. On 14 December German communications were picked up which informed the British that the twenty-seven vessels of the battle cruiser squadron, under the command of Rear Admiral Franz Hipper, were on the move. What they didn't pick up on was the fact that additionally, the entire eighty-five ships of the German High Seas Fleet, under the command of Admiral Friedrich von Ingenohl, were leaving from their base as well. The intention was for Ingenohl to sail the ships under his command to Dogger Bank, a large sandbank in a shallow area of the North Sea, about 100 kilometres off the east coast of England. From their position of safety, they could then assist Hipper's battle cruiser squadron should they come under attack from the Royal Navy.

Once further coded messages had been translated and the full extent of the German plans were understood by the British, the decision was taken to allow the raids on the North East coast of England to go ahead and then attack the German vessels as they tried to escape. That was the plan.

Despite the British subsequently deploying the First Battle Cruiser Squadron, under the command of Vice Admiral David Beatty, the Second Battle Squadron, (Vice Admiral Sir George Warrender), the First Light Cruiser Squadron (William Goodenough), light cruisers and destroyers commanded by Commodore Tyrwhitt at Harwich, submarines and destroyers (Commodore Keys) and the Third Cruiser Squadron out of Rosyth (Rear Admiral William Pakenham), all the German ships made it safely back home to their home ports.

The raid had both negative and positive connotations. The British public was united in disdain at Germany's attack on a civilian population and in their criticism of the British Royal

Remember Scarborough Recruitment Poster.

Scarborough – Men of Britain – Recruitment Poster.

Navy for not preventing it. They did not of course know at the time of the decision by the British authorities to let the raid go ahead, in the hope of sinking the German vessels as they escaped. In turn the British government seized on the incident and used it as part of a propaganda campaign for Army recruitment.

Scarborough's mayor, Mr C.C. Graham, was proud to announce within forty-eight hours of the German bombardment on his town, 'notwithstanding the suddenness and severity of the attack, the inhabitants conducted themselves in a manner wholly to their credit.'

Amazingly, even whilst the attack was taking place, milkmen and postmen calmly carried on making their deliveries. It was business as usual for them, proud men determined not to let the Germans intimidate them. Sadly, it was this old fashioned, stoic attitude that led to the death of postman Albert Beal, killed whilst delivering his bundle of letters. He was just approaching 'Dunollie', a large residence in Filey Street owned by Mr J.H. Turner, when he was struck by one of the shells. A servant who was tidying in the house's library was also killed in the blast of one of the sixteen shells which fell at the front and back of the premises.

Remember Scarborough! *by vintageartprinters*
Zazzle

Mr Fletcher, a local milkman, had an extremely lucky escape whilst undertaking his morning deliveries in the Seamer Road area of the town. One of the German shells exploded close to where he had left his horse and cart, killing the unfortunate animal instantly and damaging his cart. A piece of shrapnel ripped through his mackintosh, luckily leaving him and his milk unscathed.

In St Martin's Church the Archdeacon had already begun his first service of the day, when the sacred building was struck

Dunollie, Filey Road, Scarborough.

by not one, but three of the shells which had rained down on the town. Despite this most unwelcome of interruptions, the Mass continued with the clergyman commenting to his concerned congregation that they were as safe inside God's house as they were anywhere else.

The local hospital was also hit and damaged by one of the shells, but there was no panic, only a calmness, with patients who were waiting to be seen by the medical staff, waiting in line whilst those who been brought to the hospital as victims of the bombardment were seen and treated before them.

The Times newspaper reported:

> *Nothing could be more praiseworthy than the manner in which the town passed through its ordeal and has returned to its normal life. The people of Yorkshire are proverbially hard to impress, and the stranger who came in to Scarborough in ignorance would have nothing but the broken buildings to tell him that this quiet seaside town had been subject to an experience unknown to an English town for more than a hundred years. Even the Admiralty announced that such incidents will not affect the naval*

policy, has evoked practically no criticism. Scarborough accepts its risks.

The events at Scarborough had been felt not just by the town but by an entire nation who were united in their grief and determination to overcome. The town even received a message of support and sympathy from King George V:

The people of Scarborough and Whitby have been much in my thoughts during the past week, and I deeply sympathise with the bereaved families in their distress. Please let me know as to the condition of the wounded. I trust they may have a speedy recovery.

Mr C.C. Graham, the Mayor of Scarborough sent the following response on behalf of the townspeople:

May it please your Majesty;

Sir Hugh Bell, Lord Lieutenant of the North Riding of the County of York, has communicated to me your Majesty's gracious message of sympathy with the bereaved families in Scarborough in their distress consequent upon the recent bombardment of this town by part of the enemy's fleet, and I humbly beg that your Majesty will accept the thanks of the people of Scarborough for such message, which will be greatly appreciated.

The town's lighthouse, which stands on Vincent's Pier having been completed in 1735, was one of the buildings damaged in the German raid. The shell which damaged the tower was a parting shot by one of the two departing German vessels as they left the waters off Scarborough, before moving on to their next target which was nearby Whitby.

The castle which overlooks Scarborough is from a long forgotten era, when it protected the town from a different enemy and threat. By the time of the First World War it was nothing more than a ruin, its only enemy being the hordes of holiday

The Scarborough Lighthouse.

1914 – STARTING OUT 17

The damaged castle.

The Old Barracks at Castle Hill.

makers and day trippers united in their quest to conquer the paths leading up to the castle so as to be able to enjoy its breath-taking views.

The damage to the castle wasn't a fatal blow, only a minor wound, and it managed to stand firm, ensuring that the once proud structure didn't require bulldozing and raised to the ground. This was in part due to the strength and thickness of its 10ft outer walls. The nearby old barracks at Castle Hill did not fare so well, but thankfully it no longer housed any military personnel, being merely a store.

The Grand Hotel on the sea front, commanded views that many of its guests had willingly paid to come and see. During the bombardment it was struck by some thirty artillery shells fired from the attacking German ships and, despite a large amount of damage, nobody at the hotel, staff or guests, was injured.

One of Scarborough's other well-known establishments, the Royal Hotel, which first opened its doors for business in 1830

The Grand Hotel.

The Royal Hotel.

1914 – STARTING OUT 21

6 *Belvoir Terrace.*

and boasted many famous guests including Winston Churchill, was also shelled and badly damaged during the German raid.

Three of the bedrooms at 6 Belvoir Terrace were totally destroyed, causing major damage to the large property. Fortunately, nobody was killed but a woman who had been in one of the bedrooms at the time of the attack was blown into another room, such was the force of the explosion, and very badly hurt.

The residents of both 7 and 8 The Crescent were extremely lucky when both properties were struck by shells. The occupants of number 8, Mr and Mrs Micklethwaite, who had been looking out of their upstairs windows, actually saw the German shells heading their way, which gave them sufficient time to take refuge in the lower part of the house, a decision which quite possibly saved their lives. Next door at number 7, Mrs Leas was also blessed with good fortune, when she got up and moved from the room in which she had been sitting just moments before. As she left a shell entered the room and exploded, wrecking the fittings and furniture. How she survived is a miracle.

The shop and home of Mr G.H. Merryweather, a 'purveyor of reasonably priced food', in Prospect Road, was the scene of a tragedy. Mr Merryweather told his wife, Emily, that the town was being attacked by the Germans. She took it upon herself to round up some of her friends and neighbours so that she could take them to the safety of the cellar under their shop. Having located her neighbours, she returned with them to her home, just as one of the shells hit the front of the property and exploded. The only person who was injured in the blast was Emily Merryweather. As she fell to the floor, she cried out, 'I am wounded.' That nobody else was injured was a miracle due to how close they had all been stood to each other. Emily was placed in a carriage and was on her way to be seen by a doctor, but sadly, she died en route.

A house at 79 Commercial Street, situated about a mile inland, was another of the properties struck by one of the German shells. Although badly damaged, this story has a happy ending, because although one woman was badly injured

Merryweather shop in Prospect Road.

when she was struck in the back by a piece of shrapnel, her 90-year-old mother was uninjured. What makes the story even more amazing was that the two women had been trapped amongst the debris for more than seven hours before they were discovered and rescued by members of the St John's Voluntary Ambulance Brigade. During this time they had neither food or drink and were huddled together amidst the ruins of the damaged property, the younger woman having to deal with the pain of having a piece of shrapnel in her back all that time.

Below is a list of those residents of Scarborough who died as a result of the German bombardment of the town on Wednesday, 16 December 1914.

George James **Barnes**, a 9-year-old schoolboy, lived at Wykeham Street.

Alfred **Beal** lived at 50 Raleigh Street, with his wife Emily. He was 41 years of age and a postman.

Albert Featherstone **Bennett** lived at 2 Wykeham Street in 1914, although at the time of the 1911 Census, he had been

79 Commercial Street.

2 Wykeham Street.

living with his parents, Christopher and Joanna Bennett, and his elder brother, also Christopher, at 30 Norwood Street, Scarborough. He was 22 years of age and a Driver (1290) in the North Riding Battery of the Royal Field Artillery, having enlisted on 7 August 1914 at Scarborough and posted to Hull. His Army Service Record shows that he was killed in action at Scarborough.

Johanna **Bennett** was Albert's mother and also lived at 2 Wykeham Street. She was 58 years of age and a housewife.

The Bennett's story was particularly poignant, because by the end of the war the only member of the family who was still alive was Christopher senior, who was a luggage porter at Scarborough railway station. His other son, also named Christopher, who was wounded in the explosion, was to become a casualty of the war just like his brother and mother. Christopher junior had followed in his brother's footsteps and become a Driver (8280/761361) in the Royal Field Artillery. Aged 37, he died of his wounds on 21 January 1917 and is buried in Puchevillers British Cemetery.

Margaret **Briggs** was born at Brighouse, Yorkshire in 1885, but lived at 31 Filey Road, Scarborough, where she was one of four servants to Mr John Harry Turner, a solicitor. She was 29 years of age.

Ada **Crow** lived at 124 Falsgrave Road, where she was a servant to Mary Beatrice Morehouse. She was 28 years of age.

Edith **Crosby** was 39 years of age and a single woman who lived at 1 Belvedere Road, Scarborough, where she was a domestic servant to octogenarian sisters Satina and Louisa Tindale.

Alice **Duffield** lived at the Esplanade. She was 38 years of age and a housewife.

Leonard **Ellis** was a widower. In 1894 he had married Mary Isabel Kidd in Scarborough, but she had died in 1901 aged 29. He never remarried. The 1901 Census shows them living at 28 St Thomas Path, Scarborough, with their two children, Hilda and Charles. By the time of the 1911 Census he was living at 7 George Street, Scarborough along with his two children, which was the home of his aunt, Mary Haines. By the time of his death on 16 December 1914, he was 47 years of age and living at Londesborough Road, Scarborough, still working as a chemist's porter.

Son Charles, who was born on 30 November 1898, enlisted in the Royal Navy just four months after his father's death, on 26 April 1915, at the tender age of 16. Having joined as a Boy 2nd Class, not only did he survive the war, but he went on to serve in the Navy for twenty-three years, finally retiring as an Able Seaman, a rank he held for twenty years, on 1 October 1938. During those years he had served on more than a dozen different ships. No doubt his parents would have been proud of him and what he had achieved.

Harry **Frith** lived at 1 Bedford Street, Scarborough, with his wife Eliza and their son Ernest Harold Frith. Harry was 45 years of age and worked as a grocer and a delivery driver.

Ernest enlisted in the Army on 25 January 1917, when he was two month's shy of his eighteenth birthday, but he wasn't mobilized until 17 April 1917, when he was posted to the 6th Training Reserve Battalion as Private (60687). On 1 December 1917 he was transferred to the 7th (Reserve) Battalion, Prince of Wales's Own (West Yorkshire) Regiment, which at the time was stationed at Rugeley in Staffordshire. On 5 February 1918 he was transferred to the regiment's 4th Battalion and on 3 April he was once again transferred, this time to the 2nd Battalion, and was sent out to France the following day. Three weeks after arriving there he was reported as missing in action on 24 April.

On 16 September 1918 the War Office, decreed that the early report of Ernest being reported as missing in action, had been accepted as the official date of his death. He has no known grave and his name is commemorated on the Pozières Memorial in the Somme region of France.

By the end of the war Eliza Firth had lost both her husband and her only son.

John **Hall** was 65 years of age and an architect. He lived at 28 Westbourne Park, Scarborough with his wife, Mary and their two daughters, Frances and Gertrude. There were also three other children, who had married and left home – a daughter Maud, and sons Hewitson and John.

Harry **Harland** was a shoemaker. He was on his way home to see his wife and children were safe when he was hit in the back with shrapnel. He died ten days later aged 30.

Bertha **McIntyre** was 42 years of age and lived at 22 Westbourne Park, Scarborough, the home of Ellen Thornton. The 1911 Census shows her as being 37 years of age and a 'lady's helper', and records her surname as being spelt 'McEantyre'.

Emily Lois **Merryweather**, aged 30, lived at Prospect Road, Scarborough.

Mary **Prew**, a 60-year-old widow, lived at 22 Belle Vue Street, Scarborough. Her son Charles, who was a farm labourer, his wife Emma, and their 5-year-old son, also named Charles, all lived with her.

John Shields **Ryalls** who lived at Westbourne Park, was only 14 months old, still a baby.

George Harland **Taylor** lived at North Street and was 15 years of age and a boy scout.

John Christopher H. **Ward** was a 9-year-old schoolboy and lived at Wykeham Street, Scarborough, although the 1911 Census showed him as living at 30 Norwood Street, Scarborough. He lived there with his grandfather, Christopher, and his grandmother Joanna Bennett, who was also killed in the bombardment, along with her son Albert, John's uncle. As already noted in the earlier entry for Joanna, their other son, Christopher, was also killed during the war.

In the aftermath of the German attack, many platitudes were given to the town of Scarborough and its people; one such came from the First Lord of the Admiralty, Winston Churchill. The Mayor of Scarborough replied to his eminent friend, in a letter:

Dear Sir,

On behalf of the inhabitants of Scarborough, I have to thank you for the kind message of sympathy conveyed in your letter to me of the 20th inst., and which will be greatly appreciated.

It is evident that the enemy did not dare to face our Fleet, and so attacked this undefended town.

In this war Scarborough has taken her part in the great struggle that is now proceeding. Whilst we deplore the loss of life and property, and mourn for our dead and sympathise with our wounded, we are nevertheless as fully determined as ever that the war must be fought to a successful finish.

Our surprise at the attack was the greater as we were led to believe from the plucky commander of the Emden *that the German sailors understood something of the glorious old traditions of the sea. It is evident from our experience of Wednesday that this is not so, some newcomers into the honourable profession first learn tricks, and lastly traditions.*

As the commanders get older in the service they will find the Iron Cross pinned on their chest, even by King Herod, will not shield them from the shafts of shame and dishonour.

Yours faithfully

C.C. Graham Mayor.

What the mayor obviously wasn't aware of at the time of writing his letter of response, was the suggestion that the Royal Navy actually knew of the likelihood of such an attack somewhere on the British mainland, so that they could engage and destroy the German vessels as they escaped across the North Sea. Not only did Scarborough lose eighteen men, women and children, but every single one of the German vessels returned home to Germany safely. If the mayor had known this at the time it is doubtful whether he would have responded in the same manner.

The question which comes immediately to mind about the attack on Scarborough and its neighbouring towns in the early hours of 16 December 1914, is why? What was its purpose?

What were the Germans hoping to achieve or gain from such an attack? I believe in part it was an attempt to try and draw out small numbers of vessels of the Royal Navy, engage them with their battle cruisers, and destroy them. But whilst the German battle cruisers *Derfflinger* and *Von Der Tann* were carrying out their bombardment of Scarborough, the light cruiser, *Kolberg* was laying her cargo of mines in the North Sea, about six miles off Scarborough and the North East coast. She managed to do this totally unimpeded by vessels of the Royal Navy. It was this opportunity to lay so many mines in the shipping lanes of the North Sea used by the Royal Navy and Mercantile Marine, as well as Allied shipping, that many historians claim was the real reason behind the attack and bombardment of Scarborough.

Within two days of *Kolberg* having laid her mines, three Allied ships, the **Elterwater**, **Princess Olag**, and the Norwegian vessel, the **Vaaren**, had all struck mines and sunk in the same area where it was known that the *Kolberg* had been mine laying. What wasn't known however was just how big the mined area was and how many mines had been laid.

The Admiralty brought down a group of minesweeping trawlers from Grimsby to undertake the dangerous task of locating and sweeping the mines so that a safe passage could be taken through the mine field. The work began on the morning of 19 December 1914 and quickly produced results with eighteen mines being discovered and destroyed. Over the next two weeks more and more were discovered and destroyed, but at a cost. Two of the mine sweepers that had been sent down from Grimsby to get rid of the mines, also fell foul of their destructive powers. The **Orianda** was the first to be struck by a mine and sunk, but miraculously only one member of her crew was killed, Deck Hand (546DA) James Wilson. Next was the **Passing**, which at the time was one of the newest and biggest fishing vessels in the country. She was under the command of Lieutenant Godfrey Craik Parsons of the Royal Navy. The **Passing**, along with the other vessels of her group, had earlier in the day exploded eight mines and managed to dislodge a further six more from their mooring ropes and raise them to the

HM Trawler Passing.

surface. The ***Passing*** also struck a mine which blew a massive hole in her bow, but because the ship had been built with a series of water-tight compartments, she stayed afloat and made her way to Scarborough where she was repaired.

There then followed a spate of sinkings as the number of vessels striking mines, which had been laid by the *Kolberg*, increased in the waters of the North Sea off the coast of Scarborough.

HM Trawler ***Garmo*** struck a mine on 20 December 1914 which resulted in the deaths of six of its crew, with a further nine being injured. The Skipper (38146), Thaddeus Gilbert, who was 61 years of age and a member of the Royal Naval Reserve, was the only one whose body was recovered and he was buried at the Manor Road Cemetery in Scarborough. The five other crew members who perished were, Second Hand (578SA) James William Thornton. Trimmer Cook (146TC) John Hare, Deck Hand (1999DA) Walter Robert Sparrow, Able Seaman

(SS/2084) Thomas William Berry and Able Seaman Thomas George (SS/2550). None of their bodies were recovered and their names are commemorated on the Chatham Naval Memorial.

HM Trawler *Boston*, struck a mine and was crippled, eventually sinking at Filey Brigg. Although every attempt was made to locate and destroy the German mines, more ships were being sunk. On Christmas Day 1914 a further four ships were sunk. These were: the *Gem, Therese-Heyman, Eli* and *Night Hawk*.

The *Gem* was torn apart by the force of the explosion and ten of her crew were killed. The *Therese-Heyman* was lost with her entire crew. The *Night Hawk* lost six of her crew, and although sunk, the *Eli* did not sustain any fatalities.

Boxing Day saw the loss of two more vessels. The *Linara* and the Dutch steamer, the *Leersum*. New Year's Eve saw the loss of the Danish vessel, the *M C Holt*. Another of the trawlers sent down from Grimsby to clear the mines, HM Trawler *The Banyers* struck a mine on New Year's Eve and sank, losing six of her crew in the process.

According to the website www.wrecksite.eu, the carnage didn't stop there. What had been aptly named the Scarborough Minefield, carried on wreaking havoc amongst the unsuspecting vessels that passed the Scarborough coastline as they made their way through the North Sea. These vessels, some of which weren't identified as victims of the minefield until years later, are as follows:

26/12/1914. *Glenmorven*. Cargo Vessel. All hands lost.
07/01/1914. *Elfrida*. Collier.
15/02/1915. *Membland*. All hands lost.
24/02/1915. *Deptford*. Collier.
01/03/1915. *Sapphire*. Hull Tawler. One crew member lost.
15/03/1915. *Hanna*. A Swedish steamer.
26/05/1915. The *Condor* was a Scarborough based trawler. All nine members of her crew were lost when she hit a mine and sank in the North Sea. The body of the skipper, Robert Heritage, was recovered and he is buried at the Dean Road Cemetery in Scarborough. The rest of the crew were all lost

at sea and their names are commemorated on the Tower Hill Memorial for Merchant Seamen. They are:

Chief Engineer, Frederick Nathan **Mills**
Second Engineer, James Robert **Hunter**
Cook, Robert James **Appleby**
Second Hand, John Chamberlain **Barker**
Third Hand, Arthur Houghton **Wright**
Deck Hand, Robert Duncanson **Cammish**. There were five men with the name Robert Cammish living in either Filey or Scarborough in the 1911 Census who were all fisherman.
Deck Hand, John Thomas **Carsey**
Trimmer, Thomas **Donkin**

As can be seen by the list of ships and the men who died whilst serving on board them, the bombardment of Scarborough on 16 December 1914 continued to claim the lives of many more men who were simply doing their jobs and serving their country.

CHAPTER 3

1915 – Deepening Conflict

The year really couldn't have started worse, when about 0220 hours on 1 January 1915, HMS *Formidable* was sunk after being struck by two torpedoes fired by the German submarine, *U-24*, under the command of Kapitänleutnant Rudolf Schneider. Out of a complement of 780, the *Formidable* lost thirty-five officers, including the ship's captain Noel Loxley and 512 of its men.

The Battle of Neuve Chapelle, a British offensive in the Artois region of France, took place between 10 and 13 March 1915. Once again the British forces were ably supported in their endeavours by their Indian counterparts and, although it was recorded as an Allied victory, casualties were estimated at 11,200, whilst German casualties were in the region of 10,000.

The Second Battle of Ypres, which in essence comprised four smaller battles, commenced on 22 April. It is a battle that saw the first use of poisonous gas on the Western Front by the Germans. The battle finally ended on 25 May 1915.

German submarines began their blockade of Great Britain in an effort to prevent much needed supplies of food and equipment from reaching their intended destination.

The Gallipoli campaign began on 25 April 1915 and continued for more than eight months, finally coming to an end on 9 January 1916. By the time it was over, British Empire forces had incurred 160,000 battle casualties. Another 3,778 died of disease and some 90,000 men had to be evacuated from the peninsula due to sickness.

RMS Lusitania *published as a postcard in Europe (Wikipedia).*

In May the Germans, having only weeks before shocked the world with their use of poisonous gas, took matters one stage even further. On Friday 7 May the German submarine, *U-20* sank the British ocean going liner, RMS *Lusitania*, by torpedoing her which caused an internal explosion on board the ship. She went to the sea bed approximately eleven miles off the south coast of Ireland. A total of 1,198 passengers and crew lost their lives, including 128 American citizens. Two years later the Americans entered the war on the side of Britain and her Allies. The shift in public opinion about the war in America can be traced back to the loss of US citizens with the sinking of the *Lusitania*.

The first German Zeppelin airship to carry out a raid on London and the surrounding areas did so on the night of 31 May.

The Battle of Loos, which is as synonymous with 1915 as the Battle of the Somme is with 1916, took place between 25 September and 13 October 1915. It saw six divisions of British and Indian troops up against three German divisions. Despite being at a two to one disadvantage in manpower terms, Germany won the day and when the fighting had stopped and the smoke settled, had incurred an estimated 26,000 casualties, whilst the British and Indian forces had suffered more than double that, with 59,000.

British nurse Edith Cavell was shot by the Germans in Brussels on 12 October for helping British and Allied servicemen escape from the country, which at the time was occupied by German forces. Like the sinking of the *Lusitania* there was an international outcry about Cavell's execution, but all to no avail. Britain certainly used her death for propaganda purposes to encourage more of her young men to enlist in the Army.

The dates and incidents mentioned above, are just the tip of the iceberg in relation to the number of battles and political manouverings that continued throughout the course of the year, which resulted in tens of thousands of men being killed and wounded as the war continued.

The Commonwealth War Graves Commission website records the names of 151,803 men and women who died throughout 1915. These figures also include the names of a few civilians who were working alongside their military counterparts at the time of their death. When I entered the name of Scarborough into the 'Additional Information' box of the website, the names of eighty-seven individuals with some kind of connection with the town, came up. The following is a list of them:

John **Monkman** was a 29-year-old man who was born in Scarborough. When the war broke out he was a Trimmer in the Mercantile Marine, and was serving as part of the crew of the steam trawler *Rio* when he died on 26 January 1915. He has no known grave and his name is commemorated on the Tower Hill Memorial in London.

Charles James **Fox**
Bernard David **McLaren**
G. **Garton**
Cecil **Langsford**
Joseph **Young**

Henry Purcell **Jaques**, a Petty Officer (203908) in the Royal Navy, was aged 31 when he died when HMS *Formidable* was sunk on 1 January 1915.

James William **Clarke**
Joseph William **Rowbottom**
John **Tester**
James Jackson **Bayes**

R.R. **Byers**
Frank **Bryce**
Robert **Heritage**
G.E. **Shepherd**
D. **Dawson**
A. **Cosford**
Edward **Found**
Joseph **Young**
E. **Moore**
Charles Frederick **Whitaker**
Charles William **Taylor**
Royal Edmund **Fleming**
William **Trotter**
Thomas **Mills**
William **Bakerv**
George Albert **Laybourne**
Claude Stanley **Dell**
Ernest **Jackson**
George Thomas **Thorpe**
Robert **Smithson**
Robert **Jude**
Robert **Rowe**
Roy Henderson **Robertson**

J. **Owston** was a 21-year-old Able Seaman with the Mercantile Marine when the SS *Shipcote* was presumed sunk and lost with all hands returning from Archangel in Russia on 13 November 1915.

Alfred **Peck**
Robert William **Percy**
John Thomas **Carsey**
Arthur Houghton **Wright**
W. **Nicholson**
Thomas William **Brown**
Thomas **Donkin**
Robert James **Appleby**
Robert James **Smith**
Robert Duncanson **Cammish**

John Chamberlain **Barker**
Walter **Beach**
G.W. **Smith**
George William **Anderson**
William **Hastings**
J. **Kay**
J.W. **Fearn**
Richard **Thompson**
William Harwood **Brown**
John **Megginson**
Hugh Wharton Myddleton **Parr**
Frederick Leo **Hunter**
Laurence **Denison**
William **Hodgson**
Albert Victor **Walters**
Herbert Gladstone **Howlett**
John Francis **Webster**
Ernest Scott **Petch**
Henry Green **Norris**
Ernest William **Hood**
Albert Edward **Bodfield**
H. **Bilham**
Thomas **Bullamore**
James William **Hodgson**
H. **Short**
William Henry **Pennington**
John **Hay**
Charles Sydney **Simpson**
John Robert **Insall**
Percy Barrett **Jones**
Robert **Leppington**
Tom **Harry**
Frederick Nathan **Mills**
Harry **Betts**
John **Leach**
Frank **Woodley**
Charles Mervyn **Payton**

The year began with newspapers across England publishing extracts from a letter purported to have been written by a German sailor who was a crew member of one of the German ships which bombarded Scarborough on 16 December 1914. In the letter the German sailor claims that during the attack, shore batteries at Scarborough returned fire against them. The following report appeared in a German daily newspaper entitled, *Berliner Tageblatt*:

> *The bombardment of Hartlepool and Scarborough signified, indeed, a triumph for the German fleet in more ways than one. Scarborough was the most important harbour on the English coast between the Thames and the Humber, and was protected by strong batteries. It was a busy commercial port in time of peace, and exported a considerable amount of grain. Many such cargoes might perhaps have been sunk during the bombardment.*

The major fault with this claim, which made it easy to debunk, was the fact that there had been no such guns in Scarborough since 1905.

Major A.B. Brockwell of the Royal Artillery had been the Captain Commandant of Scarborough Castle Hill between 1875 and 1885 and retired from the Army in 1890. He confirmed that when he arrived in Scarborough in 1875 the armaments that were in place at Scarborough Castle Hill consisted of a number of 32-pounder smooth-bore guns. They were so old and antiquated that they were insufficient even for practice. The War Office then removed the guns and replaced them with six 64-pounders and two 40-pounders. These guns remained until around 1895 to 1896 when Marine Drive was built. The guns were then removed and taken to Burniston Road Barracks which at the time was the depot for Scarborough's Artillery Militia. In addition to this the battery, which was located on the side of Castle Hill, was also removed. The Burniston Road Barracks then became a Royal Artillery Depot, despite some major opposition from the local community.

Both the Scarborough Artillery Militia and the 1st East Riding Artillery Volunteers were disbanded under the Territorial scheme which had been brought in by Lord Haldane, resulting in Scarborough being totally devoid of any such artillery pieces since 1905.

I can imagine that on 16 December 1914 the majority of the population of Scarborough were wishing that they still had some of the artillery pieces in place to defend themselves against their German invaders.

This raises the question as to what the German sailor and the *Berliner Tageblatt* newspaper were referring to, as they are both quite clearly wrong in their claims. Maybe it was simply because they didn't fully understand the geographical layout of the area and that it wasn't the guns at Scarborough which returned fire, but those from the Heugh Battery in Hartlepool which did fire on the German ships.

Having been on the receiving end of a German bombardment, the residents of Scarborough were understandably concerned for their future wellbeing, having seen how the collective might of the Royal Navy, the Royal Flying Corps and the Royal Naval Air Service, had failed to protect them. But any such worries and concerns that they had were fully addressed at a meeting in Hull on Monday, 25 January 1915. Maybe a military airfield was to be opened in the area to allow aircraft to be scrambled expediently to deal with any impending enemy threat from the sea or the skies. Perhaps vessels from the Royal Navy were to be stationed permanently nearby, allowing constant patrols of the seas off the coast of Scarborough, or maybe artillery and anti-aircraft batteries were to be installed in the town to provide the protection which wasn't in place on 16 December 1914.

Mr Smith, Scarborough Corporation's chief engineer, travelled to Hull on 25 January 1915, to witness tests of steam driven siren whistles that were to be installed at Scarborough and used to warn of any impending German air raids. The whistles in question were not just any old whistles, but brass organ valve whistles, which made a very loud noise. One of these whistles was installed at the town's icehouse. So the only piece of equipment that was going to be deployed in Scarborough – and then only to advise residents of an imminent enemy attack not to actually defend them – was a very loud whistle.

The early hours of Friday, 26 February 1915 saw, what at the time, was described as Scarborough's worst ever fire, when the Remnant Warehouses, situated at the corner of Market Street and Queens Street, were discovered ablaze following an explosion from within the premises. By the time the fire had run its course, the warehouses had been completely destroyed, as was the Wesleyan Chapel. Adjoining buildings and properties in both Market and Queen streets were completely gutted. The sound of the explosion caused confusion and concern to lots of local residents, who were uncertain as to whether the town had once again become the target of a German naval attack or Zeppelin raid. Some people left their properties either to find out what had happened or to find shelter and safety from what they believed was an enemy attack.

Once again the town's sense of togetherness in a time of need came to the fore, with the elderly and infirm assisted from their properties by the younger and more able-bodied members of the community. Thankfully there was little wind which helped to prevent the fire from spreading any further.

The Scarborough Fire Brigade, along with volunteer fire fighters from local businesses, soldiers and members of the public, all fought the fire valiantly but only the walls of the Wesleyan chapel survived, whilst some of the nearby business premises sustained major damage. The overall cost of the damage caused by the fire was estimated to be in the region of £80,000 to £90,000.

First Aiders from the Scarborough branch of the St John Ambulance service, attended to sixteen men who were involved in trying to put out the fire, but thankfully none of them had been seriously injured. The cause of the explosion and the subsequent fire turned out to be as a result of nothing more sinister than a faulty gas appliance.

One sad note in the aftermath of the fire was the arrest of Jonathan Leake, 26 years of age and a private in the Yorkshire

Dragoons. He was charged with stealing a number of gold rings set with pearls, rubies and diamonds, from the premises of clothier, John Jackson of Queen Street. Mr Jackson had to leave his property hurriedly during the fire and on his return later in the day, discovered the theft of the rings. Private Leake, who had been involved in trying to put out the fires, had seized his opportunity, but his treachery was discovered when he tried to sell one of the items at a nearby pawnbrokers. The other stolen items were discovered at his billet after his arrest.

The morning of Wednesday, 17 March 1915 saw a train crash in Scarborough, which resulted in the death of a railway guard and serious injury to another member of staff and two passengers.

A train arrived at the excursion platform at Scarborough station from Whitby at a few minutes past eight o'clock. It appears that the train drew up alongside the platform as usual, after coming through the tunnel, so that the engine could be coupled on to the other end, in order to pull the train into Scarborough station. Then, inexplicably, instead of the engine getting on to another line, it came back along the same line and crashed into the train. The guard, Robert Sample, who was in his usual location in the train's 'van', was killed instantly by the force of the collision. Both Mrs Whitworth and Mr William Steel, who were both in one of the train's last carriages, were battered and bruised and suffering from shock and had to be carried from the train. The train's fireman, Edgar Major, was also badly injured, suffering both head and leg injuries.

Robert Sample, having worked for the railway company for some thirty years, was well known by regular users of the train on the North-Eastern line. On 24 November 1906 he was the guard on a train which crashed at Ulleskelf railway station. An empty coal train en route from York to Gascoigne Wood was stationary at Ulleskelf when the York to Leeds express train crashed into the rear of it. The driver and fireman of the passenger train were both killed in the accident whilst the guard, Robert Sample, and several passengers, were injured. Robert, who was 65 years of age at the time of his death, left a widow Emily and a son Arthur Robert Richard Sample living at 23 Royal Avenue, Scarborough.

The subsequent Board of Trade inquiry into the crash, took place on Thursday, 24 March 1915 and was conducted by Colonel Pelham George von Donop, of whom more later.

The driver of the Whitby train Mr J.W. Smith told the inquiry that his engine was being shifted from one end of the train to the other, but by mistake it was sent back again on the same line and in doing so ran straight in to the back of the standing train in the darkness.

Signalman Bielby said that he was attending to a mineral engine and told his signal lad to attend to the points so that the engine of the Whitby train could be moved from one end to the other. Bielby admitted that he had no authority to allow the lad to pull the levers, but that it was not infrequently done. After he heard the noise of the crash he noticed that the lad had inadvertently moved the wrong lever. Bielby confirmed that a normal night shift was eight hours in duration, but that since the outbreak of the war, this has been increased to eleven hours. Mr J.B. Harper, the Assistant General Superintendent for the railway, informed the inquiry that lines were being kept open twenty-four hours a day to try and assist with the war effort on the home front which also put extra pressure on the company's staff.

Back to Colonel von Donop. He was quite a character by all accounts, having been commissioned as a lieutenant in the Royal Engineers on 15 December 1871. He was also an extremely proficient sportsman representing the Royal Engineers in two FA Cup finals in 1874 and 1875. He was a good enough tennis played to have taken part at Wimbledon in 1882 and at cricket he played against the MCC at Lord's in 1870.

Arthur Sample, aged 24, attested in the Army on 30 November 1915, eight months after his father's death and became Gunner (143166) in the Royal Garrison Artillery, but he wasn't mobilized until 6 March 1917, when he was posted to the No.4 Depot. On 17 April he was posted to the 407th Siege Battery and on 23 April he was promoted to the rank of acting bombardier. He also went on to serve with the 514th and 166th Siege Batteries before he was demobbed on 28 September 1919 at Ripon, North Yorkshire, having reached the rank of corporal. By the time the war was over, Arthur, was a married man living at 16 Esplanade Gardens, Scarborough, with his wife Elsie (Maltby), whom he had married at Scarborough in August 1917.

On Thursday, 25 March 1915, a case was heard in the divorce court in Scarborough, concerning Mr H. Lee Morgan, a relatively well-known actor of the day, and his estranged wife, Annie Maria Morgan. The petitioner in the case, Mr Morgan, alleged that his wife had committed adultery with Mr Benjamin Pearce in Bristol. The case was undefended.

Mr Morgan informed the court that he and the respondent had married at Birkenhead in 1881, where they continued to live for some years. Being a travelling actor, Mr Morgan's work took him all over the country, meaning that he and his wife were apart from each other for long periods of time. Eventually, she moved and went to live in Bristol and the couple simply drifted apart. Mr Morgan next saw his wife again on 30 May 1913, by which time neither of them had seen each other for almost fifteen years, and the respondent said to him that she thought he was dead.

Mr Morgan produced a witness who gave evidence to the court that the respondent and co-respondent had been living openly as a couple at Lower Ashton, Bristol, purporting to be Mr and Mrs Pearce. This was in a time that living with each other, out of wedlock, was not socially acceptable to the majority of society.

Mr Morgan was awarded a divorce on the grounds of his wife's adultery.

Easter in 1915 was over the weekend of Friday 2 to Monday 5 April. Easter Sunday was a relatively busy day for the town as visitors took full advantage of their leisure time. The Yorkshire Dragoons attended a church parade, including their military band, which was stationed in the town. After the church parade they played on St Nicholas Cliff, in front of the Grand Hotel, which drew a good crowd, both young and old alike, which was excellent news for the regiment's recruiting sergeants, who had a captive audience of potential suitable recruits.

In the afternoon the band continued with its musical displays, this time located on the South Foreshaw Road, at the bottom of Blands Cliff, where there were hundreds of spectators. What also helped the occasion was the opening up of the Castle Yard, Alexandra Gardens and St Nicholas Gardens, all of the locations having previously being closed to the public for many months.

The Bank Holiday Monday was particularly good weatherwise with sunshine throughout most of the day, but still this wasn't enough to draw the crowds to Scarborough. Some people visited the town in their motor cars, but the train station was noticeably light when compared with pre-war Easter Bank Holidays.

Although not over crowded with civilians, there was a definite military feel around the town. The Scarborough companies of the North Riding Volunteer Regiment undertook a leisurely eight-mile route march, taking in the nearby villages of Ayton and Seamer. The men were under the Command of Major S. Firth and were accompanied, on foot, by the mayor Mr C.C. Graham. The band of the Scarborough National Reserves headed the procession, whilst members of the St John Ambulance brought up the rear.

Taking full advantage of the good weather, the band of the 3rd Battalion, West Yorkshire Regiment, undertook a parade around the town as part of a recruitment drive.

Tuesday, 6 April 1915 saw an announcement from the Admiralty that there was every likelihood that herring fishing in the area of the North Sea, would not be allowed that season. This related to net fishing and a decision that would greatly affect the fishing communities of Yarmouth, Lowestoft, Scarborough, Grimsby, the entire Yorkshire coast as well as many of the Scottish ports along the east coast. Trade for these fishing communities at that time of the year could be frenetic. Scarborough for example, usually had between two to three hundred herring boats fishing out of its harbour for a period of six to eight weeks at a stretch.

The herring fishing trade was not only worth large sums of money but also provided work for hundreds of people, and not just the fishermen who did the hard graft out at sea in all kinds of weather. Because of the reduction in the number of vessels fishing for herring, it resulted in smaller catches and a rise in the price of the fish, which was good news for the fishermen, if not the consumers who would end up paying more for the fish that they put on their dinner tables.

As the war continued into its second year the British government had already commandeered a large number of herring drifters and although the directive in relation to herring fishing caused suffering to the boat owners and their crews from Scarborough and its neighbouring communities, it had the knock-on effect of placing more vessels at the disposal of the authorities. Although frustrated by the decision, most accepted the position in which they found themselves, understanding the dangers they faced by continuing fishing in either the areas of the North Sea or the English Channel, where the chances of being attacked by German submarines increased on an almost daily basis.

In 1914 it was a very bad year for the herring industry, with only about 1,000 tons of trawled herrings being landed, mainly due to the outbreak of the war. By way of comparison, in 1913 that figure had been more than 10,000 tons.

The Battle of St Julien, which took place between 24 April and 5 May 1915, was one of the four actions which made up the Second Battle of Ypres. It was memorable for many reasons, one of which was the deployment of poison gas by the German forces. Some of the men involved in the fighting at St Julien, were from the 5th Battalion, Yorkshire Regiment, whose main headquarters was in Scarborough. According to the Commonwealth War Graves Commission website, eighty-eight men of the Yorkshire Regiment were killed during the fighting. Of these, thirty of them were from the 5th Battalion.

One of them was 17-year-old Private (1626) George Thomas Thorpe, who was actually too young to be fighting when he first arrived in France on 18 April 1915. Sadly, the brave young man only survived for eight days, before he was killed in action on 26 April 1915, despite recruitment rules stating that to enlist in the Army and fight abroad, recruits had to be 19 years of age or over. It was permitted to enlist at the age of 18, but those doing so then had to remain in the UK until they were 19, before they could serve abroad. Anybody under the age of 18 could not join the Army.

George has no known grave and his name is commemorated on the Ypres (Menin Gate) Memorial.

As was commonplace during the First World War, regimental war diaries almost never included the names of men from the other ranks who were killed in action or who had died from their wounds. They were simply referred to as men from the other ranks or ORs. It was only officers who had their names recorded. A good example of this coincides with the day George was killed in action. Two other men from the 5th Battalion were killed the same day and a further two died of their wounds. Below is the entry in the War Diary of the 5th Battalion, Yorkshire Regiment for 26 April 1915:

> *Same position. (Nr the hamlet of Fortuin on the edge of Fortuin to Wieltje road, just to the NE of Ypres). Reported position again to Brigade. Ordered to remain. 2/Lieut. E Majolier Acting Adjutant. Heavy shelling as with previous day with considerable sniping. Closely adjacent farmhouses destroyed by enemy's incendiary shells. Slight relief in local area when Lahore Division went into action during afternoon on the slopes to west of our position. Trenches further improved. Further casualties. At night advanced and occupied line of trenches in relief of London Regiment in Horseshoe.*

It is sad to think that five young men of the 5th Battalion died on 26 April 1915 and neither the circumstances of their deaths nor their individual names warrant mention in their battalion's war diary. Maybe it was a normal at the time, but looking back at it, it comes across as being terribly disrespectful to their memories.

George Thorpe was born in Hull in 1898 and the 1911 Census, records that he was living with his mother Louisa, a widow, and his younger sister Leneth, at 3 Darling Yard, James Yard, Scarborough, although his mother later moved to 4 Sails Yard, Oxford Street, Scarborough. His father Arthur Henry Thorpe, who had worked as a mason, died in 1898 aged 40, only a matter of weeks after Arthur was born.

It must have been blatantly clear in some of these cases that the youngsters trying to enlist were not 18 years of age, but some recruiting sergeants were of the opinion that if a young man wanted to enlist and go do his bit for King and Country, and was physically fit to do so, why stop him. The minimum height requirement was 5ft 3ins, with a minimum chest size of 34ins.

What compounded the issue of underage boys slipping through the recruitment net, was the fact that recruitment officers were paid two shillings and six pence, around £6 in today's money, for every recruit they signed up. It is easy to imagine how much money these recruitment officers stood to make by turning a blind eye. It is estimated that 250,000 boys and young men who were under the age of 19 enlisted in the British Army during the course of the First World War. By May 1916 rewards were only paid if a man enlisted voluntarily in advance of his call-up.

Lance Corporal (632) Claude Stanley Dell was another from the 5th Battalion who was killed during the Battle of St Julien on 25 April 1915. His parents Frederick and Emma Dell lived at 147 Falsgrave Road, Scarborough. His name is also commemorated on the Ypres (Menin Gate) Memorial.

Private (2034) Frederick Leo Hunter was just 19 years of age when he died of his wounds at No.3 Casualty Clearing Station on 26 April 1915. He is buried at the Old Military Cemetery in the town of Poperinghe, near Ypres. Like George Thorpe, he had only arrived in France on 18 April 1915 and was dead eight days later.

His parents, Frederick and Ellen Hunter, lived at 'Ivydene', 109 Victoria Road, Scarborough, and prior to that at 81 Eastborough, Scarborough. Frederick was the eldest of three children. He had a brother Cuthbert and a sister Winifred. Frederick's father had his own bakery and confectionary business, where he and his mother also worked. It did sufficiently well enough for the family to be able to employ a servant who also worked as an assistant in the shop.

Cuthbert's story is interesting. Born on 27 December 1897 in Norwood, London, he enlisted in the Royal Navy on 19 December 1916, when he was 19 years of age, as a Cook's Mate (M/24637), and served on board three different vessels, the last of which was HMS *Heela*, a Depot ship. His last date of service according to the Royal Navy Register of Seaman's Services, was 14 February 1919, it would appear due to having been demobbed. Five months later on 26 July, at Whitehall, London and still only 21 years of age, Cuthbert enlisted for twelve years with the 2nd Battalion, Scots Guards, becoming Guardsman 19544. His Attestation papers on joining record that he was demobbed from the Royal Navy on 17 January 1919.

Less than a year in to his army service he had obviously had a change of heart and requested to be discharged from the Army on payment of a £35 warrant under Article 1130 (1), of paragraph 392 (xiv) King's Regulations, his last day being 10 June 1920.

Private (2004) Harry Betts, was 31 years of age and a married man, who immediately before the war had lived with his wife, Gertrude, at 4 Mill Yard, Mill Street, Victoria Road, Scarborough. He was a tailor by occupation and according to the 1911 Census, he and Gertrude were then living at 20 Garibaldi Street, Scarborough, along with their three daughters and a 65-year-old lodger John Cooles. Harry Betts died of his wounds on 1 May 1915 and is buried at the Boulogne Eastern Cemetery in the Pas de Calais.

At least three other Scarborough men of the 5th Battalion, Yorkshire Regiment, are known to have been wounded during the Battle of St Julien. Private (2012) Charles Linn, who was the honorary secretary of Scarborough Football Club, was invalided out of the Army as a result of his wounds. He was awarded a Silver War Badge (13221) which indicated to others that he was a man who had been wounded whilst serving his country but who was no longer physically fit enough for war service.

Private (1847) Benjamin Watson, 19 years of age and the youngest of three brothers, of 42 Hampton Road, and Private (1403) Albert Bruce of 179 Falsgrave Road were all admitted to hospital, but none of their injuries were life threatening. The fact that neither Benjamin or Albert are shown as having been issued with a Silver War Badge indicates that both of them eventually returned to active service.

At the end of April 1915 Lieutenant Frank Tagwell, a member of the North Riding County Council, and a practising architect in Scarborough, was reported as one of those wounded, as were Corporal H. Maliby of 99 Victoria Road, Scarborough; Private J. Lambert of 60 Commercial Street, Scarborough; Private J. Agae of 77 Longwestgate Street, Scarborough and Private C. Tate of 30 Commercial Street, Scarborough.

On the one hand it could be regarded as bad news, receiving confirmation that a loved one has been wounded, because the chances are that the extent of the man's wounds would not have been fully described, just that he had been wounded. But on the other hand, at least it wasn't the delivery of a telegram relaying the sad news that a loved one had been killed in action, had died of their wounds or were missing in action and therefore it was not known whether they were dead or alive.

Monday, 3 May 1915 saw the return to Scarborough of two local men, both of whom were members of the 5th Battalion, Yorkshire Regiment. Second Lieutenants, C.H. Rose and E.G. Stuart Corry, both saw action at the front. With them was Second Lieutenant J.V. Towsend of Filey.

The officers and men of the 5th Battalion had fought with such tenacity and determination that they had been dubbed the Yorkshire Gurkhas. The nickname was also possibly connected to the Yorkshiremen's lack of height amongst their ranks. The battalion had left Newcastle on 17 April 1915, arriving in France later that same evening, and within a week they were in the thick of the fighting, with their position sustaining an almost continuous German artillery bombardment.

Another Scarborough man, Private (15) Ben Watson, of 42 Hampton Road, also of the 5th Battalion, Yorkshire Regiment carried out a heroic deed during the fighting near St Julien. He was injured as a result of his efforts and was invalided back to the UK and sent to hospital in Beckenham. Despite his injuries he found time to write home to his parents to put their minds at rest. Although quite bashful concerning his achievement, the truth finally came to light when the man whose life he had saved, spoke of his heroics to the press, in the hope he could find him and say thank you.

Private S. Randall of the 2nd Battalion, Montreal Canadian Division, explained that it was a young man by the name of Ben Watson of the 5th Battalion, Yorkshire Regiment, who saved his life at St Julien on 25 April 1915, despite being severely wounded himself:

> *I was lying wounded in a farm used as a field hospital near Ypres when the Germans got the range, and shelled the building so suddenly that within a quarter of an hour it was in ruins and on fire. This boy seeing my danger came in and dragged me out under heavy fire. While he was so engaged about thirty lost their lives. When I regained consciousness I was little the worse except for a piece of shrapnel through my chest. He must have a heart like iron. I hope he will soon be better, and once more I thank him from the bottom of my heart.*

Before the war Watson had worked at Nesfield's Brewery and the son of the man who owned the firm, the late Captain G.C. Barber, had coincidently also been his commanding officer. Watson knew that Captain Barber had been killed in the same action where he was wounded.

One of Watson's brothers, James Watson, had also served with him in France as part of the 5th Battalion and had survived the fighting.

Mrs Watson informed the press that she had previously had a son killed during the Boer War. Ben was the youngest of her three sons and described as being as brave as a lion, and she was quite certain that if his injury permitted him to, he would return to his comrades and the fight at hand. Ben never did make it back to his colleagues, his wounds being such that on the 7 January 1916, he was discharged from the Army as no longer physically fit enough for war service.

Friday, 7 May 1915 saw the sinking of one of the world's biggest passenger liners, the Cunard Line's RMS *Lusitania*. It sank approximately eleven miles off the Old Head of Kinsale Lighthouse, off the southern coast of Ireland, when it was struck by a torpedo fired by the German submarine, *U-20*. There was international disbelief and outrage at the sinking of a civilian passenger liner, without any prior warning and without first allowing the ship's passengers to take to the life boats. A total of 1,198 passengers and crew lost their lives, 128 of whom were Americans. The sinking of the *Lusitania* would eventually be one of the reasons why America came in to the war on the side of the Allies. Germany justified the sinking of the *Lusitania* at the time by claiming she was carrying war munitions, which therefore made her a legitimate military target. Not only was this denied at the time but by subsequent British governments down the years.

However, an entry on Wikipedia claims that in 1982 the then head of the North America Department of the British Foreign Office, admitted that a large amount of ammunition was in fact still on board the wreck of the *Lusitania*. It would appear that it was a case of the British authorities finally having to make the admission before salvage teams made the discovery and in doing so were at risk of causing a massive, and quite possibly, fatal explosion.

One can't help but wonder two things about this startling piece of information, firstly, did the American authorities know about the munitions on board the *Lusitania*, as the vessel was en route to the United Kingdom from America? It is a fact that somebody must have known. The second question is, if the American authorities did not know, but found out in the immediate aftermath, would they have subsequently entered the war on the side of the Allies?

The website www.immigrantentrepreneurship.org includes the following:

> *In fact, as late as 1910, about nine percent of the American population had been born in Germany or were of German parentage, the biggest percentage of any ethnic group. Moreover, as most German-Americans lived on the east coast or in the Midwest, there were numerous regions in which they made up as much as 35 percent of the populace.*

It is quite clear to see that it was not a foregone conclusion that America would enter the war on the side of the Allies, and that it is also quite conceivable that they could have quite easily entered the war on the side of the German Empire. If that had taken place, the outcome of the war, more than likely would have turned out quite differently.

One of the stewards on the *Lusitania* was 42-year-old Mr Joseph James Bostock, a married man, who had previously worked as a solicitor's clerk. His wife Harriet and their three children lived in Stoke-on-Trent, Staffordshire. His brother, Mr Leonard Herbert Bostock, lived at 2 Britannia Street, Scarborough, with his wife, Sarah, their two daughters, Irene and Florence, along with their niece, Frances Adams. His sister, Mrs Thomas E. Appleby, lived at Adamson's Cottage, Burr Bank, Scarborough.

On Tuesday, 25 May 1915 Corporal Lewis Atkinson, of the North Riding Battery, 2nd Northumberland Brigade, Royal Field Artillery wrote a letter to his wife. His parents, Mr and Mrs Byron, lived at and ran, the Bell Hotel, Bland's Cliff, Scarborough. The letter read as follows:

> *Yesterday was Whit Monday, one that I shall never forget if I live to 100. We were in action, and we knew it. I never*

had such a time. You mention in your letter about the gasses. Well, I got some. I can feel it yet in my stomach. I am otherwise quite alright, but the gas put me out of action. We have now been in action ten days, and we came out this morning, for how long, I cannot tell you. I may tell you candidly, I am not anxious for any more of just yet awhile.

The letter continued with Corporal Atkinson explaining more about the action in which he suddenly found himself. His sleep was rudely interrupted at about 2.30am, by the commencement of a German artillery bombardment, which found him in a state of undress in his dug out. He managed to put on his trousers and socks, but in the sudden panic of the situation, he was unable to locate his boots. He then made a decision which undoubtedly saved his life. No sooner had he left his dugout, without his boots, than an incoming shell landed on top of where he had been just a matter of seconds before. He made his way to the section billets which were situated about 300 yards away from his dug out, losing one of his socks in the process. But he managed to locate himself a pair of rubber boots, which made his movement slightly more comfortable.

Well, we were in action and our guns were blazing away for all they were worth. I had to keep shouting the orders for one of the officers to the gunners, as he was getting hoarse, and it was difficult to make the men hear with the guns going off. Then I got orders to go and see how the guns were working. They were both going fine, but the gases kept falling on us, and we had not all got respirators. Well, the most awful thing of the morning was as follows. I had only left one gun about a minute earlier, when such a terrible crash came, then another, and one of the gun detachments was wiped clean out. Five of them and such a sight I never wish to see again. Amongst these were Tommy Carr, Algie Robinson, of the Londesborough Vaults, also Joe Rowbottom. Mrs Brammal, at the Ship Inn, will know

> *him as Milky Joe. Poor fellows. They were killed instantly. It knocked all of the stuffing out of me. What with that and the gases, it was awful. I could not get my breath. Well, when they had found the range they knocked the top clean off the buildings we were in, but thankfully nobody was hurt or injured.*
>
> *At night time, I was one of those given the job of helping to bury the dead, as well as making the crosses for their graves, and may they all rest in peace, which I hope, will be in heaven.*
>
> *I guess you will know where this took place. What a day. Phew! I thanked God when it was all over and I was still alive.*

Throughout it all, his only thoughts were with his family and he prayed that he would be spared for their sakes. Luckily for them and him, he was.

The letter writer was Corporal (1037) Tom Adamthwaite Carr, aged 36, who was born in Scarborough on 4 January 1881. He was the only son of Edward and Jane Carr, who lived at 1 Beaconsfield Villa, Scalby, Scarborough. When he enlisted in the North Riding, Royal Field Artillery, a Territorial Army unit, for four years on 6 May 1912 in his home town, Tom, was a local secondary school teacher.

Even though Tom's unit was part of the Territorial Army, which meant that they were intended for home use only he, like many of his colleagues, had agreed to also serve in foreign theatres of war, if required to do so.

Algie Robinson, who is mentioned in his letter, was Gunner (1682) George Robinson. Before enlisting in the Army, Gunner Robinson, was the manager at the Londesborough Theatre Vaults, in Scarborough. Joe Rowbottom was Gunner (1308) Joseph William Rowbottom, aged 27, whose parents, Fred and Maria Rowbottom, lived at 8 Park Road, Scarborough, with their two daughters Doris and Phylis. Before the war Joseph had been a milkman.

All three men were part of the North Riding Battery, 2nd Northumberland Brigade, Royal Field Artillery. Neither Carr nor Robinson have a grave, but their names are commemorated on the Ypres (Menin Gate) Memorial, and Rowbottom was buried at the Ypres Town Cemetery Extension.

On Monday, 31 May 1915 news reached Scarborough of the death of other local men who had been killed or died whilst serving on the Western Front. Gunner (1015) James William Clarke, who was also serving with the 2nd Northumberland Brigade, Royal Field Artillery, was the only son of John and Mary Clarke, of 6 Lower Albion Street, Scarborough and the grandson of Mr J. Clarke, an auctioneer in the town. He was killed in action on 24 May 1915. His body was not recovered and his name is commemorated on the Ypres (Menin Gate) Memorial in Belgium.

Tom Adamthwaite Carr.

Major C.H. Lemmon, who was the commanding officer of the North Riding Battery, Royal Field Artillery, wrote to Mrs Clarke concerning the death of her son:

> *He was one of a gun detachment which about 7am, was engaging German Infantry with rapid fire. A hostile battery opened fire, and the third or fourth shell exploded on the right gun wheel. Clarke was killed instantaneously, and he was buried with his comrades the same night near the spot where he so bravely met a soldier's death.*

Private 2970 Thomas Harry, aged 40, who served with the 5th Battalion, Yorkshire Regiment, was killed in action on 27 May 1915, having enlisted less than five months previously. His widow Ethel lived at 30 'C' Block, Cavalry Depot, Canterbury and his parents at 11 St James Street, Scarborough, their previous home having been at 27 Roscoe Street in the town.

News was also received of the death of Private 1914 John W. Coulson, of the 1st/5th Battalion, Yorkshire Regiment, from Scarborough. He was wounded in action on 29 April but died of his wounds in hospital the next day. He is buried at the Boulogne Eastern Cemetery in the Pas de Calais.

A particularly interesting case came before the magistrates at Scarborough on Wednesday, 2 June 1915. The defendant in the case was Brigadier General Norman Tom Nickalls who had been summonsed for assaulting a clerk, Mr Thompson Horsman, on 25 May at an Army recruiting office at the Scarborough Labour Bureau.

Nickalls admitted the offence but claimed that he was provoked by the man he had struck and therefore felt that he was justified in his actions. The complainant's solicitor Mr C. Royle countered with the statement that nothing justified an assault, unless it was being used to protect oneself whilst being attacked by an assailant, and that at no time was Nickalls either threatened or attacked at the time when he determined to attack the complainant.

Mr Royle described the incident to the court, explaining that on the day in question, Mr Enos Thompson Horsman was with a friend on horseback in Scalby Road. Just after the band had passed, Nickalls, who was also on horseback and in company with a lady, turned to Horsman and said, *'Doesn't that make you think you ought to be in them?'*

In response, Horsman replied that he knew what his duty was, that he was already serving his country as a recruiting officer, and in that capacity he was responsible for having enlisted some 400 men for various types of war work. He added that he had applied for his own release on three occasions, so enabling him to enlist, but it had been refused.

Nickalls did not appear to believe him, suggesting that the role could just as easily be carried out an elderly gentleman or a woman. *'It is a lie; you have never asked,'* he retorted. *'It seems to me that you don't want to go.'*

'In order to prove who is the liar, I will show you these papers,' said Horsman.

He placed his hand in to his pocket with the intention of producing the papers he had been sent by the government in relation to his application to join the Army. But before he could do so, Horsman alleged that Nickalls struck him across the face with his stick, bloodying his nose and cutting his lip.

Nickalls admitting striking Horsman but denied using a stick to do so. Instead he claimed that he used the back of his left hand, catching him in the mouth and on his teeth as he did so, a mark on his knuckles suggested as proof of his actions. Nikalls also admitted, in essence, the content of the words Horsman claimed he had used, but alleged that it was Horsman who had first used the word, 'liar' which was what caused him to lose his temper and strike out. He contended that if a man in his position was called such a name in public, he had no other course of redress, and while he agreed that his response might not be legally correct, he proffered that to be called such a name was sufficient provocation to illicit such a response.

Mr Royle in cross-examination asked Nickalls if he felt calling a man a 'slacker', a word he had used to describe Horsman, might also be sufficient provocation to make a man angry. He agreed that could be the case. Mr Royle closed by pointing out that despite this slur, Horsman had not responded in such a way towards him.

On hearing all the evidence and submissions from both sides, the magistrates then retired for twenty minutes to consider the case. On their return, the Chairman of the Bench, Alderman V. Fowler addressed the court: *'The events which had led up to the assault did not in any way justify the violence, and that they cannot be parties to a mere dispute being dealt with by blows.'*

Nickalls was found guilty as charged for having assaulted Horsman, and was fined two guineas with costs. Both men shook hands with each other as they left the court.

Ironically, soon after the court case, Horsman had in fact been granted his release and had subsequently enlisted in the Army on 26 June 1915 at Buckingham Gate, London, when he became Private (4994) in the 3rd/14th (County of London) Battalion, The London Regiment (London Scottish), before being transferred to the regiment's 1st/14th Battalion on 10 April 1916. On 17 July 1918 he was transferred to the 260 Area and Employment Company, Labour Corps. He survived the war and was demobilized at Ripon on 11 January 1919, although his Army Service Record then states that he was killed in action, which is incorrect.

Horsman lived at The Garlands, Seamer Road, Scarborough with his parents, Enos and Sarah Horsman, and his brother Samuel Beecher Horsman.

Samuel, who had been an assistant teacher before the outbreak of war, also served. He enlisted at Helmsley on 9 November 1915, before rising to the rank of Sergeant (C/12137) in the 21st Battalion, King's Royal Rifle Corps. Samuel was admitted to the Northamptonshire War Hospital, Duston on 3 December 1916 and released ten days later, at which time he was admitted to the VAD Hospital, Kettering, to recover and recuperate from his sickness. He remained there for the next month, finally being discharged 14 January 1916.

On 1 August 1917 at the start of the Third Battle of Ypres (Passchendaele) the 21st Battalion was near the Klein Zillebeke road. The weather conditions were extremely poor which caused movement to be slow due to the heavy conditions of the muddy ground. Throughout the day many casualties were incurred with some still lying in the open in no man's land. During the course of the night of 1 August parties of stretcher bearers worked tirelessly to recover these men so that they could receive the urgent medical treatment that they required. It is more than likely that Samuel was one of these men, because the War Diaries for the 21st Battalion, King's Royal Rifle Corps, show that they did not incur any casualties during this period. The entry in the diary for 7 August 1917, which was the same day that Samuel died of his wounds, reads as follows:

> *The Battalion was re-organised and refitted. Baths were provided at Elzenwalle.*

That was it, plain and simple, exact and to the point, but sadly there was no mention anywhere of Samuel's death.

Nickalls had been educated at Eton and commissioned into the 17th Lancers in November 1886. He served in the Second Boer War during 1901 and 1902. At the outbreak of the First World War, he was put in charge of 63 Infantry Brigade of the 21st Division. Nearly four months after his court appearance, he was killed in action on 26 September 1915 during the Battle of Loos.

A Chinese woman who had travelled to Scarborough from Hull to hawk and sell her wares in the town, found herself appearing in front of the local magistrates on Saturday, 5 June 1915, for failing to register herself with the authorities, as required to do so under local byelaws. The case was adjourned to allow her to return to Hull. The landlady with whom she was staying, was fined five shillings for failing to notify the authorities that she was staying with her. Neither lady was named in subsequent newspaper articles written about the case.

It was reported in local newspapers on Friday, 18 June 1915 that the body of Mr Robert Heritage of 54 Quay Street, Scarborough, the skipper of the Scarborough trawler, the *Condor*, which had been missing for more than two weeks, had been washed up on the shore at nearby Speeton. It was suspected that the *Condor* struck a mine whilst out fishing and sank on 29 May 1915. Eight other members of the crew were also lost when she sank. They were:

    Mr J. Barker – Second Hand.
    Mr A. Wright – Third Hand.
    Mr A. Cammish – Deck Hand.
    Mr J. Casey – Deck Hand.
    Mr Tom Donkin – Trimmer.

Mr Robert Appleby – Cook.
Mr F. Mills – Chief Engineer.
Mr J. Hunter – Second Engineer.

All the men, except Mr Mills who lived in Hull, were from Scarborough. The vessel was owned by the Ramsgate Steam Trawling Company.

Skipper Robert **Heritage** was 70 years of age at the time of his death. He was married to Eliza with whom he had five grown up children. The youngest of his sons, James, was a member of the Royal Naval Reserve between 1908 and 1955. As he was born on 3 November 1880, this would have meant that he was 75 years of age at the time of his last service date. His service number was DA/18576.

Tom **Donkin** was only 18 at the time of his death. He had followed in his father's footsteps by deciding on a life at sea, as his father was a retired sailor, although in what capacity he worked, isn't clear. Tom and his father Charles Donkin lived at 66 Commercial Street, Scarborough with Charles's daughter, Mabel and her husband William Tycho Sheader.

William served during the war as Private (316129) with the 35th Battalion, Northumberland Fusiliers, having enlisted on 5 December 1916. He was subsequently discharged from the Army on 18 February 1918, for no longer being physically fit enough for war service, due to wounds or sickness. He was issued with Silver War Badge No. 508359, but there is a note on the record which records the issue of his award stating, 'Badge and certificate returned undelivered by GPO.' William survived the war and died in September 1948 aged 60.

The 1911 Census shows two men with the name of Robert **Appleby**, who lived in Scarborough and were both fishermen. One of them, aged 61, lived at 4 Coverley Court, Lower Conduit Street, Scarborough and the other man lived at 8 Castle Terrace, Scarborough, and was 54 years of age. Neither man is shown as having died on 29 May 1915.

I found variations and possible matches for the other members of crew, but I could not find anything conclusive about any of them.

In early July 1915 Major Walter George Raleigh Chichester-Constable managed to upset nearly every resident of Scarborough, with comments that he had made at a recruiting meeting held in Hull. His words of wisdom which ignited the touch paper were: 'Scarborough was a blot on the kingdom. Filey was not so bad, but Scarborough was a disgrace.'

The major had previously been in charge of the $2^{nd}/5^{th}$ Battalion, Yorkshire Regiment, and it is believed that he may have felt that men from the town were not coming forward and enlisting as quickly as he felt they should. Maybe his remarks were connected to his time with the Yorkshire Regiment in Scarborough, a position from which he retired some weeks before his unexpected outburst in Hull, which left him with some kind of misplaced grievance against the town.

Understandably his comments did not go down at all well with the town's residents, especially as many believed them to be totally unfair. Many local young men had left the town to go off to war, serving within all branches of the military. The community as a whole saw Major Constable's words and accusations as slanderous to them and their town which had already known the horrors of war at first hand with the bombardments of 16 December 1914.

The major went on to reach the rank of lieutenant colonel. His son, Major (45766) Cyril Hugh Joseph Chichester-Constable MC, who served with A Company, 2nd Battalion, Royal Warwickshire Regiment, during the Second World War, was killed in action on 27 May 1940. He is buried at the Wormhoudt Communal Cemetery in the Nord region of France.

Men from Scarborough had not only rallied to the call to arms and enlisted in one of the numerous British Army regiments, but many had taken to the seas, either as part of the Royal Navy or the Mercantile Marine as part of the fishing fleets or those engaged in mine sweeping operations. Many young men had also left the town to seek work elsewhere, as the only real form of employment in Scarborough was within the fishing industry. These same men had then enlisted in the military, not in Scarborough, but in their adopted towns up and down the country.

A postcard arrived at the offices of the Scarborough Post Office in early July 1915. The content of the card explained one of those coincidences which sometimes occur at the most unexpected of times and in the least expected of places.

Five men from Scarborough were responsible for sending the card which they had felt compelled to write and send after all of them had met up in Gallipoli. When the war broke out all the men who were working as telegraphists in the local Post Office, enlisted in the Army and joined the Royal Engineers, but in different battalions. They undertook their basic training in different parts of the country and then met up unexpectedly when they arrived in the Dardanelles. The postcard read:

> *Kindest thoughts and regards from the Scarborough lads gathered together for an afternoon's convivial – George Wright, W E Garton, A Hardcastle, J H Basil Taylor, S Coultas.*

Their unexpected meeting took place in a dugout at Gallipoli. All of them had been serving in different parts of the peninsula with their individual units, unaware of each other's presence until they met up.

George William Wright was born in Huntingdonshire in 1878 but ended up living in Scarborough. He was a married man and lived his wife Margaret and their three children at 21 Lyell Street, Scarborough. The British Army's Medal Roll index cards show that George was Sergeant (72019) in the Royal Engineers, having first arrived in Egypt on 28 April 1915. On 15 June 1916 he was commissioned as a lieutenant, also with the Royal Engineers. For his war-time service he was awarded the Distinguished Conduct Medal. His war-time campaign medals were applied for on 25 April 1921, at which time his home address was 'Holbrook', Nansen Street, Scarborough.

J.H. Basil Taylor had worked at Scarborough Post Office in August 1908 and by the time he left to enlist in the army, he had worked his way up to being a telegraphist. It was reported that the month after the five men met at the Dardanelles, Corporal Taylor was injured in the arm, resulting in his being hospitalised. His parents lived at 34 Gordon Street, Scarborough.

S. Coultas was Southwell Coultas, born in Scarborough on 16 July 1891. His official job title before he enlisted was a sorting clerk and a telegraphist. He lived at 15 Oak Road, Scarborough with his parents, Robert and Margaret Coultas and his brother, Cecil Trenham Coultas. Southwell survived the war, living to the ripe old age of 85.

I could not find any direct matches for, Hardcastle or Garton, to be able to expand on their personal stories.

An unusual case was heard before the magistrates at Scarborough on Wednesday, 18 August 1915 involving retired soldier and canteen steward, Mr William Barrowcliff of 47 Mayville Avenue, Scarborough. The charge against him was one of using threatening language with intent to put a person in fear. The incident in question took place on Sunday 8 August, when Barrowcliff and a serving soldier went to the home of Mr Pennington, at Beechville Avenue, Scarborough, at one o'clock in the morning. Barrowcliff and the soldier knocked on the front door loudly enough to wake up Mr Pennington and other persons in the house.

Barrowcliff told the court that the reason he had gone to Mr Pennington's property was because he had seen what appeared to be someone using a light to signal to somebody out at sea. He and the soldier searched the premises but found no such equipment that could have been used in such a manner.

Mr Pennington and his wife told the court that Barrowcliff had told them both to stand back or he would blow their brains out, a claim which was strongly denied by Barrowcliff. He denied the claim that he was worst the wear for drink and felt that he had every right to do what he did when he saw what he thought were suspicious lights coming from the Pennington's house. He had been medically discharged from the Army in May 1914.

Despite the information he provided to the court to justify his actions, the bench found his actions wholly unacceptable, stating that he had no right whatsoever, to act in the way in which he did. The court found him guilty as charged.

Barrowcliff was a married man with a wife, Mellicent. At the time of the 1911 Census, they lived at 41 Milton Avenue, Seamer Road, Scarborough, with their six children. His pension record caused some confusion, when compared to his court statement claiming that he had retired from the Army in May 1914 on medical grounds, as it showed that he had not in fact enlisted the army until 26 March 1915 at Scarborough, when he became Private (S/4/072688) in the Army Service Corps, where he was used mainly as a supply clerk. Although he was to be a clerk, he still had to undertake his basic military training and he was sent to Aldershot for this.

Barrowcliff was in fact medically discharged from the Army after having served for a total of thirty-seven days, but in May 1915 and not 1914. Although his pension record shows that he was medically discharged from the army, the reason for his discharge, was that it had been determined by his instructors that he was unlikely to become an efficient soldier as per paragraph 392 (iii) of the King's Regulations.

A young soldier from Scarborough appeared at Newcastle Police Court, on Thursday, 2 September 1915, having been charged with the offence of attempting to obtain by false pretences, the sum of 2s 10d from the Territorial Association. The soldier in question was 18-year-old Leonard Marchant, of 17 Trafalgar Street West, Scarborough, where he lived with his parents Tom and Mary Marchant, sister Dorothy and brother John. Leonard was a initially a gunner, in the Territorial Army (1242), enlisting at 17 years of age, on 27 November 1913 in Scarborough, when he became part of the North Riding Battery, 2nd Northumbrian Brigade of the Royal Field Artillery stationed at Gosforth Park.

Mr T.H. Smirk – a rather unfortunate name for a solicitor– prosecuted the case. He told the court that the matter had come about as a result of the defendant having made a declaration in order to obtain a separation allowance for his mother, Mary Jane Marchant, who had already been prosecuted at Scarborough

Police court where she was found guilty and fined two shillings with costs.

Marchant had stated on the declaration that before he enlisted he was a grocer earning 14s per week, and that his mother was dependent on him to the sum of 13s a week. Unfortunately for young Marchant his word was not taken at face value and when subsequent enquiries were made, he turned out to have been economical with the truth. In fact he only been earning 10s prior to enlisting, although in the last few weeks of civilian life, he had been earning 11s.

It had come to the attention of the War Office that the system of separation allowances was being abused by some and the problem was on the rise. It had become so bad that instructions were given that such matters were to be treated extremely seriously, put before the magistrates, and if found guilty, defendants were to be punished.

Marchant pleaded guilty and told the court that he had only done what he had for his mother's benefit and did not personally gain out of it in any way. When it finally dawned on him that he had done wrong, he wrote to his mother and told her to cancel the allowance.

Two people attended court to provide Marchant with character references. The first was Mr Edward Wallis, a Scarborough grocer, for whom Marchant had previously worked. He told the court that Marchant had been of exemplary character during his time working for him and that when war was declared, despite his tender years, he enlisted straight away. Also in court to support him was a Second Lieutenant Hillier. He expressed the opinion that Marchant had no intention of defrauding the authorities and that further more, he had acted on the advice of others, who were older and a lot wiser than Marchant was, who still saw life through juvenile eyes.

Having listened to both sides of the argument the chairman of the bench said that in ordinary circumstances such an offence would be punishable with a period of incarceration in prison, however, in view of the defendant's previous good character, he would be given the option of paying a fine of 20s or being sent to prison for fourteen days. A relieved Marchant took the option of the fine.

His embodied wartime service began on 5 August 1914, but it was nearly another two years, 3 July 1916, before he found himself in France when he saw service as a gunner (761216) with both the 316th and 317th brigades, Royal Field Artillery. He was wounded on 20 October 1917, when he received a severe injury to his right femur, but he remained in France until 24 May 1918 before returning home to the UK. The outcome of his wounds was a diagnosis that he was suffering with ankylosis which left him with an abnormal adhesion of the right knee, which ultimately left him with limited movement in his right leg.

He was eventually discharged from the Army on 5 November 1918, just six days before the signing of the Armistice, due to being no longer physically fit enough for war service.

An unusual case was brought before the Scarborough Police court on Wednesday, 13 October 1915, when Lieutenant Colonel William Hastings Fowler, of the Scarborough Companies of the North Riding Volunteer Reserve, had to appear and explain why his men were not adhering to laid down procedures in relation to light emitting from buildings during the hours of darkness. His men had permission to assemble at the excursion station, carry out drill and military-related training on designated drill nights.

Chief Constable Windsor told the court that on the evening in question the lights at the excursion station were not only on, but were clearly visible from various nearby locations, which was not in keeping with what Colonel Fowler and his men were permitted to do, especially as the military authorities had declined to provide the required certificate that the continued use of the lights was necessary for military purposes. He added that he knew Colonel Fowler had been involved in discussions with the local railway company and the Army's Northern Command on the subject, and he accepted the colonel's statement that he had continued using the lighting after negotiations had fallen through, because he was under a misapprehension as to the Chief Constable's ultimatum. As the drills at the excursion station had been discontinued pending further negotiations between the Police and the Army's Headquarters Command at York, the Chief Constable requested that he be allowed to withdraw the summons in the case, but after a brief retirement to discuss the request in private, the magistrates adjourned the case for two weeks.

William Hastings Fowler had previously been the Mayor of Scarborough during 1905/1906.

Tuesday, 23 November 1915 saw the announcement of more casualties amongst Scarborough's fighting men.

Private (16432) Walter Borrows, who was 21 years of age, of the 2nd Battalion, Yorkshire Regiment, who lived at 12 Fairfax Street, Scarborough was shot in the head by a sniper on 18 November 1915. Although several men of the Scarborough postal staff had previously been wounded, he was the first one to be killed in the war. He was buried at the Guards Cemetery, Windy Corner, just north-west of the village of Cuinchy in the Pas de Calais.

He was the eldest son and one of six children to John and Ada Borrows. One of Walter's younger brothers, John Edgar Borrows also served in the war. He enlisted on 14 August 1915 at Scarborough, just two months before Walter was killed, becoming Private (23333) in the 13th (Service) Battalion, Yorkshire Regiment. He was nearly 20 years of age and before enlisting had been a qualified gas fitter. On 5 June 1916, having completed his basic training, he was sent out to France as part of the British Expeditionary Force, with the rank of acting sergeant. On 4 March 1917 he sustained a gunshot to the shoulder which was initially treated at No.5 Casualty Clearing Station, before he was then admitted to No.2 General Hospital. After having fully recovered from his wounds, he was given eleven days leave from 7 to 18 August 1917.

He was advised that he was to be awarded the Meritorious Service Medal on 4 June 1918 and on 30 June he was sent back to England to become a member of the regiment's training staff.

Although not entirely clear or legible, it would appear from his Army service record that he left Dundee in Scotland on 15 October 1918 and arrived in Russia on 28 November, presumably as part of the Northern Russia Expedition after the October Revolution 1917.

The 15 October 1918 was also the date of John's promotion to the rank of company sergeant major. He was demobbed on 26 July 1919 and placed on the Army Reserve. Although he had the choice of having his Meritorious Service Medal presented to him in person at an official ceremony, he chose instead to have it sent to him by registered post. He was obviously a man who didn't like a lot of fuss or to draw too much attention to himself. By this time he had moved to live at 77 Murchison Street, Scarborough.

Private 17194 Horace Appleton, also of the 2nd Battalion, Yorkshire Regiment, was killed in France on 26 September 1915, having only arrived there three months earlier. Before the war he had been a member of St Paul's Church, Scarborough. He was the youngest of three children and lived with his parents, Henry and Elizabeth Horsley, his two sisters, Sarah and Ethel. They also had two lodgers, John William Smith, a tailor's apprentice and Thomas Henry Colbert, an elementary school teacher. Henry Horsley ran his own tailoring business, where Horace was a tailor's apprentice before his enlistment.

A check of the Service Medal and Award Rolls for the British Army during the period of the First World War shows a Private (46665) Thomas Henry Colbert, who was a with the 51st (Graduated) Battalion, Durham Light Infantry. There were also at least thirty-five men who served in the First World War with the name John William Smith.

Private (16528) Harold Davies, also with the 2nd Battalion, Yorkshire Regiment, had been shot and wounded whilst serving in France. He lived at 33 Oxford Street, Scarborough and had enlisted in the Army on 19 November 1914, but as a result of his wounds he was discharged on 9 June 1916, as no longer physically fit for war service.

CHAPTER 4

1916 – The Realisation

The third year of the war would see what history would later record as two of the bloodiest and most barbaric battles of the entire conflict. The Battle of Verdun, between France and Germany, lasted for nearly a year, 21 February to 18 December 1916. Once it was over, nearly a million men from both sides had become casualties, the dead being measured in the hundreds of thousands.

Close behind, and more relevant to the people of Great Britain, was the Battle of the Somme, which began on 1 July 1916 and continued for four and a half months until 18 November and consisted of twelve smaller battles. The estimated casualties were in excess of one million but as with all such large-scale actions, getting to the actual truth of the matter wasn't always easy. It is really decided on which set of figures to believe and what methods of calculation had been used to come up with those figures. From a purely British perspective those casualty figures were nearly 420,000, of which nearly 100,000 had been killed. Of these, the Commonwealth War Graves Commission website shows that at least 157 men who had connections with the town of Scarborough, died during the course of 1916, and that 111 of those men, died during the dates of the Battle of the Somme.

One of them was Lieutenant Colonel Charles Cecil Archibald Sillery, he was one of the 21,000 men who were killed on the first day of the Battle of the Somme. He was the Commanding Officer of the 20th (Tyneside Scottish) Battalion, Northumberland Fusiliers.

Commissioned as a lieutenant on 10 March 1883 into the 5th Dragoon Guards, aged 20, it was exactly eleven years to the day that he was promoted to the rank of captain, suggesting that he was, in military terms, far from being a 'flier'. It took him a further seven years before he made it to the rank of major on 10 July 1901, when he became the commandant of the Chindit Hills Battalion, Burma Military School. He retired from the Indian Army on 10 March 1907 after having served for exactly twenty years.

The 1911 Census shows Charles living with his wife Edith, and their two sons, Charles and Anthony, as well as four servants, at 'Eversley', Royal Maze, Penarth, Wales. His occupation is recorded as being retired army officer, employed on the Staff of Territorials.

At the end of 1915 Charles was brought out of retirement by the War Office, and made the commanding officer of the 20th (1st Tyneside Scottish) Battalion, Northumberland Fusiliers, replacing the previous occupant of the role, Lieutenant Colonel C.H. Innes, who had been forced to retire from the Army due to ill health. Having completed their basic training, they left for France on 9 January 1916 and arrived at Le Havre later the same day. For the next five months the men under Charles command saw more than their fair share of action.

At 7.30am on 1 July 1916 the men of the 20th Battalion, Northumberland Fusiliers, leapt from their trenches and became part of one of the bloodiest battles that the British Army had ever been fought. Charles Sillery, despite his lofty rank, was one of those who rose up out of the trenches and made their way across no man's land as the Battle of the Somme began. He was one of the 1,646 men of the Northumberland Fusiliers – and one of the 317 from the 20th Battalion – who would not see the going down of the sun that day. He is buried at the Bapaume Post Military Cemetery about a mile outside of the town of Albert in the Somme region of France.

His brother John Jocelyn Doyne Sillery, who was 48 years of age and a major serving with 11th Battalion, Manchester Regiment, was also killed in action on 7 August 1915 during the Gallipoli campaign. His name is commemorated on the Helles Memorial. The Commonwealth War Graves Commission website shows that his address was The Grange, Scalby, Scarborough. The connection with the town came from Charles's mother's side of the family.

Mrs M.E. Danby, who was 75 years of age, lived at Powys Lodge, Westbourne Grove, an affluent residential area of Scarborough. The house was a spacious property situated near to Ramshill Road. In the early hours of Saturday, 15 January 1916, she died, burned to death in a fire, the origins of which were a tragic accident.

The previous evening had seen Mrs Danby visiting a nearby friend of hers, leaving her two maids, Miss Rosie Coates and Miss Edith Davis, in the house. Both women retired to their room about 10pm and left a lamp burning in the hall so that the house wasn't in total darkness when Mrs Danby returned home. Unheard by her maids who were both fast asleep, it appears that she eventually returned home at around 4am. Mrs Danby would then customarily carry the lamp which her maids had left in the hall, so as to be able to make her way to her own bedroom and read for a while before going to sleep.

Miss Coates and Miss Davis, whose room was situated at the back of the house on the second floor, were awoken by the smell of smoke about 8.30am on the Saturday morning and made their way to Mrs Danby's room. They opened her bathroom door to be immediately confronted with thick smoke and flames. Unable to get any further into her room, the two maids dressed quickly before leaving the house to raise the alarm.

Later the same day the charred remains of a body were recovered from Mrs Danby's room. Local practitioner, Dr Hutton stated that there could be no doubt that they were those of Mrs Danby. She had lived in the town for many years, the widow of a farmer.

An inquest took place on the following Monday, with the jury returning a verdict of 'death by accidental burning'. They, along with the coroner, also expressed their sympathy to Mrs Danby's relatives.

On Monday, 17 January 1916 the First World War gained yet another victim with the death of a soldier. Nothing strange about that, but this young man wasn't killed on the battlefields – he died in the room he was billeted in at the Clarence Gardens Hotel in Scarborough.

Private (3834) Thomas Pollard was 19 years of age and serving in the 5th Battalion, Yorkshire Regiment. He was in a room with several of his colleagues examining his Lee Enfield .303 rifle, with the muzzle pointed in the general direction of his face, when the rifle accidentally went off. The bullet entered his face, almost between his eyes, and exited via the top of his skull. It continued upwards, passing through the ceilings of the two bedrooms above, before it left the building via the roof. Pollard immediately fell to the floor; his colleagues suspecting that he was probably dead from such a horrendous wound, rushed to his assistance. Miraculously, Thomas was still alive and the ambulance, which in those days came under the jurisdiction of the Police, was called to convey Thomas to Scarborough Hospital. He was operated on later the same day but never regained consciousness and was pronounced dead at 8.30pm.

Thomas was well liked by his comrades and friends, who described him as being a cheerful young fellow, somebody without an apparent care in the world, despite the war and certainly not somebody who would take their own life. He had only recently returned to Scarborough after having attended a course of musketry training at Strensall Camp in North Yorkshire.

At an inquest the day after his death, a verdict of Accidental Death was returned. Thomas was buried at the Dean Road Cemetery in Scarborough. His parents, Mr and Mrs Pollard, lived at 88 Lower East Street, Middlesbrough.

Even though there was a war going on the trials and tribulations of everyday life, still continued on the home front in towns and villages across the nation and Scarborough was no different. On Monday, 7 February 1916 a case was heard at the town's Police Court. Before the bench was John Reeves Scott aka William Alexander Welsh.

Strensall Camp 1916.

The prisoner, a clean shaven, smartly dressed man, was 34 years of age, and described in court as a company promoter of 5 Balmoral Grove, Rhyl, he faced two charges. The first was that he had stolen by means of a trick a quantity of bed linen, blankets and serviettes, to the value of £50, the goods of Messrs. W. Rowntree and Sons, between 3 and 17 January 1916. He was further charged that between 13 and 18 January he had obtained by false pretences from John Reginald Cooper of Messrs. J. Tonks and Sons, a quantity of blankets, sheets and table cloths to the value of £27 16s 9d.

It was at this stage that the man admitted that his name was in fact William Alexander Welsh. He had been arrested that morning on a warrant and brought before the court. Mr Whitfield, for the prosecution, informed the court that he would be calling a number of witnesses, some of whom did not live in the Scarborough area, and as such he would be looking for an adjournment of the case and for the defendant Welsh, to be remanded in custody until the following Monday, so as to enable him to contact all of the witnesses.

Mr J.D. Mundy for the defendant advised the court that he had no objections to the adjournment of the case, but challenged the prosecution's request for his client to be remanded in custody.

The Chief Constable of Scarborough Police was asked by the clerk of the court, what his view on the matter was.

'I object to bail, strongly.' The Chief Constable replied. He was asked for the grounds of his objection, to which he replied. *'The man is a deserter from the Army, and if the Magistrates let him go on bail, I would have to hand him over to the military authorities, and he would not be able to answer his bail.'*

Bail was refused and Welsh was remanded in custody until the following Monday. Later the court heard that Welsh, a married man with four children, had been jailed in 1913 for being an absconding bankrupt. After working as a tramcar driver in Newcastle, he joined the army in October 1914, but deserted in 1915 and went to America before returning to Rhyl. He was sentenced to 12 months imprisonment with hard labour.

The Scarborough Sea Scouts School, the first of its kind in the country, which had been established by the local education authority, stepped outside of the usual school curriculum and instead provided boys with relevant instruction to prepare them for a life at sea. The ground-breaking scheme was monitored by both the Board of Education and the local authority to ensure that it was fit for purpose and was working as it should.

The school was visited on Monday, 20 March 1916 by Lieutenant General Sir Robert Baden Powell. The forty boys at the school gave a display to their visitors, who also included Lord Londesborough, General Lord Basing, who was the commanding officer of the troops at Scarborough, the Mayor Mr C.C. Graham and other local dignitaries. Mr Graham spoke about the importance of a practical education which provided young men with relevant work-based skills. General Baden Powell also spoke about the merits and advantages of such an alternative form of education for impressionable young boys.

On Monday, 17 April 1916 two aliens, Dutchman Theodorus H.H. Van Traa, and Alfred Kraunsoe, who was Danish, appeared before Scarborough Police Court, charged with having entered a prohibited area, namely Scarborough, whilst not being in possession of an identity book. Both men denied the allegation and were represented in court by local solicitor, Mr J. Whitfield.

They had arrived in Newcastle from Bergen the previous Friday evening and, after having presented themselves to the Aliens Officer, they stayed in the town overnight. The following day they arrived in Scarborough and went to the Pavilion Hotel where they had their evening meal. On leaving the hotel, they went to Scarborough Police station to register themselves, as they were required to do so under the Aliens Act. This was where their problems began because they had arrived in the town without an identity book nor the permission of the Registration Officer, which meant that by their very presence they had committed an offence as Scarborough was a prohibited town for aliens to be without first having acquired the relevant documentation. They claimed that the Police in Newcastle had told them on their arrival that it was all right for them to come to Scarborough; although highly improbable, it didn't really matter whether they were telling the truth or not, as they had already committed the offence. They were brought before the court to answer the charge against them. It later transpired that they were not strangers to the area and were in fact well known by some well-placed Scarborough residents.

The two men were related, with the Dutch man being the other's son-in-law. The Dane, Alfred Kraunsoe, also made it known that in his home country he was a vice-consul who worked closely with his British counterparts. It was an interesting case in that although the magistrate accepted that they were not acting in an untoward manner, he was extremely conscious of the danger to the nation when people of education and understanding travelled from their own countries to enemy countries, and then on to Britain before returning to their own country via the same route, which potentially allowed them to pass on any suitable information to an enemy power. This was the very reason why the Aliens Act was in place and it did not deal with a man differently because of his social standing in society; it could never work effectively if men were treated differently because of their social position. Having listened to all of the evidence and taken everything into account, the magistrates decided that it was a serious enough case to warrant adjourning it and sending it to the county's next assizes on May 8. There it was accepted that the defendants had acted under a misapprehension and both men were dismissed under the Probation of Offenders Act.

On Wednesday, 10 May 1916 an article appeared in the Press concerning the Dell family who lived at South Villa, Loughborough Road in Scarborough. Mr and Mrs Dell had five sons who had enlisted and gone off to war.

Sydney Dell had been commissioned into the Royal Flying Corps. Another son, who had also been commissioned as an officer, had been wounded in France, whilst a third was in the Officer Training Corps and a fourth, had sadly been killed whilst serving his country.

A search of ancestry.co.uk showed a family by the name of Dell living at a house called 'Coniston' in Avenue Road, Scarborough. The parents were Frederick, a tea dealer, and his wife Emma Dell. They had five sons who all served in the army during the war but none of them had the name Sydney. One, Guy Francis Dell, who had originally enlisted in the Alexandra, Princess of Wales's Own (Yorkshire Regiment), eventually received a commission in the Royal Flying Corps as a lieutenant. He survived the war and lived to be 87 years of age.

Claude Stanley Dell had been a 'grocer's traveller' before the outbreak of hostilities, but quickly enlisted thereafter. He was 26 years of age and a lance corporal in the 5th Battalion, Yorkshire Regiment, when he was killed in action on 25 April 1915. He has no known grave and his name is commemorated on the Ypres (Menin Gate) Memorial.

Charles Henry Dell, who was the middle of the five sons, had been a grocery manager before the war. He enlisted in the 5th Battalion, Yorkshire Regiment and went on to reach the rank of sergeant (940). Charles was one of the lucky ones who survived the war physically unscathed.

Frederick Stephen Dell was a married man, having wed Amy Kate Otridge on 8 August 1903 at St John the Evangelist

Church, in Walworth, London. When the war began, already 34 years of age, he enlisted and served as Private (33280, 2578) in the Yorkshire Regiment, Yorkshire Hussars (Alexandra Princess of Wales's Own) and also in the Royal Air Force, but I am not certain as to whether that was as an aircraft mechanic or on a commission as a lieutenant.

Leighton Sydney Dell began the war Gunner (46737) in the 13th Brigade, Royal Field Artillery, first arriving in France on 14 October 1914, which suggests that he was either already serving in the British Army before the outbreak of the war, that he was on the Army Reserve, or that he was in a Territorial unit. He was certainly in India before the war, as that was where on 29 July 1911, in Madras, he married Kathleen Lucy Harmer. His brother Frederick was his best man. His Medal Rolls index card for the First World War shows that on 19 April 1915 he was commissioned as a lieutenant and transferred to the Royal Flying Corps.

On 27 February 1920, Leighton Dell applied for his wartime medals – the 1914 Star and Bar, British War Medal and the Victory Medal. It would appear that after the war Leighton Dell remained in the military as he was working for the Department of Aircraft Production and Aeronautical Supplies. On 18 February 1921 he appeared before a Field General Court Martial and was 'Dismissed the Service' with the added indignity of having to forfeit all his wartime medals. As case papers for such trials remain closed to the general public for 100 years, it is not possible to discover the circumstances surrounding his court martial. There are papers held at the National Archives on Lieutenant Leighton Sydney Dell that are available for public perusal, but until 2021 that will not include anything to do with his court martial. He died in Leeds in December 1957 aged 72.

Thursday, 8 June 1916 saw the re-opening of the Scarborough Spa. Even though there was no end in sight to the war it was felt that the time was right to re-open the spa. Mr Alick Maclean, who was the conductor of the Queen's Hall Orchestra in London for the winter season, managed to get together a group of twenty-one instrumentalists to uphold the high musical traditions that visitors to the spa had been accustomed to over the years. During the 1915 Scarborough Spa season, there had been a lady harpist as part of the orchestra which was unusual for the time, with most being men. The 1916 version of the orchestra included three female violinists, another example of the changing times for women. Such placements were virtually unheard of before the war.

The orchestra played three times a day each Monday, Tuesday, Wednesday and Saturday, as well as twice on a Sunday. Sometimes the performances were indoors and sometimes they were in the open, weather depending. The Monday, Saturday and Sunday performances also included the Lyric Quartette of male vocalists.

Other attractions at the spa during the summer season included a children's gala, which took place on the evening of Whit Monday, a juvenile fancy-dress ball and the Spa's Grand Hall, a summer costume dance, and vaudeville style entertainment.

Thursday, 13 July 1916 saw another side of war and an unexpected one at that. Two of Scarborough's fishing trawlers were sunk some 10 miles off the coast of Whitby by the German submarine under the command of Werner Fürbringer, but not before their crews were ordered to lower their small boats and then leave their vessels and board the German submarine. Bombs were then placed on board the trawlers by the German sailors and the ships sunk. The crews were ordered into their small boats and made their way safely into Whitby. They were well treated whilst on board the German submarine.

Tuesday, 18 July 1916 was somewhat of a landmark occasion in Scarborough's history, as this was the day that saw the prosecution of the town's first conscientious objector. Sidney Howard Hunt, who was 19 years of age, worked as a gardener and a florist and lived with his parents Tom and Clara Hunt and six of his siblings at 14 Avenue Road, Scarborough.

Sidney was in court for failing to report to the relevant military authorities, when required to do so under the terms of the Military Service Act. He had been conscripted into the

Army and had failed to turn up at the time and place he was instructed to. This was an offence under military law. He was fined 40s and handed over to the military authorities.

I was unable to find out anything further about what happened to Sidney during the war. He died in the Belvedere Nursing Home, Belvedere Road, Scarborough on 21 June 1954. His effects, which totalled just over £2,000, were left to his younger sister Elsie who died at the age of 95 in 1998.

Scarborough councillor Mr F.A. White, who ironically was the chairman of the lighting committee of Scarborough Council, appeared before the Scarborough Police Court on Friday, 28 July 1916, charged with having committed an infringement of the wartime lighting restrictions. As might be expected in the circumstances, Mr White was not happy with being hauled before the court to answer such an allegation. He made a vigorous protest, alleging over zealous special constables had gone out of their way to find trivial cases, such as his, to prosecute and stated that such unnecessary conduct on their part led visitors to leave the town, although he provided no examples of what he alleged. He further stated that Scarborough Corporation was spending tax payers' money in attempting to attract visitors to the town, which in turn greatly benefitted the town's economy and those businesses who relied on the money such visitors brought to the town. It was some of the town's over zealous special constables, who, Mr White claimed, were doing their best to undo the fine work being done by Scarborough Corporation by their interference.

Although the bench accepted Mr White had taken steps to prevent lights from being displayed at his property, the magistrates, perhaps somewhat uncomfortably, still imposed a fine against him of half a crown.

Mr White's outburst seemed not only to try and minimise the potential seriousness of the infringement, but to attempt to direct the blame for the prosecution at the feet of the special constables, who were doing their best to ensure the safety of the local community. Mr White's stance in this matter was somewhat at odds with his position as the chairman of the lighting committee. It is not known whether he remained in this position.

At the beginning of August 1916, an unusual case was heard before the Scarborough Police Court. Claud Lindsay Lister, a local man, was charged with having masqueraded as a captain of the Northumberland Fusiliers. He had taken the liberty of writing down his pre-planned response to the allegation in the form of six pages of foolscap paper. It appeared that he had previously served in the Northumberland Fusiliers, but by 1916, was no longer in the British Army. When questioned by a local Police detective, as to why he was wearing a military uniform that he no longer had the right to wear, his explanation was that he was in the process of having his civilian suit repaired and cleaned and that his only other suitable clothes were his old Army uniform, although he admitted to having worn it previously.

The matter had previously been brought before the Police Court for hearing, but the proceedings had been halted so that jurisdiction could be confirmed as to whether the matter should be heard before a military court or a civilian one. The War Office had determined that the case could be heard in the latter.

Lister claimed that he fought in the Matabele and South African wars, being invalided with fever in Matabele and wounded whilst serving in South Africa. He further informed the court that he had held the rank of lieutenant and was in command of a squadron of mounted infantry and that on the formation of General Baden Powell's South African Constabulary, he became one of the first to be gazetted and was the Assistant Commissioner at Klerksdorp in the Transvaal.

After all the evidence had been presented to the court the magistrates found Lister guilty as charged, but were lenient in their sentencing. The military uniform was ordered to be destroyed by the Police and a fine of £5 was imposed with a month imprisonment if payment could not be made.

Lister was fortunate as the court had given serious consideration to jailing him, but had decided to replace a prison sentence with the fine, in part as he had shown no opposition or argument to the burning of the uniform.

The 1911 Census showed him lodging with Eleanor File and her sister, Mary Ann Frith, at 6 Edridge Road, Croydon, Surrey, with his occupation shown as a retired Army pensioner. The British Army Lists which cover the period 1882 to 1962, record that Lieutenant Claud Lindsay Lister, who was born on 1 December 1870, served with the Kaffrarian Rifles for the years 1912, 1915, 1916, 1917 and 1918, which if correct, and I have nor reason to believe that it is not, would suggest that his possession of the uniform was genuine.

Monday, 7 August 1916 brought the sad news of another wartime death, but this wasn't of a soldier on the battlefield, but of a hard working father of four children, in the supposed safety of his own home. Tom and Mary Marchant had been married for twenty-one years and had four surviving children, daughters Mildred and Dorothy and sons Leonard and John, together they lived at 17 Trafalgar Street West, Scarborough. Tom Marchant worked as a coach trimmer and on the surface all was happy in his life, but sadly something had gone drastically wrong, so much so that he felt that his only option was to take his own life.

At five o'clock in the afternoon on 7 August John Marchant, the 15-year-old son of Tom Marchant, was the first one home, or so he thought. He came in via the front door and there was a note pinned on the kitchen door which said, 'Don't come in alone.' Unfortunately, he chose to ignore the advice and found his father dead lying on the kitchen floor. Tom Marchant was covered by two tablecloths with a gas pipe stretching from the gas cooker to his mouth. He had been last seen in good health and spirits at midday the same day and the reason for his death was left unexplained.

Over the two days, 24 and 25 September 1916, Scarborough once again suffered at the hands of the Germans. This time eleven of its larger fishing trawlers were sunk by a solitary German submarine, *U-57* which was under the command of Kapitänleutnant Carl-Siegfried Ritter von Georg. During that same time frame *U-57* sank ten other Allied vessels. However, although the vessels were sunk, none of the 126 men on board them were killed, as Ritter von Georg, allowed each of the crews to remove themselves from their vessels before they were sunk. The eleven vessels all met their watery graves an estimated 20 miles north-east of Scarborough. They were the *Tarantula, Marguerite, Fisher Prince, Seal, Otter, Harrier, Gamecock, Sunshine, Nil Desperandum, Otter Hound* and *Quebec*.

The knock-on effect for the local fisherman of Scarborough, who sailed the seas to earn their living, was that they could no longer do so. With their ships now on the sea bed, they were no longer able to fish for the foreseeable future as there would be no opportunity to replace any of the boats until the war was over. The only three vessels of the Scarborough fishing fleet to have survived the surprise onslaught, were the *Penguin, Ben Hope* and the *Scorpion*.

The German submarine captains were, by September 1915, under strict orders to ensure the safety of the crews of the vessels which they sank. Germany had already had a big scare when it came to the sinking of Allied shipping, when one of her submarines, *U-20*, under the command of Kapitänleutnant Walther Schwieger, sank the Cunard passenger liner, RMS *Lusitania* on Friday, 7 May 1915. Germany had begun enforcing her policy of unrestricted submarine warfare on 18 February 1915, in the seas around the British Isles, having declared them a war zone.

On 17 September 1916 an unnamed Scarborough man, who was serving his country in the Royal Artillery, wrote the following about some of the fighting he had witnessed during the Battle of the Somme:

> *The first line and support trenches, previous to the bombardment, were of solid construction, riveted with timber, or stakes and brushwood. They varied in depth from seven to twelve feet, and in width from three feet six inches to six feet. The communication trenches were so much damaged by our fire that it was difficult to determine their original appearance. They were apparently ten feet deep and six feet wide.*

The dug outs were generally situated ten to twenty feet below the floor of the trenches, and in some cases thirty feet deep. They were elaborately lined with wood, and were fitted throughout with electric light and bells, and fitted with splendid pieces of furniture.

They varied in size, some being constructed for five or six men, others for more, and although the trenches leading to them were pretty well knocked in, the dug outs for the most part remained undamaged.

In one dug out, evidently one that had been occupied by a German officer, some of our infantry men came across some of his white shirts, with beautifully embroidered fronts, and in the midst of the fearful onslaught coolly took off their own somewhat dirty raiment and bedecked themselves in the shirts which had been left behind by this gentleman of culture in his hurried retreat.

All the time fierce hand to hand fighting was going on in neighbouring dug outs, and after indulging in a glass of wine and handing over a dozen prisoners, which they had pulled out of the petite maison, these two men proceeded to the next dug out, as in a game which seemed to them to excel even the most exciting wild beast hunt in the wilds of Africa.

Such is the spirit of every man in the British Army. Is there, therefore, any wonder that they push back the Prussian Guard, and make the Hun cower before them?

I always find it truly amazing that somebody, who was actually taking part in the fighting, could use such a detailed description, especially one that conjured up death and barbarity, and still managed to make it sound like normality.

Joseph and Annie Merryweather of Prospect Road, Scarborough received a letter from a hospital in France on Sunday, 15 October 1916 which brought with it a mixture of emotions. The letter was from a nurse who was tending to their youngest son, Harold. The good news was that he was alive, the bad news being that because of the severity of his wounds, the doctors had to amputate one of his legs above the knee. The letter read as follows:

> *Your son, Corporal H Merryweather, of the Yorkshire Regiment, expressed a wish for me to write to you re the nature of his wounds. When admitted in to hospital his wounds were of a serious nature, a compound fracture of the thigh, extending to the knee joint, which had to be opened, as it was in a septic condition.*
>
> *The surgeon had great hopes of saving the leg. This Morning (Wednesday) October 11th, it haemorrhaged, so the surgeon had to amputate the leg above the knee. He has just recovered from the anaesthetic, and at once asked me to write to you. At present his condition is very satisfactory, although he is suffering from a certain amount of shock.*
>
> *He has been a most ripping patient, like his name, always bright, cheerful, and smiling. We are all very sorry that he had to part with his leg. He was very brave about it, and thought it would be for the best. As he has suffered a great deal of pain with it, he said that he would not worry.*
>
> *I am sure you must be very proud of him for he has proved himself a hero as well as doing his bit for his country. I hope he will soon be himself again.*

Sadly for Mr and Mrs Merryweather more bad news was very soon to come. Their youngest son Private (372945) William Alfred Merryweather serving in the 8th (City of London) Battalion, Post Office Rifles, who was 27 years of age, had been killed in action on 7 October 1916. His body was not recovered and his name is commemorated on the Thiepval Memorial in the Somme region of France.

It would appear that the Merryweathers had not heard the news of William's death before they had received the news of Harold having been wounded. The boys' father, Joseph

Merryweather, was a grocer and a sub postmaster, who ran his own business.

Harold Merryweather had joined the Army after the outbreak of the war. He had been the organist before the war at St John's Road Primitive Methodist Church in Scarborough and was employed by Messrs. W. Rowntree & Sons, whilst William had been a grocer's assistant in his father's shop.

I have not been able to establish whether the eldest son, George Hardwick Merryweather, also served during the war, but if he did he survived. Like William, he was also a grocer's assistant in the family business. At the time of the 1911 Census, the Merryweather family had been living at 1 to 4, Blenheim Street, Scarborough where they occupied a total of twenty rooms.

On 17 October 1916 a letter was written by Mr W.R. Rea, the MP for Scarborough to Prime Minister Lloyd George. The following letter was received in reply from Mr F.L. Stevens, an under secretary and civil servant. The exchange of letters had come about as a result of the billeting of soldiers in Scarborough.

Dear Sir,

Mr Lloyd George wishes me to inform you that he fully realises the privations which the inhabitants of Scarborough have suffered as a result of the war, but that he knows that you will readily understand that it would not be in the interests of the State to quarter troops in any place except as military considerations dictate.

Mr Lloyd-George wishes me to add, however, that if at any time military exigencies should permit, you may be assured that your representations will be borne in mind.

Yours truly,

Mr F.L. Stevenson.

This was a very nicely worded letter, which in essence actually said, 'Really. The country is at war, and you are moaning and complaining about having to have British soldiers billeted in your town. Please!'

A soldier by the name of Walter Benson appeared before Scarborough Magistrates on Wednesday, 1 November 1916, charged with having stolen items of jewellery to the value of £45, at a lodging house he was staying at owned by Miss Grace Frost at Albemarle Crescent, Scarborough.

The magistrates heard how Benson had taken rooms with Miss Frost for a few days, claiming that his name was William Stanley, and that he was a sergeant major from the School of Musketry at Hythe. On the morning after the day Benson had began lodging with Miss Frost, she went out for the morning, leaving her jewellery in a small box on her dressing table and Benson in her home. By the time she returned home, Benson had gone and so had her jewellery. He was subsequently arrested at York, by which time he had disposed of the items in Bristol, Wolverhampton, Birmingham, Leeds and Manchester.

The Chief Constable told the court that Benson was a very plausible man and he could see how people could be taken in by him. He wasn't a sergeant major and never had been; he was just a private. Other than that, he would give no more information about himself. Despite his best attempts at shrouding his past in a cloak of mystery, it was established that he was a married man with two children, whom he had deserted. He was a wanted man in three different towns and was convicted of committing a similar offence in Newcastle in 1913 under the name of William Patrick Dawson.

Despite wearing three wound stripes on his arm, indicating that he had been wounded in action on three separate occasions, and being in possession of a Distinguished Conduct Medal, he had never served in a foreign theatre of war and was not entitled to wear any of those items.

The Chief Constable added that the man was an accomplished liar and a thief. Benson was found guilty on all charges against him and sentenced to twenty-four weeks in prison with hard labour.

As there were at least fifty-seven men with the name William Benson who served in the British Army during First World

War, I have been unable to find out anything further about this particular man.

The death of Lieutenant and Quartermaster John Bernard McReynolds was sad news for his family who lived at North Marine Road, Scarborough. He was serving with the 11th Battalion, East Yorkshire Regiment, when he was killed in action on 12 November 1916, just six days before the end of the Battle of the Somme. He was buried in the British Cemetery at the village of Couin in the Pas de Calais region of France.

He was an old army man having completed his term of service with the Territorial Army at Scarborough. When war broke out he was appointed as a serjeant major with the 11th Battalion, East Yorkshire Regiment and was subsequently promoted internally, receiving his commission as a lieutenant.

The 1911 Census shows that he was living at 102 Gordon Street, Scarborough. He and his wife Eliza had five children, two daughters and three sons. Despite this, he is shown as having been admitted to the Royal Chelsea Hospital as a pensioner on 4 April 1912 yet discharged only eight days later on 12 April. Although this is what the Royal Chelsea Hospital Pensioner Admissions and Discharges list for the period 1715 to 1925 records, it does appear somewhat at odds, as part of the entry criteria to become a pensioner at the Royal Chelsea Hospital is that a man has to have reached 65 years of age, have no living dependents and have fallen on difficult times. McReynolds was only in his early forties and was married.

It was announced in late November 1916, that Lieutenant John R. Sturdy of the Suffolk Regiment, but who had previously served with the Indian Cavalry in both India and France, had been awarded the Military Cross for gallantry. The citation for his award read as follows:

> *For conspicuous gallantry and bold leading of his platoon. He led a bombing party against the enemy under heavy rifle fire, and in pitch darkness, causing them to retire with great loss. His initiative saved what might have been a serious situation.*

He was a Scarborough man, living with his parents William and Lydia Sturdy, at 16 Commercial Street, along with his brother Thomas and his two sisters Eva and Lydia.

John had been engaged to a local lady who sadly had been killed during the German bombing of Scarborough on 14 December 1914.

The deputy coroner Mr J.R. Wilkinson had by the very nature of his job to deal with death and its causes on an almost daily basis and it could be said that in such circumstances it would be hard not to become blasé about death. However, Saturday, 9 December 1916 was the day when he held an inquiry into the tragic death of 4-year-old Mary Aldous, the daughter of Mrs Annie Hornby of 3 Dixon's Yard, Cross Street, Scarborough.

On 7 December Mary was left indoors with another young child whilst Annie popped out for a few minutes. When she left young Mary was sitting on a stool in front of the fire, but there was no guard around it.

A neighbour of Mrs Hornsby was informed by some boys that there was a child on fire in Mrs Hornsby's home. The woman called out to a passing man by the name of William Bland who hurried into the house and took off his coat. He discovered the girl standing in the doorway of the property, enveloped in flames from head to toe. He quickly smothered her with his coat, immediately extinguishing the fire. William Bland then took out his knife and carefully cut away what was left of the child's smouldering clothing. Mary was then taken to Scarborough Hospital where her wounds were treated in a gallant effort to save her life. Despite these attempts, she sadly died later the same day.

The jury returned a verdict that the girl's death was as a result of shock resulting from the severity of the sustained burns.

Remarkably, by today's standards that is, no comment or observation was made in relation to the mother, Mrs Annie Hornby, having left Mary on her own, other than in the company of another young child, in front of an open fire.

Annie had married Samuel Artley Hornby in Scarborough 1903. Although a local man, Samuel is shown as having being in the New Zealand Army Reserve between 1916 and 1917 when he was 40 years of age. After the war both Annie and Samuel are shown on the 1919 electoral rolls for Wellington. Perhaps the only way that they could rebuild their lives after the tragedy of Mary's death was to get away from it all and so they emigrated to New Zealand.

Saturday, 29 December 1916, saw Mrs Jubb of 35 Elmville Avenue, Scarborough leaving for Switzerland to visit one of her sons who had been in hospital there since June. After having being wounded in action and then captured by the Germans, he was sent to neutral Switzerland for medical treatment. His condition had not improved that much and he was awaiting an operation having been shot in both legs. Another of her sons, H. Jubb, was also in hospital, but in Malta, where he was suffering with malaria. He was a Sapper in the Royal Engineers.

CHAPTER 5

1917 – Seeing it Through

According to the Commonwealth War Graves Commission website, 1917 saw the deaths of 294,834 British and Commonwealth military personnel. I then added 'Scarborough' in to the 'Additional Information' box on the search engine and this brought up 268 men who were either from, or who had connections with, Scarborough. It was actually 266, because two of the men were named 'Scarborough.' Benjamin Oman Scarborough was just 16 years of age when he was killed on 10 December 1917, when the Steam Trawler *Arnadavat* on which he was a deck hand, was sunk when it hit a mine which had been laid by the German submarine *U-17*. Benjamin's father, Robert Scarborough, the ship's skipper, also died. Both men were from Aberdeen in Scotland. The names of both men are commemorated on the Tower Hill Mercantile Marine Memorial.

The year was scattered throughout with a plethora of battles, offensives and events resulting in such a large number of deaths.

Below are just a few of the significant dates from the year:

1 February 1917 – Germany's policy of unrestricted submarine warfare begins. The policy included the sinking of both British merchant shipping and clearly identifiable hospital ships, as well as those vessels from neutral countries that were discovered in waters around the British Isles.

8 March 1917 – Russian Revolution begins. This followed the signing of the Treaty of Brest-Litovsk between the new Bolshevik government of Soviet Russia and the Central Powers of Germany, Austria-Hungary, Bulgaria and the Ottoman Empire, which ended Russia's involvement in the First World War, freeing up more German troops that could be moved to the Western Front.

6 April 1917 – The United States of America declares war on Germany, possibly saving Britain and her Allies from defeat.

9 April 1917 – Start of the Battle of Arras when British forces attacked German defensive positions close to the French city of Arras. The fighting, which continued until 16 May 1917, resulted in more than 150,000 British casualties, for what were marginal gains and a battle which basically ended in a stalemate. The battle was in effect a diversionary attack to try and tie up German forces to assist the French Nivelle Offensive.

During the time frame of the battle, a total of fifty men, who were either from Scarborough or who had a connection with the town, lost their lives. Of these at least twenty have no known grave and their names are commemorated on the Arras Memorial.

14 April 1917 – Start of the Battle of Vimy Ridge, part of the Arras campaign, when four Canadian divisions stormed and captured the ridge in two days of fierce fighting.

7 May 1917 – First night time air raid on London.

7 June 1917 – Start of the Battle of Messines which lasted until 14 June 1917. It was an offensive carried out by the Second British Army, near to the village of Messines. The British began the day by detonating nineteen mines under the German front line trenches. They then employed the tactic of a creeping barrage, which helped the infantry achieve their objectives with speed and surprise, as they overran the German positions.

31 July 1917 – Start of the Third Battle of Ypres, also known as the Battle of Passchendaele. This attritional battle which lasted for three months and six days, became synonymous with the horror of the Western Front as appalling weather conditions turned the battleground into a muddy swamp in which men and horses drowned. British and Empire casualties reached 275,000 with German casualties estimated at 260,000. When the campaign ended less than 5 miles of territory had been captured.

Third Battle of Ypres.

16 August 1917 – Start of the Battle of Langemarck, a brief encounter during the Third Battle of Ypres. The fighting at Langemarck was the Allies' second general attack of that battle.

20 September 1917 – Start of the Battle of Menin Road Ridge. This was one of the early British attacks during the Third Battle of Ypres and lasted for five days. Although seen as British victory, the Allied forces still managed to incur some 20,000 casualties.

20 November 1917 – Start of the Battle of Cambrai. Although it started out as a British offensive operation, it resulted in the German defenders not only consolidating their positions, but mounting a counter-attack. By the end of the fighting, each side had incurred more than 40,000 casualties. It was notable as the first battle in which the British used tanks in force.

Tank at Cambrai.

James Crampton – Shot at Dawn

James Crampton was born in 1877 in Scarborough, Yorkshire, the last of six children of George and Elizabeth Crampton. On 4 February 1917 Private (34595) James Crampton of the 9th Battalion, York and Lancaster Regiment was shot at dawn for desertion. He was 39 years of age.

James Crampton had been a reservist and was called up at the outbreak of the war, re-joining the 6th Battalion, Yorkshire Regiment as Private (8245) and served with them throughout the entire ill-fated Gallipoli campaign, before being transferred and arriving in France on the first day of the Battle of the Somme on 1 July 1916. The following month he deserted, managing to stay at large until his capture three months later on 17 November 1916. After a brief trial, in the form of a Field General Court Martial, at which he was found guilty of the offence of desertion, he was sentenced to death by firing squad. He was duly executed on 4 February 1917 and is buried at the Poperinghe New Military Cemetery, which is situated in the West-Vlaanderen region of Belgium. The cemetery, with seventeen graves, contains the largest number of executed British soldiers from the First World War, anywhere in the world.

The 9th Battalion's war diary for 4 February 1917, reads: *'Battalion at Infantry Barracks at Ypres. Lewis gunners practised,'* but absolutely nothing about Private James Crampton being executed by firing squad, or that it was colleagues of his who had been tasked with carrying out the execution.

The Army Register of Soldiers Effects 1901 to 1929 has his name spelt as Grampton, but underneath is written, 'alias Crampton' It also shows that because of the circumstances of his death, a war gratuity was not awarded, although what he was due in pension rights was awarded to his family members.

The 9th Battalion's war diary for 16 August 1916, the day that Private Crampton deserted, has the one solitary entry which says, *'In reserve area.'* The entry for 23 January 1917 reads as follows. *'Disposition as 21st. Situation normal. Casualties 1 OR killed. 2nd Lieutenant W.G. Lapham, joined the Battalion.'* No mention of Private Crampton's court martial.

James Crampton's court martial took place on Tuesday, 23 January 1917 at Ypres. The three officers who had been selected to sit in judgement were Captain E.V. Price, from Private Crampton's 9th Battalion, York and Lancaster Regiment, Lieutenant E.W. Barcliff, 11th Battalion, Sherwood Foresters and Captain O.F. Dowson of the Army Service Corps.

Five witnesses were called by the prosecution, against Private Crampton, who in his own defence took the somewhat staggering decision to make no comment. This meant that in his defence all he had was the evidence of his character as seen through the eyes of another man, in the form of Lance Corporal E. Guymen, also of the 9th Battalion, York and Lancaster Regiment, a man who had also served with him in the 6th Battalion, Yorkshire Regiment throughout the Gallipoli campaign.

The five witnesses for the prosecution were, Lieutenant A.A. Chapman, Company Sergeant Major G. Oldfield, Corporal W. Mason, a Private Goulding, and the sergeant who had taken the roll call on the night of 17 August 1916.

The charge which Private Crampton faced was, 'When on active service deserting his Majesty's service.' This was a charge that resulted in an automatic plea of Not Guilty, usually with a reason of mitigation, because to plead guilty meant almost certain death by firing squad.

Looking at the five prosecution witnesses in more detail we find that Company Sergeant Major G. Oldfield, who was in the same battalion as Private Crampton and who, on 16 August 1916, had instructed him and Private Goulding that they had being detailed to work with the Royal Engineers for the day at a nearby railhead. Company Sergeant Oldfield survived the war and was demobbed and placed on the Army reserve as from 31 January 1919.

Private Goulding also gave evidence at the court martial to confirm that he and Private Crampton had been tasked by Company Sergeant Major G. Oldfield to work with the Royal Engineers on 16 August 1916, but on their arrival they were told that they were not required and returned to their battalion. Private Goulding explained that he saw Private Crampton later the same day when he left their location with another soldier who subsequently returned on his own.

The sergeant from the 9th Battalion, Yorks and Lancaster Regiment, who had taken the roll call at 9pm on the evening of 16 August 1916, gave evidence that he discovered that Private Crampton was not in his dug-out.

Corporal W. Mason of the Military Police had been on duty at the town hall at Armentières when Private Crampton was brought in by Lieutenant Chapman of the New Zealand Pioneers. Both Corporal Mason and Lieutenant Chapman were called as witnesses to give their accounts in relation to Private Crampton's arrest and subsequent detention. Surprisingly, the sergeant whom Lieutenant Chapman had sent to the house in Armentières to ascertain if Private Crampton was staying there, was not called as a witness. Taking into account he was the person who initially identified and detained Private Crampton, I would have assumed that he would have been the most obvious and relevant witness to give evidence at the court martial.

Lance Corporal E. Guymen, a colleague of Private Crampton's in the 9th Battalion, who had served with him in the Yorkshire Regiment in Egypt, provided a statement in relation to Private Crampton's character. The picture that was painted of James was of a troubled soul. Lance Corporal Guymen explained to the court that the general feeling amongst the rest of the men in the company, was that 'he was gone in the head'. Private Crampton was, according to Lance Corporal Guymen, a bit of a loner, and that it was not uncommon for him to go off on his own suddenly and un-announced.

It is absolutely incredible looking back at this case now, 100 years after the events actually took place, to think that a man could go on trial for his life with no legal representation, with nobody having apparently examined his medical record and only one witness to provide a character reference for him.

Lieutenant Colonel R. Ratcliffe, who was the commanding officer of the 9th Battalion, York and Lancashire Regiment, attached a report to the court papers, the decision of which had to be confirmed and ratified by Field Marshal Sir Douglas Haig, before the sentence of the court could be carried out. The report included some alarming comments about Private Crampton, such as 'the man never seemed to understand quite what he was doing', and was according to his officers, 'mentally deficient' and had always been, 'a source of trouble, never seeming to understand the most simple of instructions that were given to him, and being of a very forgetful nature.'

To most fair minded individuals who possessed even a modicum of compassion, alarm bells would have sounded immediately upon reading Lieutenant Colonel Ratcliffe's report, but sadly it would appear, his fate had already been decided. No compassion was forthcoming and the execution of Private Crampton went ahead as per the finding of the court on 4 February 1917 in the courtyard of the Town Hall at Poperinghe.

1917 – SEEING IT THROUGH

The 'Shot at Dawn' Memorial at the National Memorial Arboretum, Staffordshire. (Picture by Harry Mitchell via Wikimedia Commons.)

During the First World War, a total of 346 British soldiers were executed for committing military offences which were deemed so serious, that death was the only reasonable punishment. Of these, 306 men were subsequently given pardons by the British Government.

The first British soldier to face a firing squad during the course of the First World War was Private (L/10061) Thomas James Highgate, of the 1st Battalion, Queen's Own (Royal West Kent) Regiment. The war was only thirty-five days old when he was shot by firing squad on 8 September 1914.

Thomas had been on the Army Reserve since 4 October 1912 as Private 6045 with the 3rd Battalion, Queens Own (Royal West Kent) Regiment. He enlisted in the Regular Army at Guildford on 5 February 1913 when he was still three month's shy of his eighteenth birthday. His Army Service Record has survived and makes for very interesting reading. It starts by noting he had reached 18 years of age on 4 May 1913. On 28 February 1914 Thomas deserted. The next part of his record has a burn mark running through it and is only partly visible. It would appear that he was either captured, or returned to his unit on 4 May 1914 and faced trial by a District Court Martial on 22 May 1914. He was found guilty and sentenced to forty-two days detention due to run until 2 July 1914, but on 26 June, he was returned to duty, with the final week of his detention remitted for good behaviour. The next entry is dated 8 September 1914 and says, 'Died gun shot wounds.' It would appear that at a later date, and definitely in another's hand writing, 'F.G.C.M for desertion, British Expeditionary Force,' has been added.

His record also shows that he was awarded the 1914 Star, British War Medal and the Victory Medal, but they were later forfeited because of his act of desertion.

His Company Conduct Sheet records that he was dealt with on five occasions whilst he was serving in Dublin, for having a rusty rifle on parade, being absent from tattoo and for exchanging a duty with a fellow soldier without permission to do so.

A very interesting typed letter appears near the back of Thomas's Army Service Record. It is dated 12 October 1914 and it has been sent by the War Office to the officer in charge of No.10 District, Infantry Record Office at Hounslow:

Sir,

I am commanded by the Army Council to inform you that the Deputy Adjutant General, 3rd Echelon, reports that No.10061 Private Thomas James Highgate, 1st Battalion, Royal West Kent Regiment, was shot for desertion on the 8th ultimo after trial by a Field General Court Martial.

I am to request that you will cause the number, name and Regiment to be verified, and the next of kin to be informed. Lord Kitchener's note of sympathy will, of course be omitted from the communication to the relatives who should simply be informed that the man was killed on the 8th ultimo.

I am Sir,

Your obedient servant.

What an extraordinary letter! To receive such a correspondence must have been so confusing. The shock and numbness of knowing a loved one was dead was bad enough, but to then later appreciate the enormity of what the letter was actually saying, and without knowing what the true circumstances were that had led to his death, must have been hard to bear.

Although this man has absolutely nothing to do with Scarborough it feels right to include his story as this was the very first man executed during the First World War, and with his Army Service Record having survived, it gives a flavour of what it must have been like for Private James Crampton.

More than 200,000 men of the British Army faced a court martial during the First World War. Of these 20,000 were found guilty of an offence under military law which carried a possible death sentence as the outcome, but of these only 3,080 were originally sentenced to death. A number of those who were executed were under a suspended sentence for having already committed a previous offence, but all the same, 304 British soldiers were shot dead by firing squads, which was a traumatic experience for those ordered to take part in them.

1914 – 4 executions
1915 – 55 executions
1916 – 95 executions
1917 – 104 executions
1918 – 46 executions

The vast majority of the executions were for either desertion or cowardice, although eighteen of them were for acts of murder.

There were four types of court martial which dealt with soldiers and officers who were in breach of military law. The lowest form of trial was that of a Regimental Court Martial which was for men of the lower ranks, or non-commissioned officers, and dealt with the most minor of offences.

Next was the District Court Martial, which could only deal with breaches of military law that could not result in a sentence of more than two year's detention. This type of court required a 'bench' of seven officers if the offence was committed at home, but only five officers if overseas.

Then came the really serious one, the Field General Court Martial which could impose the death penalty. This type of court was more often used in wartime. For the death penalty to be imposed, all three sitting officers had to agree.

Last but by no means least came the General Court Martial which was where commissioned officers were sent for trial and men from the other ranks who had committed serious offences such as murder. If the case was heard 'at home', at least thirteen commissioned officers were required to hear the proceedings, but if the case was overseas, only five commissioned officers and a Judge Advocate were required.

There is a school of thought that suggests that the British soldiers who were executed by firing squad by their own colleagues, were killed in part so that senior British Army officers could set an example to other soldiers not to think about doing the same thing.

The end of January 1917 saw more bad news being delivered to some of Scarborough's families, concerning the deaths of their loved ones.

Private (23967) Joseph Henry **Sails**, who was 35 years of age and serving with the 12th Battalion, Yorkshire Regiment, was killed in action by an exploding German shell on 20 January 1917. He was buried in the military cemetery on the outskirts of the French village of Rancourt in the Somme region of France.

Private Sails was an experienced soldier who had fought in the Second Boer War, also known as the South African War. He was a married man and left a widow Ann, whom he had married in 1905, and their four children, whose home was at 112 Nelson Street, Scarborough, although prior to that the family had lived two doors away at 108 Nelson Road. Before the war he had worked for the North Eastern Railway Company in Middlesbrough.

Joseph was the youngest of three sons born to Thomas and Sarah Sails. One of his brothers was George Tyco Brookbanks Sails, a tailor by trade, who also served during the First World War. He enlisted at Newcastle-upon-Tyne on 16 July 1916 when he was 38 years of age. It was noted at his medical examination that he had flat feet, but not a sufficient defect to cause his rejection as a soldier. He was a married man with three children, the youngest of whom had been born just a month before the outbreak of the war.

He was initially a private (266484) with the 5th Battalion, Northumberland Fusiliers, later posted to the regiment's 2nd/4th Battalion. He was further posted to the 19th Battalion on 27 December 1917, before eventually being transferred to the 945th Area Employment Company, Labour Corps on 24 January 1918 and later appointed as the company tailor, an obvious choice taking into account his civilian occupation. He survived the war and was demobbed on 26 February 1919.

Some parts of George's Army Service papers were slightly confusing, as on different pages of it his enlistment date is shown as 9 November 1915, 29 November 1915 and 9 November 1916.

John William Sails, the son of Thomas and Sarah Sails, died in 1893 when he was 18 years of age.

Christopher Candler **Bennett** was 27 years of age and a driver (8280/761361) in C Battery, 317th Brigade, Royal Field Artillery. He died on 21 January 1917 as a result of complications following an operation for a serious wound he had suffered in action.

Christopher had sadly lost four members of his family when their home at 2 Wykeham Street had been struck during the German bombardment of Scarborough on 16 December 1914. They were his mother Joanna, his nephew, John Ward, another relative, George Barnes, aged four, and his brother Albert Bennett, who Christopher had made a valiant effort to save. He was himself a serving soldier at the time of his death with a Territorial unit of the Royal Field Artillery.

Christopher had also rendered assistance to many others in the immediate aftermath of the German bombardment, including a 90-year-old lady.

Private (41235) Francis Ernest **Kennedy**, who was 21 years of age when he enlisted in the Army on 22 January 1916, was in the 17th Battalion, Highland Light Infantry when he died of his wounds on 16 January 1917. He was buried at the Etaples Military Cemetery, in the Pas de Calais region of France.

Maurice Lotherington Rowntree, aged 36 years and a married man, found himself before the magistrates at Scarborough Police Court on Tuesday, 13 February 1917, charged with being an absentee from the Army.

He was a well-known member of the Society of Friends and a lecturer at the Swarthmore Religious and Social Settlement in Leeds. He put his case, speaking with an eloquence that one would naturally expect from such a learned gentleman. He found it to be tremendously tragic that the splendid heroism of the nation's troops should be devoted to works of destruction, adding that it was the logical outcome to an un-Christian system of life. He believed that if people really trusted in the love of God, then whatever might come, he believed, that the power of true righteousness and liberty would triumph over all obstacles.

He finished his fine words by saying that war would never bring anything other than the peace of death.

The magistrates, as if mesmerised by his words, stated that it was an exceedingly sorrowful duty which they had to perform that day, but however much they might sympathise with Mr Rowntree's views and opinions, his arguments were outweighed by the law of the land. He was found guilty, fined two shillings and handed over to the military authorities.

I could find no record of Maurice having enlisted in the Army, or any other branch of the military, during the First World War.

An unusual case came before the magistrates at Scarborough Police Court on Friday, 23 March 1917 in the form of five local women who had all been charged with professing to tell fortunes. They were: Mrs Emily Jane Buckle, otherwise known as Madame Cora, from 28 Nelson Street, Scarborough; Mrs Alice Rumford of 87a Longwest Parade, Scarborough; Emily Louisa Hawkswell, otherwise known as Madame Louisa of 5 Mill Street, Scarborough; Madame Lucy James, of The Market Hall, Scarborough and Mary Morley, otherwise known as Madame Morlee, of 3 Museum Terrace, Scarborough.

Buckle, James and Morley all pleaded not guilty to the charges against them, with the latter also being the only one of the five women to be legally represented, by Mr G.E. Royle. The witnesses in the case were two women, one of whom was the daughter of a Police constable, whilst the other was the wife of another constable.

The defendant James told the court that she had lived in Scarborough for eighteen years and believed in Palmistry. In the case of Madame Morlee, the Chief Constable, Mr H. Windsor, informed the court that he knew the defendant had been invited to a garden party at Londesborough Lodge, and told people's fortunes by way of amusement only. He added that she had connections with some of society's richest and finest individuals and that she advertised her 'abilities' in newspapers. The Chief Constable stated that he found her claims to be a danger to both local residents and visitors to the town. She had admitted to him, both in writing and verbally, that she had premonitions, allowing her to see things that were going to happen.

Madam Morlee said that she had practised her skill for some twenty years, and no matter what the outcome of the case against her was, she would continue to do what she described as, her calling, as she honestly believed in the truth of the science which she practised. She had two previous convictions against her for the same offence.

The defendants Rumford and Hawkswell had both used cards and crystal balls to ply their individual trades.

After all of the arguments and evidence had been heard in the case, the magistrates fined Madame Morlee £7 10s, an extremely hefty fine for the day, and informed her that if she was charged and convicted of a similar offence in the future, she would more than likely be sent to stand trial before the Quarter Sessions, which could ultimately result in her having to serve a custodial sentence.

The remaining four defendants were all found guilty and fined one guinea.

The unidentified body of a man was found out at sea on Monday, 23 April 1917 and was brought in to Scarborough. The only article found on him was an aluminium cigarette box with the word 'Scarborough' inscribed across the middle of it. The dead man's clothing consisted of knee-length sea boots, which were marked as having being manufactured by R. Coggins & Sons Ltd, Raunds, Northampton, the type that were common to sailors working on fishing vessels, blue serge trousers, made by D. Hill, Carter & Co, Ltd, of North Shields, a striped cotton shirt, a blue-coloured jersey, and blue woollen socks.

It had not been possible to ascertain how long the man's body had been in the water, although it was in relatively good condition. The deceased's age was guessed as being about 30. He was 5ft tall with a proportionate build, dark complexion, with short dark brown hair.

Because of the maker's names found in the deceased's boots and trousers, it was assumed that the man was British and that he was from one of the numerous fishing trawlers which had been sunk in the region, either by striking a mine or by German torpedo. There were no outstanding cases of fishing vessels having accidently lost a man overboard.

A meeting of the Scarborough Town Council took place on the evening of Monday, 14 May 1917. At the start of the meeting, the Mayor Mr C.C. Graham, addressed those present and advised them about the loss of one of their own. Second Lieutenant Percy **Moore**, the 22-year-old son of Councillor Abraham Moore, had been serving in the 12th Battalion, East Yorkshire Regiment. He was killed in action on 3 May 1917 and was buried at the Aubigny Communal Cemetery Extension, south of the village of Aubigny-en-Artois.

Percy was one of five children born to Abraham and Amelia Moore of 1 Stepney Road, Scarborough. Abraham was a building contractor and had been a town councillor for many years. His other son, George E. Moore, also served during the war as a corporal (GS/3351) and acting lance sergeant with the 13th Battalion, Royal Fusiliers, and was commissioned on 25 April 1917, just ten days before Percy was killed. George survived the war and on his return to Scarborough went to work for his father in the building industry. He remained in the town for the rest of his life, passing away on 18 April 1978 at the age of 84.

Miss Edith Elizabeth **Taylor** was born in Scarborough in 1870. She went on to become a Red Cross nurse during the First World War, during this time her family home was at Rothsay House, Prince of Wales Terrace, Scarborough. She died on 5 June 1917 of septic pneumonia, which it is believed that she caught from a patient whilst working at a military hospital in Scarborough, possibly the Westwood Hospital.

Nurse Taylor's funeral took place at St Martin's Church, Scarborough, with full military honours, including the draping of her coffin in a Union Flag, which was carried to the church and subsequently to the graveyard by a number of soldiers, non-commissioned officers and officers. Also present were some of her colleagues and other members of the Red Cross, the St John Nursing Division, along with the St John Ambulance Division.

A service was held at St Martin's Church, with the Rev. St Clair Topper, Vicar, and the Rev. Cecil Cooper, the vicar of Scarborough, officiating. Edith's late father had been the Medical Officer of Health for Scarborough. Edith was the eldest of four children born to John and Elizabeth Taylor.

At the time of her death she was a wealthy spinster leaving in her Will the sum of £6,242 9s 6d, the monies being split between Harold Burn Hopgood and Noel Cecil Dowson, both of whom were solicitors.

Edith's elder brother, Marshall Dowson Taylor, had served during the war as a private (210926) in the Labour Corps, which in itself was an interesting fact, because by that time he was a naturalized citizen of the United States of America, having qualified as such on 2 February 1909 in Los Angeles, California, where he lived at 310 South Alvarado Street. In 1917, by which time he had lived in America for some fifteen years, he applied for a passport for both himself and his wife, Ethel, stating on the application that he needed to return to England to care for his elderly mother for a period of one year. He sailed from New York on board the SS *Adriatic* on 12 July 1917 en route to England, where he arrived on 28 July at the Port of Liverpool.

Two months later on 14 September 1917 he arrived in France having being commissioned as a second lieutenant in the 53rd Santal Indian Labour Corps. He was by now 46 years of age. Having survived his wartime experience, he returned to America.

A report in one of the region's local newspapers dated Saturday, 23 June 1917 reported a man's suicide that had taken place in Scarborough earlier the same day.

Robert **Hume** had enlisted in the British Army in 1915, even though by that time he was 51 years of age. He saw service in Salonika, but was eventually medically discharged, suffering with asthma and bronchitis. He had only been living in Scarborough a short while and was staying at the Royal Northern Sea Bathing Infirmary, under a scheme which had been put in place by the countess of Londesborough. The main criteria for staying there was that a man had to be a displaced ex-soldier.

On the morning of 23 June he was found dead at the Infirmary, having apparently committed suicide by cutting his own throat. I was unable to establish what regiment he had served with.

Saturday, 4 August 1917 saw the death of Mr George Taylor after a protracted period of illness, at his home 2 Grosvenor Road, Scarborough. He was 84 years of age. He filled the positions of Clerk of the Peace for the borough of Scarborough, as well as the Registrar of the Court of Record, and the position which saw his name in the local newspapers on a regular basis, Scarborough's Coroner.

Mr Taylor was born in Willerby near Scarborough in 1833 and was privately educated in both Leeds and York, before commencing his training as a solicitor in 1856. Having qualified, he began legal practice in Scarborough in 1860. His first experience of holding a position in local politics came in 1879, when he was elected as a member of the Scarborough Town Council, to represent what was then known as the South Ward. This was a position he held for just two years before resigning to take up the position of Clerk of the Peace and Registrar of the Court of Record, which at the time was more widely used than it was during the years of the First World War.

It wasn't until 1893 that he was further appointed as the Scarborough Borough Coroner, after having held the position of Deputy Coroner for many years under Mr R. Collinson, the man whom he replaced.

Mr Taylor had at one time commanded the local volunteer artillery corps, providing him with a keen interest in anything to do with the military. In his younger days he had kept an interest in the country pursuits of shooting and riding out with the local hunt.

Mr Taylor left a widow, Mary, thirteen years his junior, and two children, a daughter, Katherine, and his son Edward Stewardson Taylor, a captain in the Yorkshire Regiment. In his Will Mr Taylor left the sum of £3,226 3s 6d to his widow, Mary.

Submarine attack

Tuesday, 4 September 1917 was almost a repeat of 16 December 1914 for the residents of Scarborough. But this time the artillery bombardment didn't come from ships of the German Imperial Navy, but from one of their submarines, whose guns have a range of around 3 miles. Once again it was a devastating attack which started at around 6.45pm, lasted for about ten minutes, and resulted in thirty shells raining down on Scarborough. By the time the attack was over three of the town's residents had been killed with another five injured.

It was a lovely evening, the weather was fine and the skies were almost cloud free. Quite a few people were out enjoying an after dinner stroll along the seafront promenade, many resting on the benches and taking in the picture-postcard views. But then the tranquillity of the evening was suddenly broken by the sound of shells exploding all around the town. At first confusion reigned but it quickly became clear that the town was once again under attack by German artillery shells, but from whence they came, nobody was absolutely sure.

Mr Thomas Temple Pickup who lived at 2 Queens Terrace, Scarborough, aged 64, was killed close to his home. Mrs Elizabeth Scott, who lived at 108 Hoxton Road, Scarborough, was killed when a fragment of shrapnel hit the side wall of 109 Hoxton Road and smashed in her bay window. The wife of a local Police constable, she died later of her wounds.

Alice Appleby, who was 17 years of age and lived at 8 Whitehead Hill, Scarborough, was badly injured when one of the German shells exploded near to where she was walking on the South Foreshore Road, which left her with a broken arm and leg.

Mrs Annie Bestwick of 109 Victoria Road, Scarborough, was injured when one of the shells came crashing through her attic window.

One shell landed in the middle of the road in Albert Street, the blast so powerful that it knocked out the windows in four of the adjoining properties. A house in St Nicholas Street that was damaged had also suffered a similar fate in the December

1914 attack. Other shells caused damage in Pavilion Square, St Thomas's Street, Eastborough, the Spa Grounds and Cambridge Street. One landed at Scarborough's cricket ground, which was situated in North Marine Road, whilst a group of women were playing lawn tennis but thankfully none were injured. The roof of platform one at Scarborough railway station also saw some minor damage, but the track was not damaged and nobody was injured or killed.

Considering the number of shells that were fired by the German submarine, the number of deaths and casualties was thankfully relatively low.

On this occasion a number of Royal Navy patrol boats responded expediently and were able to return fire to the attacking submarine, which is possibly why the bombardment lasted for only ten minutes. The reason behind the first attack on Scarborough in 1914, was not totally apparent, and this one even less so, as there was no conceivable military target that the submarine could have been aiming for.

The two victims of the latest German bombardment of the town, were buried on the afternoon of Saturday, 8 September 1917 at Scarborough cemetery. As would be expected in the circumstances, a large crowd gathered to mark the laying to rest of Mr Thomas Pickup and Mrs Elizabeth Scott. The Rev. Cecil Cooper took Mr Pickup's funeral, whilst the Reverend W.O. Thomas officiated at Mrs Scott's, with four members of the Scarborough Constabulary carrying her coffin to the graveside.

Thomas left a widow, Eliza, who was three years his senior. He was a cabinet maker by trade and left £194 16s 1d in his Will, all of which was bequeathed to Eliza.

Elizabeth was the wife of John William S. Scott, a Police constable in Scarborough. They had been married for twenty years and had four children, a daughter Lilian, who was the eldest, followed by sons Jack and Thomas, and the youngest of the family, Ada. Not only had Scarborough lost one of its own, but John Scott had lost his wife and four innocent children had lost their mother.

Thomas and Jessie King lived at 8 Avenue Road, Scarborough with their daughter Amy. Thomas was a retired tailor and they had three children, sons Herbert and Arthur and daughter Amy. Arthur had died, aged 21 in 1899. Thomas had died at home on 9 July 1911. Despite his parents living in Scarborough at the time of the 1911 Census, Herbert had left home many years earlier and became a school teacher. He initially attended school in Scarborough before attending Yorkshire College in Leeds where he graduated with a Bachelor of Science degree, he went on to further his education with a Masters degree. After finishing his education, he acquired teaching positions at both Dronfield and Harrogate schools. He later returned to Scarborough as the chemistry master at the town's municipal school, working there for six years between 1902 and 1908, after which he moved on to the Science Department of the Cockburn High School.

Herbert only received his commission as an officer in the British Army in 1917 when he was 41 years of age. He was engaged in special analytical work and left for France in August 1917. Sadly, he did not survive the war. He was killed in action on 6 October 1917 whilst serving as a lieutenant in the Royal Army Ordnance Corps. He is buried at the Brandhoek New Military Cemetery No.3, which is situated about 3 miles outside of the town of Ypres, in Belgium.

Monday, 1 October 1917 was an extremely sad day for the Mayor of Scarborough, Christopher Colbourne Graham, as it saw the death of his son Second Lieutenant Hugh Colbourne **Graham**, serving with the 9th Battalion, but attached to the 2nd Battalion Yorkshire Regiment. He has no known grave and his name is commemorated on the Tyne Cot Memorial, in the West Vlaanderen region of Belgium. He was 29 years of age.

Educated at both Winchester College and the University of Leeds, at the outbreak of the First World War, Hugh tried to enlist in one of Kitchener's New Army battalions, but he failed the medical on account of poor eyesight. But not a man to give up easily, he tried again and this time he was accepted by the Royal Army Medical Corps and attached to the Northumberland Fusiliers.

After passing a course for infantry officers at Bristol University, he was sent out to the Western Front, and it was during the fighting of the Third Battle of Ypres that he was killed.

At a council meeting held on Friday, 9 November 1917 Mr C.C. Graham was re-elected as mayor for a fifth consecutive year, a feat never previously achieved in Scarborough. The proposal for his election was put forward by Alderman W. Ayscough and seconded by Councillor J. Malton. After once again readily accepting the position, the mayor gave a short speech of thanks and a brief resumé of the previous year's achievements and events.

He spoke about how the number of visitors to the town had exceeded the projected expectations and commented on how the beneficial effect of these increased numbers had been felt by all concerned. He closed by accepting that although the war had not been good for the town and its people in many different ways, through those troubled times an appreciation had been gained of life in general, health as well as education.

Alderman V. Fowler was also re-elected as Mr Graham's deputy. Mr Graham was born in London in March 1857 and after having finished his education he went on to become an analytical chemist. He married Mary Johnstone Bremner when he was 26 years of age at Kingston-upon-Hull. Mary died in Scarborough in December 1910.

An unusual case took place at the Scarborough Police Court on 17 November 1917. The man in the dock was local man Thomas Shaw, his crime, feeding horses in contravention of the Horse Rationing Order. Not only were

Mr Christopher Colbourne Graham.

horses being killed in their tens of thousands, helping the British Army in the different theatres of war across the world, but those who had been lucky enough not to have been purchased on behalf of the War Office for military purposes overseas, now had to face being restricted in what they could eat, even though they still had to work in the fields and on the roads on the home front.

Mr Shaw, a riding master and a married man with two children, lived at 9 Royal Crescent Lane, Scarborough. Evidence had been provided that he owned several horses for pleasure, which meant that as result of the Act, they were not entitled to be provided with any corn at all. The Police were able to show that Mr Shaw had used several quarts of oats more than he was entitled to use during a particular time frame, despite his telling an officer when interviewed that he had only fed his horses bran and chop and had not fed them oats.

Found guilty, he was fined £10 for contravening the Horse Rationing Order and a further £10 for withholding information from the Police.

Looking at this case through today's eyes, even bringing the matter to court appears somewhat severe, let alone the size of the hefty fines, but this isn't about the here and now, it is about then, a hundred years ago, when as a nation we were at war. The longer the war went on the more precious food became, it was so much harder to come by. We are after all an island nation and with Germany doing her damnedest to starve us out by sinking as many ships as possible that were spotted in British waters, foodstuffs were at a premium and had to be rationed whether they were for human or non human consumption.

Monday, 3 December 1917 saw the announcement of the deaths of three of Scarborough's finest young men during fighting on the Western Front.

The news of the death of Lieutenant Lawrence Edward **Rowntree** had been received by his mother, Mrs Roundtree, of Low Hall, Scalby, Scarborough. His death was all the more painful for her as Laurence was her only child.

After being educated at the Friends School in Bootham, he went on to study at King's College, Cambridge. At the outbreak of the war he joined the Friends Ambulance Unit and served in France, later enlisting in the Army as a private in the Tank Corps, before being commissioned as a second lieutenant in the Royal Field Artillery. At the time of his death in action on 25 November 1917, he was 22 years of age and serving with A Battery, 26th Brigade.

He is buried at the Vlamertinghe New Military Cemetery which is situated just outside Ypres town centre. The village of Vlamertinghe was the home to both British artillery units as well as field ambulance sections.

The Commonwealth War Graves Commission has recorded his name as Laurence Edmund Rowntree. His parents, Constance Margaret Naish and John Wilhelm Rowntree, married at Barton Regis, Gloucestershire in 1892.

Second Lieutenant George Russell **Hutchinson**, who was the son of Mr C.B. Hutchinson of the Criterion Hotel, Scarborough, was reported as having been killed in action on 22 November 1917. Confusion reigned for Mr Hutchinson senior, as to the authenticity of the news of his son's death as he had received a letter from him which was dated 24 November 1917, stating that he had just come out of the lines. Despite the confusion and enquiries with the War Office over his death, the Commonwealth War Graves Commission shows him as having been killed in action on 26 November 1917 whilst serving with the 2nd/8th Battalion, (Prince of Wales's Own) West Yorkshire Regiment. The British Army Medal Rolls Index for the period of the First World War, records that he was 'deceased' on 26 November 1917, that has then been changed to read that he was in fact killed in action on 27 November 1917.

George's body was never recovered, but his name is commemorated on the Cambrai Memorial, which is situated close to the village of Louverval in the Nord region of France. The memorial commemorates the names of more than 7,000 British and South African soldiers who were killed during

The Cambrai War Memorial.

the Battle of Cambrai which took place between 20 November and 7 December 1917, and who have no known grave.

Before the war George Hutchinson had been a journalist, working on the staff of the *Leicester Mail*, but he volunteered soon after the outbreak of hostilities, arriving in France on 29 July 1915, initially as a private (11391) with the Leicestershire Regiment, before transferring to the Army Cycling Corps as a private (12898). He was commissioned into the West Yorkshire Regiment on 31 August 1917.

When his wartime service medals, 1915 Star, Victory Medal and the British War Medal, were claimed by his mother, her address was 32 Elmville Avenue, Scarborough.

Second Lieutenant John Henry Raymond **Salter**, son of Dr Charles Edward and Mrs Annie Gertrude Salter, of 34 Prince of Wales Terrace, Scarborough, had originally been reported as missing in action on 18 October 1917; this was later changed to his having been killed in action on 13 October 1917.

At the time of his death he was only 18 years of age and serving with the No.54 Squadron, Royal Flying Corps. He was buried at the Tyne Cot Cemetery which is situated in West-Vlaanderen region of Belgium.

By the end of the war, John's parents had moved to 'Moseley House', 5 Westbourne Grove, Scarborough. The family were well off enough to be able to afford to employ four servants. They had three other children, sons Geoffrey and Clive and daughter Hilary.

Geoffrey was also a casualty of the First World War. He was 20 years of age when he was killed in action on 28 May 1918 whilst attached to No.20 Squadron Royal Air Force, from the East Yorkshire Regiment. He was also a holder of the Military Cross. He has no known grave and his name is commemorated on the Arras Flying Services Memorial, which can be found in the Faubourg-d'Amiens Cemetery, in the Pas de Calais region of France.

On the evening of Saturday, 1 December 1917 Sergeant Whitty and Constable Firth forced an entrance at 156 North Marine Road, Scarborough, after a lodger staying at that address attended the Police station and explained that she had been unable to gain entrance to the property and was concerned that all was not as it should be. The lodger told the Police that she had been away on holiday and had just returned that evening.

The owner of the property was a widow, Mrs Mary Evesham. Her husband George, who was fourteen years her senior, had passed away on 15 October 1913 and had during his working life been a butler, and the licensee of the town's Criterion Hotel.

On gaining entry to the property Sergeant Whitty and Constable Firth, discovered Mrs Evesham dead on the bedroom floor in her nightdress. At the subsequent inquest Dr Hutton said that he was of the opinion that Mrs Evesham's death was down to heart failure and a verdict of death by natural causes was returned accordingly. Mary's Will had her actual date of death as being 23 November 1917.

CHAPTER 6

1918 – The Final Blow

This was the final year of the war and what a bloody one it would be. According to figures compiled by the Commonwealth War Graves Commission, a total of 284,445 British and Commonwealth soldiers, sailors and airmen who were killed between 1 January and 11 November 1918. On top of this figure was the one for the men who had been wounded, and of course, there were also similar numbers of men who had been killed or wounded whilst fighting for Germany and the other countries of the central powers.

The Commonwealth War Graves Commission records that 217 men, who were either born in Scarborough or had a connection with the town in some way, were killed during the course of 1918 up to and including 11 November. In addition, there were five men with the surname of Scarborough, who were killed during that same period.

It has to be remembered that the signing of the Armistice on 11 November 1918, wasn't the end of men dying. Between that date and the end of 1921 – the last year in which deaths were officially attributable to any connection with the First World War – a further 83,815 men of the British and Allied forces, died of illness, disease or their wounds. Of these a number of them had a connection with Scarborough. I have included the names of these men in a separate chapter at the end of the book.

As with the other years of the war, some major battles took place throughout 1918, which were just as terrible as those from previous years.

Germany knew that it wouldn't be too long into 1918 before American troops would be ready to fully play their part in the fighting on the Western Front. To this end the need for urgency was paramount on their part. They needed to come up with a plan to break the stalemate on the Western Front, what they had in mind was to punch a hole in the Allied defensive line and in doing so, separate the British and French forces and then drive the former all the way back to the coast. The Germans also realised that their plan was extremely risky and if it failed, the war would be lost. Nearly three months had gone into the planning, but there were two things that the German High Command seemed to have overlooked, firstly the dogged resistance that they might encounter, and secondly, because they intended to spread their resources over such a wide area, there was always going to be the possibility that they would overstretch their supply routes, which would be a major problem for their troops at the front waiting for additional men, equipment and food.

The *Kaiserschlacht* or Kaiser's Battle, began on 21 March 1918 when over three million shells were fired into the British front line in the Somme sector followed by an attack by thousands of German infantrymen who had been trained in new shock tactics. The Second Battle of the Somme continued until 5 April with further battles at St Quentin, Bapaume, Noyon, Rosières, Avre, and Ancre. The second phase of the offensive, which began on 9 April 1918, saw even more battles take place at Estaires, Messines, Hazebrouck, Bailleul, Kemmel Ridge, and Scherpenberg. At a critical point in the fighting on 11 April, Field Marshal Douglas Haig issued his famous special order of the day:

> *There is no other course open to us but to fight it out. Every position must be held to the last man: there must be no retirement. With our backs to the wall and believing in the justice of our cause each one of us must fight on to the end. The safety of our homes and the Freedom of mankind alike depend upon the conduct of each one of us at this critical moment.*

The third and fourth phases of the German offensive began on 27 May and 9 June. The fifth, and what would be the final phase, began on 15 July with the second Battle of the Marne, but although in the initial phases the British and Empire forces were forced to give up the territory they had won with so many lives and fall back almost to Amiens, the German efforts would ultimately be to no avail.

What history has recorded as the Hundred Days, the Allied counter offensive, in response to Germany's efforts to defeat the British and her Allies, began on 8 August 1918, with the Battle of Amiens, also referred to as the Battle of Picardy. This was one of the turning points of the war. On the first day of the battle, Allied forces gained more than 7 miles of German-held territory, which impacted the morale of both sides in very different ways, and saw large numbers of German soldiers surrender, many of whom were hungry and near exhaustion, through lack of food and sleep.

Amiens was notable for two reasons. It was one of the first major battles where armoured warfare played a major part, with the Allies putting some 400 tanks in to the fray. Secondly, it saw the end of trench warfare on the Western Front, as the desire to bring the war to a victorious end fuelled the thinking of those in command and resulted in more innovative and successful tactics.

The next phase of the Allied offensive continued with the Third Battle of Albert, which commenced on 21 August 1918. On 2 September, having realised their position was becoming even more precarious, the order was given by the German Supreme Army Command to pull all their forces back to the apparent safety of the Hindenburg Line. Besides the casualties Germany had incurred since 8 August, more than 100,000 of her men had either surrendered or been taken as prisoners of war. Even though there would be more battles, Germany already knew that the war was over and that they could no longer prevail militarily. With this in mind they wanted to instigate peace talks, but Britain and her Allies were having none of it. By now, having invested so much in to the war, both in a monetary sense and in human terms, they were only interested in accepting Germany's unequivocal surrender. They finally achieved their goal with the signing of the Armistice on 11 November 1918, and the signing of the Treaty of Versailles with Germany taking place on 28 June 1919, officially bringing to a close the First World War.

By way of comparison, let us look at what was taking place in everyday life in Scarborough.

On Wednesday, 2 January 1918 an article appeared in a local newspaper, concerning Sergeant R. **Thompson** who had served with the Royal Army Medical Corps. He had returned to his home town of Scarborough after having being medically discharged from the Army.

During his service he had some remarkable escapes. Whilst in Greece travelling towards Salonica, the truck he was in overturned and landed in a river, pinning Thompson underneath and up to his neck in water. Fortunately his colleagues managed to rescue him from his predicament, but as a result of the accident, he had broken his thigh. He then had to endure a thirty-mile drive along rough roads which made for a very bumpy and uncomfortable journey. Eventually Thompson arrived at the hospital where the medical staff treated his injury, but whilst there Thompson and his fellow patients had to endure an Austrian artillery bombardment, which killed three of his comrades and left him with a fractured arm. Eventually he was placed onboard a ship bound for the UK, but even that wasn't plain sailing. On the journey home, the hospital ship struck a mine and everybody had to abandon ship. The lifeboats were launched but the one that Thompson was in did not disengage from its coupling properly and Thompson and the others with him were thrown in to the sea, the lifeboat following close behind. They all managed to scramble back into the lifeboat, before eventually being rescued and taken back to England without further incidents. An interesting anecdote in relation to Thompson and the sinking of the ship he was on. The last, and only, hospital ship to be sunk after striking a mine in 1917, was the HMHS *Salta* which at the time of its sinking, was on the approach to the Port of Le

Havre, to pick up wounded soldiers. The date of its sinking was 10 April 1917. I can only deduce that Thompson's homeward journey was not on board a hospital ship.

On Saturday, 19 January 1918, six people were killed and at least eight others were injured in a train crash on the Midland railway in the Eden Valley, approximately sixteen miles south of Carlisle. The Scotch Express which had left London, St Pancras railway station, earlier that day, with its final destination being St Enoch's station in Glasgow, was derailed because of a landslide and ended up on its side.

One of the surviving passengers on board the train was Lieutenant A.F. Thompson, of the Royal Flying Corps who was the son of Mr A.W. Thompson, a jeweller from Scarborough. He was interviewed by the *Yorkshire Post* newspaper about his ordeal:

> *I was sitting in a compartment in the middle of the train with four others when I felt one big bump, as if the brakes had been sharply applied, and we were all thrown from our seats. Then we had a still bigger bump. I tried to get to the window to see what had happened, when I was caught on the head with some kind of woodwork and knocked to the far side of the carriage. All of a sudden the carriage tilted over at a frightful angle, and I and an officer friend who was travelling with me, scrambled out of the window. All the time steam was coming from the engine in a most alarming way. Going to the front part of the train we found the wreckage of the first two coaches stretched high across the line. People were trying to get out of the train, but there was singularly little panic. Near the smashed woodwork behind the engine some women and children were lying, and it looked as if they were past human aid. All the luggage was in the front van and it was underneath the wreckage.*
>
> *One poor fellow was pinned by iron work on his chest, and a soldier was pinned by the ankle and could not move, a little boy about five years of age presented a very pitiful sight.*

His face was covered with blood and his scalp was torn right off. Axes procured from the rear of the train were quickly brought into use by railway workers and uninjured passengers. Unfortunately, there was not a single doctor on the train, but there were a number of VAD nurses and they worked right manfully in succouring the injured and supplying restoratives to them. Two of the women dining car attendants also helped in the noble work. It is a curious thing that only a minute before the accident happened one of the passengers in our compartment made a remark about the Aisgill disaster and no sooner had he spoken than this thing happened.

The Aisgill disaster, another rail crash, had taken place in the early hours of 2 September 1913 on the Settle—Carlisle railway line when two trains collided with each other. It resulted in sixteen deaths and thirty-eight injuries.

On Saturday, 16 February 1918 there was a list of war casualties in the *Hull Daily Mail*. One of the names included on the list was Sutton, G, (17339), East Yorkshire Regiment who, it stated, had been wounded. This turned out to be Private George **Sutton** who also went on to serve as a private (157146) in the Machine Gun Corps.

He lived with his parents, Thomas and Edith, along with his four sisters and two brothers in Scarborough. The address recorded on the 1911 Census is 'Lerhmerchant' although that is not absolutely clear on the handwritten version. Although his elder brother Thomas was old enough to have served during the First World War, but I cannot find any record of him having done so.

At the end of March 1918 a tragic incident took place at the town's North Sands. Eleven-year-old Leonard Francis was playing on the beach with his younger brother, Roland, when the latter discovered an object which caught his eye but neither of the boys had any idea what it was. As the older brother, Leonard began to examine the object in more detail and it was whilst he was doing this that the item exploded, blowing off all the fingers on his left hand, except the little one. What they had found was a hand grenade. The injuries which Leonard sustained, although serious enough, could have been a whole lot worse, especially as both boys were so close to one another at the time it went off. How or when the bomb came to be on the beach is unclear, but thankfully for Leonard and his brother, it must have been quite a while, as it clearly did not explode as intended, because if it had done both of the boys would have been killed outright.

Leonard was taken to the nearby Military Hospital at Burniston Road, Scarborough, where his injuries were treated as best they could be in the circumstances.

The family home was at Burniston Barracks where Leonard's father, Daniel, a retired Army Pensioner, was the barracks warder. His mother, Nellie, had plenty to keep her busy, especially with two other young children, besides Leonard and Roland.

Stanley Newson **Witting**, was born in Leeds on 29 August 1897. After leaving school he became a bank clerk at the National Provincial Bank of England in York. With the outbreak of the First World War he enlisted at York on the 20 December 1915, four months after his eighteenth birthday. He served with the British Expeditionary Force in France and Flanders, arriving there on 25 September 1916, before initially joining the 4th Entrenching Battalion on 10 November 1916. He was transferred to the 1st Battalion, Royal Marines on 25 November 1916, but was only with them for a month, before he was sent back to the UK on 23 December 1916 where he joined No.4 Officer Cadet Battalion. On 30 May 1917 he was commissioned as a temporary second lieutenant in the 2nd Battalion, Royal Marines Light Infantry, Royal Naval Division. He returned to France on 26 January 1918, joining the 2nd Battalion, Royal Marines on 10 February. He was killed in action during fighting at Havrincourt on 22 March 1918. He has no known grave, but his name is commemorated on the Arras Memorial in the Pas de Calais. At the time of his death he was only 20 years of age.

He had an elder sister, Jessie, as well as two younger siblings, Mary and Horace. His parents, Charles and Emily Witting, had previously lived at 1 Ashville Road, and 99 Murchison Street, Scarborough, but not long before their son's death, they had moved to 10 Eaton Road, Ilkley, later moving to 'Shenley', Westville Road, Ilkley.

There was an older brother, Thomas Noel **Witting**, who was born in 1894. By the time of the 1911 Census, he was 17 years of age and living with the Proctor family at 3 Otterburn Terrace in Newcastle, where he was a bank clerk.

Like Stanley, Thomas served during the First World War, and sadly also like Stanley, he was killed. He was serving as a private (92122) with the 19th (Service) Battalion (2nd County) Durham Light Infantry, when he was killed in action on 14 October 1918 and buried at the Dadizeele New British Cemetery, which is situated in the West-Vlaanderen region of Belgium. He had initially enlisted on 2 March 1918, but was not mobilized until 22 April 1918, and served as a private (40162) in the 3rd Battalion, West Riding Regiment. His transfer between the two regiments took place on 8 October 1918, just six days before his death and two days after having arrived in France.

On 15 December 1920, a letter arrived at the Witting's home, addressed to Mr Charles Whitting. It was from the Infantry Records Office in York:

> *Sir,*
>
> *I beg to inform you that owing to the agreement with the French and Belgium governments to remove all scattered graves for concentration in proper cemeteries, it has been found necessary to exhume the body of the late No. 92122 Pte. T N Witting, 19th Battalion, Durham Light Infantry, for re-burial at **DADIZEELE NEW BRITISH CEMETERY**, 9 miles East of Ypres.*
>
> *I am to say that the necessity for the removal is much regretted, but was found unavoidable for the reasons above given.*

> *I am to assure you that the work of reburial has been carried out with every measure or care and reverence, and that special arrangements were made for the appropriate religious service to be held.*
>
> *I am, Sir*
>
> *Yours faithfully*
>
> *For Colonel i/c. Infantry Record.*

Such post-war movements of the remains of British and Empire soldiers, was commonplace across both Belgium and France, as men were often buried close to where they were killed, or in makeshift graves that sprang up next to hospitals, Field Ambulance Units or Casualty Clearing Stations, near to where the fighting was at any given time.

On Monday, 29 April 1918 an inquest was held at Bridlington by the town's Coroner, Mr Herbert Brown, on Mr John Davis Hartley, a 46-year-old fish buyer from Scarborough.

The evidence showed that on 22 April Mr Hartley and a friend, Mr George Sutton, also a fish buyer from Scarborough, had been to Bridlington for the day on business and were travelling to their homes in Scarborough, on Mr Sutton's motor bike, Mr Hartley being the pillion passenger. During the journey, according to the newspaper report, 'something went wrong' and both men were thrown from the bike. Mr Sutton escaped without injury, whilst Mr Hartley landed on his head, fracturing his skull. He was taken to the Lloyd Hospital in Bridlington for treatment but died a week later on 29 April.

A verdict of accidental death was recorded. There was however, no explanation included in the article concerning the circumstances of how the accident had come about. Even though Mr Sutton had survived without injury, and based purely on the fact that it was not included in the article, he apparently did not provide an account at the inquest of how the crash had happened. Whether the accident was because the motor bike had veered off the road, had struck an object in its path, or because of the speed it was travelling at, was not explained.

Private 59910 Henry **Fox** of the 5th (Reserve) Battalion, Manchester Regiment, who was only 19 years of age, died on Sunday, 12 May 1918 when he fell from the cliffs at Cloughton, some seven miles north of Scarborough. He was in company with several other soldiers who were on the cliffs looking for seagull's eggs. He had already managed to find two and was looking for more when he lost his footing and fell down the steep cliff.

On Tuesday, 14 May 1918 Lance Corporal (240055) Geldart Williamson of the 5th Battalion, Border Regiment, told the inquest that whilst they had been on the cliffs the previous Sunday, Fox kept looking over the edge of the cliffs to see if he could spot any eggs. Lance Corporal Williamson repeatedly told him not to. Despite his protestations Fox replied, *'There is an egg down there, and I mean to get it.'* Williamson then took hold of Fox's shoulder and pulled him away from the cliff's edge. A short while later he looked back to where he had last seen Fox but could not see him. Then he was discovered at the bottom of the cliff and died of his injuries soon after.

A verdict of accidental death was returned. Fox was buried at Scarborough's, Dean Road Cemetery.

Williamson survived the war as did his younger brother Percy, who served, with the Westmorland and Cumberland Yeomanry, the Northumberland Yeomanry and the Corps of Hussars.

Before the war Richard **Harland** was a successful solicitor, who both worked and lived in the town. He was the Honorary Secretary of the Scarborough Liberal Association, the Honorary Solicitor of the Scarborough Townsmen's Association and the representative for Scarborough with the Humane Society. He was a man who was actively involved in a wide range of activities for the benefit of his community.

His mother Marie Harland, lived locally, at 'Poplar Villa', 165 Falsgrave Road. His father, Edward, who had been an auctioneer, valuer and estate agent, had died in 1896 at the relatively young age of 46, leaving Marie to bring up six children on her own. Edmund was the eldest, then came Sarah, followed by Albert, Walter, William and the youngest member of the family, Richard.

Richard had married in July 1914, just before the outbreak of the war, and lived with his wife Lily at 14 New Parks Crescent, Scarborough. He enlisted in the Army late in the war and was eventually sent out to France at the end of March 1918 with the 254th Siege Battery, Royal Garrison Artillery. After just eight weeks at the front he was killed in action on 16 June 1918 and was buried in the British Cemetery at the village of Morbecque, in the Nord region of France.

Wednesday, 17 July 1918 saw a hearing take place at Scarborough which concluded the application by Mrs Dawson of 10 Mulgrave Terrace, Scarborough, for a maintenance order to be made in her favour against her husband, James Holmes Dawson. Mr Dawson informed the court that he had paid about 30 shillings a week towards his wife's maintenance, but she countered that he had not paid her anything since the beginning of the year, and that on top of that, she had in fact kept him.

When cross-examined by his wife's solicitor, Mr Dawson admitted he had sent a parcel of meat, fowl and butter, the total value of which was estimated to be somewhere in the region of £2, to a lady referred to in court as, Mrs Bang.

He further admitted that Mrs Bang had written a letter to him addressed, *'My own love, Jimmie'*, which contained other sentences, including, *'I looked for a letter this morning, but was disappointed. I hope there is no trouble for you love, and that Ciss, Mrs Dawson, is not nasty. If she is, you know who is never cross with you, don't you love? Come as soon as you can.'*

It was suggested to him that his 'home' was in fact at Mrs Bang's house at Bramley, something which he strenuously denied. The magistrates granted Mrs Dawson a divorce, with Mr Dawson having to provide her the sum of ten shillings per week.

A letter, by an un-named author, appeared in the *Yorkshire Evening Post*, dated Thursday, 29 August 1918, on the topic of Scarborough as a holiday destination. Some of it was complimentary, some of it not so. It would appear that this wasn't the first letter this person had written in to the newspaper. Here is a flavour of what the individual concerned had written.

It began with a reference to a previous letter which had, apparently, been quite complimentary about the town of Scarborough. The author commenting that, *'In my last letter probably I gave the impression that I was looking at Scarborough and everything in it through rose tinted glasses.'*

If that was the case, then the second attempt was certainly a lot more balanced in its praise and criticism. Scarborough is described as being a pleasant and comfortable place to have a relaxing holiday, presumably because of its location, views, scenery and fresh, bracing sea air. But the target of the author's criticism was the town's outdoor, sea water swimming pool, or bathing pool as it was referred to back in 1918. The problem with an outdoor swimming pool at such a location is its reliance on the tide for changing the water in the pool, which then follows that if the open sea doesn't break over the wall of the pool, then the water inside it does not get changed, which leads to the potential risk of infection and sickness for those who use it, whilst the smell of the pungent water was not pleasant. If the smell was an indicator of the potential health risk that the water in the pool, if left unchanged, could cause, then unintentionally gulping down a mouthful of it, wouldn't exactly have been a re-assuring experience.

There was the added issue of vegetables growing amongst the rocks which surround the pool. In particular, during a period of warm weather when the demand to use the pool would be at a peak, the aroma given off by these vegetables was not pleasant. On some occasions it was so bad that some people were refusing to use the pool.

The other issue the author of the letter raised was that of pool attendants, or rather the lack of them in 1918. During the early years of the war, *'there was a man to keep observation of the bathers. This year, no doubt because of a labour shortage, there seems to be nobody in attendance.'* The point made was that if a bather got into difficulties whilst they were in the pool, there was no attendant present keeping an eye out for such eventualities.

Another issued discussed in the letter was bathing costumes and the different types that were in use at the time. It transpires that Scarborough Corporation actually issued male bathers with a particular type of costume that they had to wear. At the time mixed bathing was either not allowed, or certainly not the norm. By way of example, the Tooting Bec Lido in South London, which was an outside pool, did not allow mixed bathing until 1931, other locations still didn't allow mixed bathing until well in to the 1940s. Before then women and girls were allowed to use the pool only one morning a week.

The changing rooms, or what passed as such in 1918, were apparently not the most secure to be found. The 'dressing boxes', as they were referred to, could not be locked which made them an easy target for any would be thief. It seems that the best course of action was for bathers to take no money, jewellery or other valuable items with them when they wanted to play or swim in the water. Although it sounds like even bathers' clothes were at risk of being stolen if they ventured too far from their dressing box for long.

Scarborough's sea water bathing pool was opened in 1915 soon after the start of the First World War. It was a recreational pool, although its original purpose was for it to act as a wave barrier to protect the cliffs and coastline from the continuous battering of the rough seas, which could be a regular feature.

September 1918 saw an unusual case heard before the Scarborough County Court. There is the added oddity that one of those who is part of this story, is the brother of a man whom I have already written about earlier in this chapter. I was only aware of their connection when I started writing the latter of the two stories.

Private Tom Kidd was a soldier in the Army Service Corps and lived at 9 Stephenson's Buildings, High Street, Bridlington. He was in court to claim £100 from Mr Albert Edward Harland who used the trading name of Edward Harland & Sons, Auctioneers of Aberdeen Walk, Scarborough. The business had been started many years earlier by his father, Edward Harland.

Mr Kidd's case was that Mr Harland had purchased furniture from his wife and then sold it on. His point was that his wife, Mrs Kate Kidd, did not have the right to sell the furniture, in the first place.

Mr Stewart, the solicitor acting on behalf of Mr Kidd, told the court that his client had joined the Army in 1914 and served in Egypt, Salonika and Palestine. Whilst he was overseas serving his country, his wife took up with a man by the name of Rodwell who claimed he was a discharged soldier. He persuaded her to move to Scarborough, bringing all her furniture with her. She moved into 5 Spring Bank, Scarborough, which she had done so via Mr Harland. After only a week, Rodwell persuaded Mrs Kidd to sell the furniture and Mr Harland bought it from her for a total of £50. Rodwell kept £40 of the money with the remaining £10 going to Mrs Kidd. Since moving to Scarborough she had taken to using the name Mrs Rodwell so as not to create any suspicion about their relationship.

Soon after the furniture had been sold, Rodwell told Mrs Kidd that he had to go to the West Riding and that on his arrival he would contact her and let her know where he was staying, but he never did.

Mr Kidd told the court that the items which his wife had sold to Mr Harland, would cost him £100 to replace. It was pointed out that Mrs Kidd had signed a receipt, of her own free will, stating that the goods were hers to sell. Mr Harland told the court that he had acted, innocently, properly and professionally in his dealings with Mrs Kidd, taking her to be the wife of the man referred to as Mr Rodwell and that he had absolutely no reason to doubt the authenticity of her claim to be in a position to legally sell the furniture to him.

In summing up the Judge said that the matter before him was an unfortunate case, that one could not but help feeling a great deal of sympathy for Mr Harland and that he had even more sympathy for Mr Kidd. The real villain of the piece was the mysterious Mr Rodwell who had deceived Mrs Kidd. The ruling was in favour of Mr Kidd, with Mr Harland ordered to pay him the sum of £85.

There were in fact a total of forty-seven men with the surname of Rodwell who had been discharged from the Army on medical grounds and who had subsequently been awarded a Silver War Badge.

A slight irony in the case was that Tom Kidd had previously been an auctioneer's assistant, although afterwards he had worked as a groom. He had married Kate Elizabeth Tranmer on 1 September 1907 at the Primitive Methodist Chapel, Bridlington and they had three children, Florence, Kathleen and Albert.

He had volunteered in his home town of Bridlington on 3 November 1914 and become a private (4328) in the Army Service Corps. He went to Egypt with the Mediterranean Expeditionary Force, leaving England on 12 July 1915, as part of the Army Service Corps' Remounts Service and arriving at Alexandria two weeks later on 26 July. He remained in Egypt until 21 November 1915 when he sailed for Salonica, arriving there two days later. He remained in Salonica for nearly two years until 6 July 1917, when he embarked on the troop ship *Menominee* then moved back to Egypt, arriving in Alexandria on 10 July 1917. Six days later he was admitted to the 31st General Hospital in Alexandria, having been diagnosed with malaria, where he remained until 9 August 1917. But twelve days later he was once again struck down with malaria and was admitted to the 24th Stationary Hospital for further treatment, where he remained until 3 September. Having finally recovered from his sickness, he remained in Egypt for a further four months before leaving on board the same vessel on 18 December 1917. He finally arrived back in England on 10 January 1918, where he was given a three-week furlough on compassionate grounds, one assumes because of his domestic circumstances having discovered his wife's affair with Rodwell.

Attached to Private Kidd's Army Service Record is the following letter sent by his solicitor to the officer in charge of records at Woolwich and dated 19 January 1918.

Sir,

I am desired by Private Tom Kidd No. 4328 of the 40th Remount Squadron, Egyptian Expeditionary Force, who is now home on leave, to write and ask you if it is possible to have his leave extended. Private Kidd was given 21 days leave in the United Kingdom and he arrived in England on the 10th instant and his leave will expire on the 31st inst.

Private Kidd was given special leave in the following circumstances. While Private Kidd has been abroad, his wife came under the influence of another man who persuaded her to sell all the furniture and other effects belonging to Private Kidd in connection with his business and break up the home and go away with him. This man got all the money and subsequently deserted the wife, leaving her stranded. In addition, this man appears to have forged Private Kidd's signature and so enable the wife to withdraw the money from the Bank, standing to the credit of Private Kidd. This money the man got.

Altogether Private Kidd has lost about £200 under circumstances which make it quite possible that he will be able to recover the whole or the greater part of the value of the furniture and effects from those who have bought them from the thief, and the amount of the money from the bank who have paid it out on a forged order.

These proceedings will take time and it is impossible to carry them on without Private Kidd's presence, and I write to know whether it is possible to obtain an extension of leave to try and bring these matters to a conclusion and recover what he has lost.

It would answer the purpose if he could be given duty in England, where he would be available when wanted and it would not be necessary for him to be on leave all the time.

I am sure the circumstances will have your sympathy. Financially, Private Kidd has been robbed of all his *savings and when he comes out of the Army he will start with absolutely nothing. His wife has also been ruined in a domestic sense, and it is desirable that he should be allowed to remain at home to see what arrangements can be made to remake the home and this, particularly for the sake of the children. I believe the wife is thoroughly repentant. Until this happened I understand not the slightest reflection could be made upon her character, and it is one of those cases where a woman seems to have become hopelessly infatuated with a man.*

The wife has been an excellent mother to the children and still is, and Private Kidd says they are still being splendidly looked after by her. In fact there seems every chance, given time, the home can be remade and the family united again.

If you are not in a position to grant leave, I shall be much obliged if you will inform me to whom I ought to write.

I am, Sir,

Your obedient servant

William J Stuart (Solicitor).

On 19 March 1918 Private Kidd was admitted to the 2nd Western General Hospital in Manchester to be treated for syphilis. He remained in hospital for thirty-six days before being released, but it would appear that he still did not have a clean bill of health as he had to go to a hospital in Bury as an out patient for an unspecified period of time. Whether or not his wife Kate knew of his infection is not known.

Private Tom Kidd was finally demobbed from the Army at Ripon, Yorkshire on 1 March 1919.

On Monday, 7 October 1918 at Scarborough Magistrates Court, Frederick Watkin David Jones, a deserter from the RAMC, was sent to prison for three months with hard labour for wearing Army badges and decorations without authority. He was wearing a discharge badge belonging to a Scarborough man which had been taken from a jacket at premises where Jones had been employed. He wore one red and three blue service stripes and three gold wound stripes although he had never been out of England. He was not entitled to the red service stripe, having joined the Army in 1916 and deserted in February.

The chairman said it was a gross case of deceit. After serving his imprisonment he would be further remanded to await escort, on the charge of being a deserter. He pleaded guilty to both charges.

In November 1918 within a matter of weeks of the signing of the Armistice, Scarborough found itself embroiled in the thick of the political arena, with the new parliamentary seat of Scarborough and Whitby coming into being as part of the North Riding of Yorkshire division. The new seat came about as a result of the Representation of the People Act 1918, after the Boundary Commission of 1917, albeit a somewhat strange moment in time to form such a body during a time of war when its final outcome was far from clear. Prior to the formation of the new constituency there had previously been three parliamentary seats which covered the same area: Scarborough, Whitby and part of Cleveland. The new Scarborough and Whitby seat covered an area with a population of about 73,000.

Mr Rowntree, the former Liberal member, had changed sides and accepted the Labour nomination to be its new Member of Parliament. The Hon. Gervase Beckett, represented the Coalition Conservative Party and had been the previous Member of Parliament for Whitby since 1906. The 1918 General Election saw those newly selected MPs being elected to Parliament on 14 December. Beckett was duly elected to represent the newly formed parliamentary seat, his previous military service no doubt helping his constituents decide who best to vote for.

When asked what people should expect from peace, he replied that in the first instance the expectation should surely be that the history of the previous four years, should not be repeated.

CHAPTER 7

VAD Nurses from Scarborough

There were an estimated 90,000 volunteers who carried out a plethora of roles for the British Red Cross during the First World War, including nursing, transport and cookery. Branches of the organisation were set up across the country, with each of these groups being known as Voluntary Aid Detachments, or better known by the abbreviation of VAD. Those men and

VAD Nurses.

women who were members of these groups were often referred to as VADs.

Women who wished to work as nurses were required to have been taught first aid and passed an exam. They also needed lessons in medical hygiene. It took a while for these well meaning volunteers to be taken seriously by the authorities, the military and the established professional nursing organisations, which led to an initial reluctance for them to be allowed to work in hospitals and involved in the overall treatment of wounded soldiers. Thankfully this attitude, and in some cases outright snobbery, abated and Voluntary Aid Detachments and the volunteers that came with them were accepted, albeit in some cases, begrudgingly, into the mainstream of wartime hospital and medical care, both throughout the UK and in many of the foreign theatres of war.

The following is a list of men and women from the Scarborough area who worked for Voluntary Aid Detachments during the war. There will have been others, not from the Scarborough area, who also worked in the town's wartime hospitals, but I have not to included them, even though their

Wounded soldiers being delivered.

efforts were no less important. My apologies to anybody I have inadvertently missed off the list.

Miss Mary Kathleen **Abraham** was 22 years of age when she first enlisted in the VAD on 16 February 1919 and she was still serving as late as 9 May 1919. She worked as a full-time nurse at the 2nd West General Hospital. Her home was at 22 Prospect Road, Scarborough.

Mary's sister, Miss Norah Inglis Symond **Abraham** started working for the VAD just before her sister on 1 February 1919. She too was employed as a nurse at the 2nd West General Hospital, Manchester and she also finished working for them on 9 May 1919, the same day as her sister.

Both of the girls, like their parents, William and Mary Abraham, were Australian by birth, born in the state of Victoria.

Mr James F. **Allan** lived at Norwood Street, Scarborough. He began working for the Scarborough Ambulance Division of the No.6 Northern District, St John Ambulance Brigade, on an 'as and when required' basis. He finished his commitment with them some time in late 1918.

Mr Bertrand **Allanson** lived at Cloughton, Scarborough with his parents, William and Mary Allanson, his elder sister Cordelia, and his younger brother, Erskine. Bertrand, started working for the VAD as a night porter at Cober Hill Hospital on 25 November 1914. His is an interesting story. Bertrand, enlisted in the Army the very next day at Richmond, in Yorkshire, becoming a Bandsman (5/43679) in the 80th Training Reserve Battalion, having been a music teacher before enlisting. He was discharged from the Army under paragraph 392 (xvi), no longer being physically fit enough for wartime military service. He then started working for the VAD again, once again as a night porter at Cober Hill Hospital, before finally finishing there on 29 March 1919.

Miss Edith Dorothy **Allen** lived at 6 Avenue Victoria, Scarborough. She worked for the East Yorkshire VAD (No.6) as a nurse, initially at the 3rd Northern General Hospital at Sheffield from 9 September 1916, where she stayed until 12 July 1917. Having volunteered for overseas service, she was then sent to

France, where she worked at the 59th General (Military) Hospital at St Omer, where she remained until 9 December 1917. From there she was sent to work at the Abbeyville No.2 Stationary Hospital for six months until 13 June 1918, when she moved yet again, this time to No.14 Stationary Hospital at Wimereux, where she was still working on 26 March 1919.

Miss Rachel **Appleyard** lived at 64 Royal Avenue, Scarborough. She spent a total of nine years working for the VAD between 1910 and 1919, with most of that time spent at the Royal Northern Sea Bathing VAD Infirmary in Scarborough, during which time she was attached to the York's 22 section, part of the North Riding Division of the VAD. Rachel's sister, Miss Sarah **Appleyard**, had the exact same story.

The girls' father, George Appleyard, was a retired harbour master, yet none of his three sons had followed in his footsteps. His eldest, Thomas, owned and ran a tobacconist shop. John, was an apprentice electrician, whilst Allan was still a student. There were at least fifteen men with the name Thomas Appleyard who served in the First World War, with at least three of them being in regiments that had obvious Yorkshire connections, not that he would have necessarily served in any one of those regiments. At least thirty-one men who served in the First World War, had the name John Appleby. There was an Allan Appleyard who was a Private (2092) in the 5th Battalion, Yorkshire Regiment, who landed in France on 18 April 1915. On the balance of probabilities, and taking in to account the 5th Battalion's connection to Scarborough, there is every reason to believe that this is one and the same person. Either way, both individuals survived the war.

Miss Eleanor **Atty** lived at 3 Bellesdene Road, Scarborough. She had a long and varied service with the VAD, which she worked for between 1913 and 1919 as a voluntary nurse. This included working at the Royal Northern Sea Bathing Infirmary in Scarborough, the Barracks Hospital in Scarborough, the St Lucas Military Hospital, Bradford and the Officers' Hospital in Scarborough. She was one of those allocated to the York's 22 section VAD of the North Riding district.

Miss Dora **Baker** lived at Culworth Lodge, Scarborough. She spent nine years working part-time for the VAD, beginning in 1910, and was part of the York 22 VAD section. She was involved mainly in depot related work in Scarborough. Dora's sister, Miss Elizabeth **Baker**, had a similar service record, which differed in so far as she had also been a nurse at the Royal Naval, Sea Bathing VAD Hospital in Scarborough.

Mr James Hedley **Baker** lived at 25 Manor Road, Scarborough. He began working for the VAD on 28 April 1917 as a chauffeur. His service card had no detailed information about what his work entailed or where it was carried out. The First World War Service Medal and Award Rolls, records a James Hedley Baker, a member of the British Red Cross and Order of St John, attached to HM Hospital Ship *Glenart Castle* between 30 August 1916 and 7 March 1919, even though the vessel was sunk on 26 February 1918, when she was torpedoed by the German submarine, *UC-56*.

Mrs Annie Jane **Bakewell** lived at Scalby near Scarborough. She worked for the VAD at Scarborough from the outbreak of the war until December 1917. She was mainly employed as a home worker, engaged in hospital-related knitting and needlework.

Mr John R. **Barton** lived at 71 Caledonia Street, Scarborough. He began working for the Scarborough Ambulance Division of the St John Ambulance Brigade, on an 'as when required' basis. This was usually when wounded Allied soldiers arrived in the town, or wounded soldiers needed transporting from one of the town's numerous hospitals and taken to the railway station or other location. He was still carrying out this work on 16 October 1919.

Miss Maud **Bastiman** lived at 70 Victoria Road, Scarborough. She began working with the VAD as a part-time unpaid voluntary nurse in March 1917. She was still working in the same capacity on 3 May 1919 by which time she was at the Military Hospital, Burniston Road, Scarborough.

Miss Ida **Battle** lived at 2 Esplanade Crescent, Scarborough. She began working for the local VAD in October 1917, as an unpaid voluntary masseuse, for which she was fully qualified. She was still serving on 3 May 1919 when she was working at the Military Hospital, Burniston Road, Scarborough.

Mrs Janet **Bayes** lived at 37 Mayville Avenue, Scarborough. She was a full-time cook and had been since January 1917, finishing on 3 May 1919, when she was working at the Military Hospital, Burniston Road, Scarborough.

Mr John W. **Beedle** lived at Cloughton, Scarborough and worked at Cober Hill Hospital as a voluntary night orderly between 1 August 1916 and 7 March 1919.

Mr Harold Gladstone **Binns** lived at 61 Esplanade, Scarborough and during the First World War he worked as a voluntary orderly for the Friends Ambulance Unit, between 18 February 1916 and 15 January 1919. At the time of the 1911 Census Harold's family were recorded as living at 94 Prospect Road, Scarborough. His parents, George and Emily Binns, had three other children, daughters, Victoria and Violet and elder son Edward.

Miss Clara **Blackburn** lived at 2 Belvedere Road, Scarborough. She worked for the VAD as a probationary nurse, did a certain amount of cooking and was also a store keeper, all of which were carried out unpaid and voluntary. She worked at the following medical establishments: The Red Cross Hospital, Foxborough Hall, Melton; the 3rd Military Hospital, Westborough, Scarborough; the Great Hermitage Hospital and the Weston House Red Cross Hospital Scarborough.

As was quite often the way, many families had more than one daughter working for the VAD during the First World War, so strong was the desire by many, to do their bit for their country and the war effort. Her sister, Miss Phoebe **Blackburn**, lived at the same address and also worked for the VAD as a probationary nurse. She started in December 1914 and was still working in the same capacity by 3 May 1919 at the Military Hospital, Burniston Road, Scarborough.

Miss Mary **Blakey** lived at 9 Albemarle Crescent, Scarborough. The 1911 Census shows that she was only a visitor to this address. After staying there for eight years, she obviously liked the area and decided to stay just a little bit longer than she had originally planned. The house was owned by retired farmer, Thomas Collinson and his wife, Elna. She worked as a full-time VAD nurse, in charge of surgery, from 25 November 1914 all the way through until 25 March 1919. This included working at both the Cober Hill Hospital, Cloughton, Scarborough, and the Royal Naval Sea Bathing Infirmary at Scarborough.

Miss Hilda **Bolton** lived at 21 Victoria Avenue, Scarborough. She was an unpaid, part-time, probationer nurse working for the VAD, starting out in the early months of the war in December 1914 and still serving on 3 May 1919. She began at the 3rd Military Hospital, Westborough, Scarborough, before moving on to the Weston House Red Cross Hospital and finally ending up at the Military Hospital, Burniston Road, Scarborough.

Miss Mabel **Botterill** lived at Garton House, Cromwell Parade, Scarborough, with her parents and three sisters, Ethel, Blanche and Gertrude. She worked as a VAD nurse for two years between 1917 and 1919 as part of the York's 22 VAD. Her time was spent at the Cober Hill Hospital, Cloughton, Scarborough. Mabel had an older brother, Arthur Botterill, who served during the first World War. A married man with two young sons, he enlisted on 10 December 1915 at York, becoming a Private (35255) in the West Yorkshire Regiment. He was discharged from the Army on 31 March 1917, his services being no longer required under King's Regulations, paragraph 392 (xxv), although there was no detailed explanation for this decision.

Miss Lena **Bouts** lived at 26 Huntriss Row, Scarborough. She was a member of the Middlesex 64 VAD and worked as an unpaid nurse at the Syon House, Red Cross Hospital at Brentford. Her service card doesn't include exactly which years she worked for the VAD.

Mr Jackson **Bower** lived at Cloughton, Scarborough whilst working for the North Riding VAD between 1 August 1916 and 7 March 1919. He was a night orderly at Cober Hill Hospital in Cloughton. Mr Jackson, was the foreman at High Farm, Burniston, Cloughton, owned by John Mennell Cockerill, and one of the other workers was Jackson's younger brother, Thomas.

Miss Ethel Mary **Cadman** lived at Willersley, Scarborough. She began as a probationary, part-time, unpaid nurse in December 1914, working at the Weston House, Red Cross Hospital in Scarborough until July 1915. Although not clear on her service card, it would appear that she took some time out, before recommencing her nursing duties on 29 September 1916 at Rubery Hill Military Hospital in Birmingham where she stayed until July 1917. The hospital was originally built as the Birmingham Lunatic Asylum in 1892. In 1915 the asylum's patients were moved out to the St Edwards County Asylum at Cheddleton, with Rubery Hill becoming the 1st Birmingham War Hospital. It was a massive location, capable of caring for 1,100 patients at any one time. During the course of the war 20,000 wounded soldiers were patients on its wards.

By the time that the British Red Cross began amassing the information for its First World War staff records, it would appear that Miss Agnes **Cain** was a patient at the Scarborough Sanatorium. During the war she was a Sister with the Queen Alexandra's Imperial Military Nursing Service (QAIMNS), beginning in 1914. She had been sent out to France early in the war with the British Expeditionary Force as part of the York's 22 VAD section. Many times she had endured German artillery bombardments which eventually resulted in her being invalided home suffering from shell shock in 1918.

Miss Gwendolin **Catley** lived at 16 Ramshill Road, Scarborough. She had begun working for the York's 22 VAD section as far back as 1913, eventually leaving in the aftermath of the war in May 1919. During her time, she worked as a voluntary part-time nurse at Cober Hill Hospital, Cloughton, the Barracks Hospital Scarborough and the Royal Northern Sea Bathing VAD Infirmary, also in Scarborough.

Mrs Emily **Catt** lived at 3 Pavilion Terrace, Scarborough. She started out as an unpaid probationary nurse in December 1914 at the 3rd Military Hospital, Westborough, as well as at the Weston House Red Cross Hospital, both in Scarborough, and by May 1919 she was working at the Military Hospital, Burniston Road, Scarborough.

Emily's daughter, Miss Margery **Catt**, also worked in a nursing capacity, although she only held a certificate in basic First Aid rather than actual nursing. Between 17 January and 19 December 1918 she worked as a masseuse as part of the Middlesex 38 VAD section, of the Prince of Wales's Hospital for Officers, in Staines, Middlesex.

Miss Ady Edith **Chambers** lived at 64 Gladstone Road, Scarborough. She was a member of the York's 22 VAD section and worked at the Barracks Hospital, the Officers' Hospital and the Royal Northern Sea Bathing Infirmary, all of which were in Scarborough. She was on duty at the time of the German naval bombardment on 16 December 1914.

Mrs Edith Mary **Clare** lived at 2 South Street, Scarborough. She held the rank of Superintendent of the York's 22 VAD section and was involved in the training of staff. She worked for the VAD unpaid between 1914 and 1919. Edith's husband John was a chemist with his own shop. They had a boarder, George Henry Sebring, who was John's assistant, and a servant Isabel Rennison who did the cooking.

Mr James William **Clark** lived at 82 High Field, Falsgrave, Scarborough and worked full-time on the 'Medical Board'. His service card, does not include much in the way of detailed information of where and when he worked. He did not begin working in his position until 19 November 1918, eight days after the signing of the Armistice.

Miss Lois **Clarke** lived at 'Boa Vista', Scalby, Scarborough. She was an unpaid, probationer nurse, who worked at the Military Hospital, Burniston Road, Scarborough between March 1917 and 3 May 1919.

Miss Gwyneth **Cliff** lived at 6 Lonsdale Road, Scarborough. She was a VAD nurse, working with the London 96 section of the St John Ambulance Brigade, between 7 November 1914 and 3 May 1919. She started out at the Gifford House Auxiliary Hospital in Roehampton and was there until May 1915, after which she went to France with the British Expeditionary Force, where she spent most of her time with the No.18 Stationary Hospital. She was still serving as late as 19 May 1919.

Mr Harold **Cliffe** lived at Rothbury Street, Scarborough and worked with the No.6 Northern District, Scarborough Ambulance Division of the St John Ambulance Brigade between 16 May 1916 and 1919. He was called upon 'as and when' he was needed for ambulance related work in and around the Scarborough area, ferrying wounded soldiers to and from other hospitals and the railway station.

Mr Joseph **Coates** lived at Burniston Road, Cloughton, Scarborough. Between 25 November 1914 and 15 March 1919 he was the quartermaster at the town's Cober Hill Hospital. He also helped out as a night time hospital orderly and was in charge of the dressing station in case of there being a German invasion. In his day time job Joseph was an insurance agent. He was a married man with a young child.

Miss Violet **Cobbs** lived at 7 West Street, Scarborough. She worked for the York's 22 VAD section as a part-time nurse between 1916 and 1919 at the Officers' Hospital in Scarborough.

Mr Harold **Cole** lived at Market Street, Scarborough and worked for the Scarborough Ambulance Division of the No.6 Northern District of the St John Ambulance Brigade. He was used on an 'as and when required' basis. He was still working for them in 1919.

Mrs Doris **Collier** lived at 27 Moorland Road, Scarborough and worked for the VAD between 15 July 1916 and 1 August 1917, as a nurse and a cook. She worked at the following locations between the following dates: Weston House Hospital Scarborough 07/12/14 to 29/08/15; Bethnal Green Military Hospital 15/07/16 to 01/08/17; The Military Hospital Scarborough 04/03/18 to 21/07/18. Doris worked as a nurse at the first and third locations and as a cook at Bethnal Green.

Miss Elsie Cutsworth **Collins** lived at 22 Ramshill Road, Scarborough, and worked for the York's 12 VAD section between 26 April 1917 and 14 June 1919. She worked as a nurse at the Military Hospital in Tooting between 26 April 1917 and

26 November 1917 and the Military Hospital York between 1 January 1918 and 14 June 1919.

Miss Marianne Isabel **Coombes** lived at 8 St Nicholas Street, Scarborough and worked for the York's 66 VAD section as a nurse between 10 March 1916 and 24 June 1917, although her service card does not give any details of where she was located.

Miss Mary V. **Coopland** lived at 71 Newborough, Scarborough. She was a voluntary part-time nurse between 7 December 1914 and 26 March 1919. Initially she worked at the Weston House Hospital until 29 August 1915. It would appear that she then had a break of nearly two years, before she began working at the Military Hospital, Burniston Road, Scarborough on 25 June 1917 and was still there at 26 March 1919.

Mrs Laura **Copplethwaite** lived at 2 The Crescent, Scarborough. Between October 1914 and 3 May 1919 she served as an unpaid probationer nurse at both the Royal Northern Sea Bathing VAD Infirmary and the Military Hospital, Burniston Road, Scarborough.

Miss Margaret **Costello** lived at 31 Rothbury Street, Scarborough. She worked for the York's 22 VAD section between October 1918 and February 1919 at the Officers' Hospital, Scarborough as a full-time head cook. The 1911 Census shows Margaret working as a cook at The College, Scarborough, in the capacity of a servant.

Mr Thomas **Coulson** lived at Silphs, Scarborough. Between 25 November 1914 and 15 March 1919, he worked as a voluntary section leader at the Cober Hill Hospital, Cloughton, Scarborough. He also covered as a night orderly as and when required to do so.

Miss Alice **Cowton** lived at St Thomas Vicarage, Scarborough. She worked for the VAD between 1 December 1914 and 2 January 1917 as a full-time voluntary head cook at the Cober Hill Hospital, Cloughton, Scarborough.

Miss Helen Cecilia **Crawhall** lived at the Ganton Vicarage, Scarborough. She worked as a sister for the York's 32 VAD section at the 16th Durham VAD Hospital, Shotley House,

Shotley Bridge, but for only two months between 17 October and 31 December 1918.

Mr Robert M.B. **Cuff** lived at Esplanade Road, Scarborough. He was a medical officer and lecturer on first aid, nursing and hygiene. He worked on a voluntary basis between 1913 and 1919 for the York's 22 VAD section, and for his important work he was made an honorary life member of the British Red Cross. A general practitioner by profession, he had previously resided at 40 Filey Road, Scarborough, a single man with two servants.

Miss Natalie Vera **Cursham** lived at Trinity Road, Scarborough. She worked for the York's 22 VAD section as a full-time waitress at the Officers' Hospital in Scarborough between 1918 and 1919. She was paid a wage of 24 shillings per week. She lived with her grandmother, Sarah Anne Hamburger, a woman of 'private means', Sarah's sister Caroline Clapham, along with three servants.

Miss Amy Augusta **Dale** lived at 1 New Parks Crescent, Scarborough. She began working as a VAD nurse on 7 December 1914 and was still serving as of 26 March 1919. Her places of work were the 25th Durham VAD Hospital, Ashburne, Sunderland, the Highfield Auxiliary Hospital, Norton, Malton and the Military Hospital, Scarborough. She was also the secretary to the York's 80 section of the North Riding VAD. Amy was awarded three white service bars, due to her five-year wartime service.

Her sister, Miss Margery **Dale**, also began her wartime service as a voluntary VAD nurse on 7 December 1914. Her first post was at Highfield Auxiliary Hospital, Norton, Malton. The other hospitals she worked at included Weston House Hospital, Scarborough, the 25th Durham VAD Hospital in Ryhope Road, Ashburne, Sunderland and the Military Hospital in Burniston Road, Scarborough. Her last day as a VAD nurse was on 24 June 1917.

Although her VAD service card recorded her name as Margery Dale, her actual name was Helen Marjorie Dale. Marjorie and Amy lived with their widowed mother, Catherine Dale. There was a third sister, Jessie, who died in 1894 aged 24.

They also had an older brother, Sydney Dale, who was a married man with three children and by the outbreak of the war, was living in Manchester and working as an electrical engineer and draughtsman. Their father, Benjamin Hague Dale, who was 21 years older than his wife, Catherine, had passed away on 8 August 1887.

Mr Edwin **Davy** lived at 27 Westbourne Grove, Scarborough and was an engineer by profession. It was in this capacity that he worked for the VAD in Mesopotamia between 15 August 1916 and 1 May 1919, as a motor launch engineer. At the start of his role he was earning £2 per week and by the time he had left and returned to England he was earning £3 10 shillings per week.

Miss Ethel **Dawson** lived at 17 Holbeck Hill, Scarborough and during the First World War she was a volunteer nurse who worked for the York's 22 VAD Section at both the Royal Northern Sea Bathing Infirmary, in Foreshore Road, and the Officers' Hospital in Scarborough. She was a VAD nurse for seven years between 1912 and 1919.

Miss Grace **Dawson** lived at 29 Esplanade Gardens, Scarborough. She worked as a voluntary nurse for the York's West Riding 66 VAD section for 18 months between 16 September 1916 and 30 December 1917. During this time she was at the Oswestry Military Hospital between 19 September 1918 and 16 April 1917 and the Royal Naval Hospital at Chatham between 29 June 1917 and 30 December 1917.

Miss Ida **Dawson** lived at 5 Barwick Terrace, Scarborough. She worked for the York's 22 VAD section as a qualified nurse between 1912 and 26 March 1919. She was at the Royal Northern Sea Bathing Infirmary in Foreshore Road, Scarborough between 1914 and 1916 and was on duty on 16 December 1914 when the hospital was hit by three artillery shells fired from ships of the German Imperial Navy, positioned 10 miles out in the North Sea. She also worked at the Royal Chelsea Military Hospital and was at work during every raid on London by either German Zeppelins and Gotha bombers and did not once leave her post.

Mrs Elizabeth **Dennis** lived at 117 Trafalgar Square, Scarborough. During her wartime experience as a voluntary

VAD NURSES FROM SCARBOROUGH 149

Bagthorpe Military Hospital Nottingham.

3rd General Hospital Sheffield.

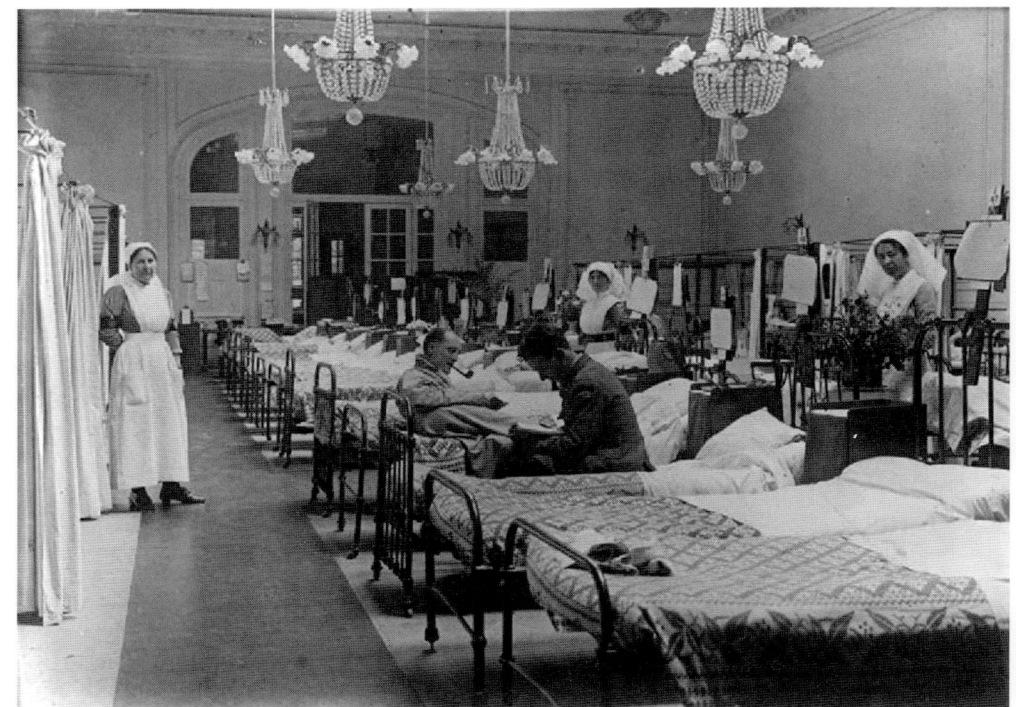

Duchess of Westminster Hospital Le Touquet.

nurse, she worked at the Bagthorpe Military Hospital in Nottingham, between 31 May 1916 and 30 June 1917, before moving on to the 3rd Northern Hospital in Sheffield, between 24 October 1917 and 17 April 1918.

Mr Jas Reid **Dick** lived at 4 Filey Road, Scarborough. He served as both a medical officer and a lieutenant with the British Red Cross Society at the Duchess of Westminster Hospital in Le Touquet, France. He served for five months between 24 July 1915 and 25 December 1915.

Miss Ada E. **Ellis** lived at Granville Square, Scarborough. She served as a voluntary VAD nurse with York's 92 VAD section between 11 September 1915 and 23 October 1917. Initially she worked at the Military Hospital in Egypt until 30 March 1916. On her return to the United Kingdom, she began working at the Military Hospital at Kinmel Park, in Rhyl, Wales.

Miss Christine **Eyre** lived at 14 Park Avenue, Scarborough. She was a member of the York's 22 VAD section and served as a nurse at the Royal Northern Sea Bathing Infirmary in Foreshore Road, Scarborough between 1910 and 1919.

Mrs Margaret **Farrar** lived at Harley Street, Scarborough. Between 7 December 1914 and 29 August 1915 she worked as a voluntary cook at the Weston House, Hospital, Scarborough, and then between 18 June 1917 and 26 March 1919 she served as a voluntary nurse at the Military Hospital, Burniston Road, Scarborough.

Mr Edward **Fenwick** lived at 13 Harley Street, Scarborough. During the First World War, between October 1914 and 16 October 1919, he worked for the Scarborough Ambulance Division, which was part of No.6 Northern District, St John Ambulance Brigade. As well as driving ambulances, he also helped out during air raids and with pier related duties, on an 'as and when required' basis.

Miss Irene **Field** lived at 135 Columbus Ravine, Scarborough. She became a part-time, volunteer probationary nurse in June 1918, working at the Military Hospital, Burniston Road, Scarborough. She was still there as of 3 May 1919.

Miss Dorothy **Foster** (Mrs Melvill) lived at Wynbrook, Scalby, Scarborough. Between November 1914 and August 1915 she was a voluntary ward nurse at Hovingham Hall Hospital, Malton, Yorkshire.

Miss Jeanette **Fowler** lived at Langford House, Westwood, Scarborough. In November 1916 she started working for the VAD as a voluntary probationer nurse at the Military Hospital, Burniston Road, Scarborough and was still there as of 3 May 1919.

Miss Hilda **Garbutt** lived at 2 New Parks Crescent, Scarborough. Between 7 December 1914 and 29 August 1915 she worked as a voluntary VAD nurse at the Weston Hospital and the General Hospital, both of which were in Scarborough.

Miss Clara **Gaunt** lived at Wheatcroft Avenue, Scarborough. She worked at the Military Hospital, Burniston Road, Scarborough, as an unpaid probationer nurse between February 1918 and 3 May 1919.

Mr Benjamin Wilson **Gibson**, lived at 19 Harley Street, Scalby Road, Scarborough. Between 14 August 1916 and 4 April 1919 he was a motor launch engineer, working in Mesopotamia. He was Mentioned in Despatches, as reported in *The Times* on 22 February 1919.

Miss Rose **Gilbert** lived at 6 Grange Avenue, Scarborough and between 9 November 1916 and March 1919 she worked as a nurse for the VAD at medical establishments in Grimsby, Egypt and Herne Bay.

Mrs Janet Elizabeth **Giles** lived at 4 Filey Road, Scarborough. She was a nursing sister between 27 December 1914 and 1 October 1916. She was then promoted to matron and continued in that capacity from 2 October 1916 until 31 January 1918, at the Duchess of Westminster Hospital at Étaples in France. She was Mentioned in Despatches on 29 May 1917 and was awarded the Royal Red Cross 2nd Class military decoration on 1 January 1918.

Dr Leonard Thomason **Giles** was the husband of Janet Giles, and was a surgeon with the VAD between 5 November 1914 and 4 May 1916.

Miss Violet M. **Godfrey** lived at 5 Montpelier Terrace, Scarborough. She was a VAD nurse between 27 November 1915 and June 1916 at the Military Hospital in Malta and between 26 August 1916 to 26 March 1917 at the 4th London General Hospital, Denmark Hill.

Mrs Annie **Goule** lived at 26 Nanson Street, Scarborough. Between October 1914 and May 1917 she was the part-time cook at the Red Cross Auxiliary Hospital, Skegness, as part of the North Lincoln Red Cross No. 48 section.

Miss Jane Ann **Graham** lived at 24 Avenue Victoria, Scarborough. She started working for the VAD in 1915 but her service card doesn't show when she stopped working for them. Her main job appears to have been bandage making along with some nursing.

Miss Blanche Louise **Hargreaves** lived at 5 Alma Square, Scarborough. Between 2 January 1917 and 15 March 1919 she worked as a full-time VAD Nurse at the Cober Hill Hospital,

Cloughton, Scarborough. Her sister, Miss Norah **Hargreaves**, worked at the same hospital as the head cook between 13 October 1917 and 15 March 1919.

Mrs Lily Curlew **Harland** lived at 14 New Parks Crescent, Scarborough. She worked as a full-time nurse at the Red Cross Hospital at Masham, Yorkshire, between 16 September 1918 and 26 March 1919. She had also lived at 64 Falsgrave Road, Scarborough.

Miss Gertrude **Harrison** lived at 141a Victoria Road, Scarborough. Between 27 June 1916 and 5 February 1919 she worked as a full-time VAD nurse at the 2nd Northern General Military Hospital, Beckett's Park, Leeds. She had previously worked as a part-time nurse at the Weston House Hospital, Scarborough.

Her sister Miss Mabel **Harrison** also worked for the VAD during the war, as a chauffeuse at an unnamed military hospital in France between 29 August 1919 and 21 January 1920.

Mr Wallace **Harrison** lived at 7 Elder Street, Scarborough. He initially worked as a cook for the British Red Cross, Unit No.5, based in Boulogne, France, for less than two months between 29 October and 14 December 1914. He returned to Boulogne on 18 May 1915 in the same capacity and remained there until 22 January 1919.

Mr James W. **Hawkins** lived at Garfield Road, Scarborough. He worked for the Scarborough Ambulance Division of the No.8 District of the St John Ambulance Brigade between 9 June 1916 and 16 October 1919. His job was in transport and he worked 'as and when' he was required to do so.

Miss Edith Myrtle Letitia **Heffer** lived at Belgrave House, Westbourne Park, Scarborough. She worked for the VAD as a nurse between 3 May 1917 and 15 March 1919, at the Cober Hill Hospital, Cloughton, Scarborough.

Miss Alice **Hick** lived at 32 Westbourne Grove, Scarborough. In December 1914 she began working as an unpaid, part-time probationary nurse at the 3rd Military Hospital, Westborough, Scarborough, as well as at the town's Weston House Red Cross Hospital. Her last position was at the Military Hospital,

Burniston Road, Scarborough where she was still working in May 1919.

Mr Mark Ray **Hick** lived at 7 Westbourne Grove, Scarborough. He was 34 years of age when he began his short career working as a volunteer for the British Red Cross Society's Motor Ambulance Department, between February and May 1915.

Mr Norman Walker **Hick** lived at Athol House, Fulford Road, Scarborough. He had the remarkable job title of 'Searcher'. This involved him going out into no man's land and other locations where there had been fighting, to search for wounded or missing men. His time working with the VAD is shown on his service card as having commenced on 14 November 1917 but it does not show when he finished.

Mrs H.F. **Hill** lived at Morningside, Newby, Scarborough. She was another who had a short time working for the VAD, in fact less than one month, between 13 January and 11 February 1916. She was unpaid and mainly worked from home making garments and other medical related clothing.

Mrs Jessie **Holgate** lived at 30 Ashville Avenue, Scarborough. She was a voluntary VAD nurse between 7 December 1914 and 26 March 1919. She worked a total of 4,260 hours at the Weston House Hospital and the Military Hospital, both of which were in Scarborough.

Miss Kate **Holmes** lived at 57 Gladstone Street, Scarborough. For the five years between December 1914 and March 1919, she worked as part-time nurse at the Military Hospital, Burniston Road, Scarborough.

Miss M. Kathleen **Hornby** lived at 7 New Parks Crescent, Scarborough. She worked as a voluntary VAD cook between 7 December 1914 and 29 August 1915 at the Weston House Hospital, Scarborough.

Mrs Eva Mary **Humpleby** lived at 63 Garfield Road, Scarborough. She was a 'house member' for the VAD between 14 May and 16 June 1917 at the Military Hospital at Eaton Hall in Chester.

Mr Richard P. **Hutton** lived at Dean Road, Scarborough. He was a VAD member who was utilised as an ambulance driver on an 'as and when required' basis. He was part of the Scarborough Ambulance division which was in turn part of the No.6 Northern District of the St John Ambulance Brigade. He served between 3 June 1917 and 16 October 1919.

Miss Alice **Jacklin** lived at 11 Trafalgar Square, Scarborough. She worked for the VAD from the outbreak of the war all the way through until the end of the war and beyond as an unpaid volunteer. She filled the roles of both Superintendent and Commandant during her war-time service with the VAD. This included being the Superintendent of nursing at the Beverley Auxiliary Hospital. Her duties had also been organising and teaching new students for both the St John Ambulance and Red Cross organisations.

Mr Henry **Jackson** lived at Suffield Nigs, Hackness, Scarborough. He worked for the VAD as one of their numerous volunteers between 25 November 1914 and 27 May 1918, employed as a night orderly, helping with the transportation of wounded soldiers to and from Scarborough railway station from Cober Hill Hospital at Cloughton, Scarborough. On leaving the VAD he joined the Army.

Miss Kitty **Jackson** lived at Cayton, Seamer, Scarborough. She was a probationary VAD nurse working on a part-time basis at Wykeham Abbey Hospital in Yorkshire between March 1917 until as late as 26 March 1919.

Miss Mary **Jackson** lived at Cross Gates Farm, Seamer, Scarborough. During the First World War she served as a part-time VAD nurse at Wykeham Abbey Hospital in Yorkshire between August 1915 and the end of the war.

Miss Zoe **Jameson** lived at 17 Holbeck Hill, Scarborough. She served as a nurse for the VAD between 1912 and 1919. During that time she worked at the Royal Naval Sea Bathing VAD Hospital as well as the Officers' Hospital, both of which were at Scarborough. Her duties at the latter were on a part-time basis.

Miss Alice B. **Jeffrey** lived at 38 Columbus Ravine, Scarborough. She was a voluntary part-time VAD nurse at both the Weston House and Military Hospital in Scarborough between 7 December 1914 and 26 March 1919.

Mr Frank W. **Jennings** lived at St Thomas Street, Scarborough. He was an ambulance driver working for the Scarborough Ambulance Division of the No.6 Northern District, St John Ambulance Brigade. He worked on an 'as and when required' basis. His service number was F5684A.

Miss Charlotte **Jepson** lived at 15 Princess Royal Terrace, Scarborough. She was an unpaid, probationary nurse as well as doing some of the cooking when required. She started working for the VAD in December 1914 at the 3rd Military Hospital at Westborough, Scarborough. From there she moved on to the Weston House Red Cross Hospital, also at Scarborough, then to the Ullesthorpe Auxiliary Hospital in Leicester, before ending up at the Military Hospital, Burniston Road, Scarborough, where she was still working as of 3 May 1919. When war broke out, Charlotte was already 55 years of age. She lived with her older sister Frances and their one servant.

Miss Edith Mabel **Jobson** lived at 13 Crown Terrace, Scarborough. She worked as a full-time clerk at the Officers' Hospital in Scarborough, where she began working in October 1918 and was still there as of 26 March 1919.

Mr Mark **Johnson** lived at Hackness, Scarborough. He worked at the Cober Hill Hospital, Scarborough, starting there on 25 November 1914, where he remained until 7 March 1919. His main duties were as a night orderly and to undertake collecting and dropping off wounded soldiers, to and from the local railway station.

Mr Philip James **Johnson** lived at Hackness, Scarborough. During the war he worked at Cober Hill Hospital at Cloughton, Scarborough, beginning there on 25 November 1914 with his last day being 7 March 1919. He was a voluntary night orderly and would also drive an ambulance to and from the railway station when required. He was a married man with three young children and his job was as a labourer and mason.

Miss Doreen **Lance** lived at 'Windyholme', Seacliff Road, Scarborough. She worked for the VAD between 1917 and 1919, at the Cedar Hall, British Red Cross Hospital and the Officers' Hospital in Scarborough. Doreen was the eldest of three children born to George and Mary Lance. George was a wholesale grocer earning enough money from his business to be able to employ two servants.

Miss Hilda **Lange** lived at 69 Westborough, Scarborough. Her service card shows that she worked for the VAD between 12 January 1916 and 4 September 1919, but it does not record in what capacity. We do know, however, that she worked at the 2nd Western General Hospital in Manchester, but in which particular section, is not recorded. The hospital was spread over twenty-four locations and in total had 17,020 beds, for both officers and men. By way of example, the section that was situated in Leicester Road, was housed in one of the city's secondary schools which had a capacity of 150 beds which were for men from the other ranks.

Mr Thomas **Leadley** lived in Suffield, Scarborough. He worked for the VAD as a night orderly at Cober Hill Hospital, Cloughton, Scarborough, between 25 November 1914 and 15 March 1919.

Mrs Mary **Linton** lived at the Old Mill, Cloughton, Scarborough. She worked for the York's 22 VAD section between 1916 and 1919, by both lending and driving her own motor vehicle for VAD use.

Miss Grace **Lowish** lived at 150 North Marine Road, Scarborough. She was something of a heroine, although not a lot seems to have been made of her bravery. Grace was a nurse who worked for the York's 22 section of the VAD between 1914 and 1919. On 16 December 1914 when Scarborough was bombarded from the sea by ships of the German Imperial Navy she was on duty at the Royal Northern Sea Bathing Infirmary in Scarborough and, despite the hospital having been shelled during the bombardment, she carried on with her work regardless.

Mrs Eugenie **Ludlow** lived at 154 Falsgrave Road, Scarborough. She worked for the VAD as a trainee nurse between 23 September 1914 and 28 October 1915. Where she worked isn't recorded on her service card, but presumably it was in one of the Scarborough hospitals.

Miss Gwynneth **March** lived at 18 Alexandra Park, Scarborough. From January to November 1917, she worked as a part-time, probationary nurse and continued in post after that date, having satisfied her superiors that she was up to the job. She was still working as at 3 May 1919 at the East Leeds Military Hospital.

Miss Rowena **Mason** lived with her parents John and Ethel Mason, her brothers Herbert and Alfred and her sister, Ruth, at 9 New Parks Crescent, Scarborough. She worked as a full-time VAD Nurse at the Cober Hill VAD Hospital at Cloughton, Scarborough, between 9 October 1917 and 1 May 1918. Her brother Herbert Townsley Mason had been a mechanical engineer before the war but on 7 January 1915 at the age of 26 he enlisted in the Canadian Army at Edmonton. He survived the war and returned to Canada where he died on 10 November 1976 at the age of 87.

Miss May **Mattingley** lived at Langford House, Westwood, Scarborough. During the war she was a voluntary, probationary nurse who worked at the Westwood Auxiliary Hospital, as well as the Military Hospital, Scarborough, between November 1916 and July 1918.

Mrs Hilda M. **Maufe** lived at 37 Princess Royal Terrace, Scarborough. She worked for the VAD as a full-time waitress at the Officers' Hospital in Scarborough for five months between October 1918 and February 1919.

Miss Laura **Maw** lived in the High Street, Cloughton, Scarborough. She worked as a full-time VAD nurse on the surgical wards at the Caber Hill Hospital, Cloughton, Scarborough between 25 November 1914 and 15 March 1919.

Miss Martha Alice **McNab** lived at 4 Montpelier Terrace, Scarborough. She worked for the VAD as a matron between 24 December 1914 and 15 March 1919. During that time she was at both the Cober Hill, Hospital at Cloughton, Scarborough and the Sea Bathing Infirmary at Scarborough.

Mrs Lottie **Mellon** lived at 1 West Park Terrace, Scarborough and she worked as a full-time VAD nurse at the Castle Military Hospital in Dublin between August 1917 and December 1918.

Mrs Mabel **Micklethwait** lived at Plain Tree Farm, Stationdale, Cloughton, Scarborough. She served as a VAD nurse between 7 December 1914 and 26 March 1919. During that time she worked at the Weston House Hospital, the Bradford War Hospital, Dressing Station, Thompson's Munitions Works, Warminster Red Cross Hospital and the Military Hospital, Scarborough. She worked at the Red Cross Hospital, Warminster, between October 1917 and January 1918, during which time she was a sister.

Her daughter, Miss Winifred **Micklethwait**, was also a full-time VAD nurse, working at the Military Orthopaedic Hospital, Du Cane Road, Shepherds Bush, London, between 6 December 1916 and 6 January 1918.

Mrs Flora **Morton** lived at the Military Hospital, Burniston Road, Scarborough whilst she worked there from August 1914 to 3 May 1919 as the store keeper and acting matron. She was awarded the Royal Red Cross 2nd Class military decoration in July 1918. This award is given to those who show exceptional services in military nursing.

Miss Emily **Mottersdale** lived at 37 Tindall Street, Scarborough. Between November 1914 and April 1915 she worked at the Hovingham Hall Hospital, Morton, Yorkshire, as a part-time ward nurse.

Miss Agnes **Muil** lived at 15 Cromwell Road, Scarborough. Between December 1914 and 3 May 1919, she worked as a voluntary probationer nurse, at the Military Hospital, Burniston Road, the 3rd Military Hospital, Westborough and the Weston House Red Cross Hospital, all in Scarborough.

Mrs Nora May Oakes **Murray** lived at 44 Gladstone Road, Scarborough with her husband John, a physician and surgeon. During the First World War, she worked at the Military Hospital, Burniston Road, Scarborough, as a part-time, voluntary probationer nurse. She began in March 1917 and was still working there on 3 May 1919.

Mrs Benita Marie **Newsum** was another person who was not from Scarborough but who worked in the town during the war years. She was the full-time head cook at Cober Hill Hospital,

Cloughton. Scarborough between 15 December 1915 and 15 December 1916.

Miss Evelinda **Nickalls** was from Scarborough although I am not certain of her address. She served with the VAD as a full-time nurse working on the wards, at the Grove House Auxiliary Hospital, Harrogate, between June and October 1917. Prior to this she had worked at the 2nd Tennyson's Hospital on the Isle of Wight.

Miss Mary Ethel **Norwood** lived at 22 Manor Road, Scarborough, with her elderly mother Mary Norwood. She signed up as a VAD Nurse in the early months of the war and began working at the Weston House Hospital, Scarborough on 7 December 1914 continuing until 29 August 1915. Later in the war she went to work as a nurse at the Military Hospital, Burniston Road, Scarborough from 14 February 1918 until 26 March 1919. Mary had an older brother, John Percy Norwood, who on 20 September 1909, applied to be made a Freeman of the City of London.

Miss Lizzie Weale **Pain** lived at 94 Trafalgar Road, Scarborough, with her mother Caroline Pain. She was a dressmaker by occupation. She started working for the VAD in December 1918 and was still serving on 3 March 1919. Her role was that of a full-time cook in the Officers' Hospital, Westwood, Scarborough. She worked at another hospital at Burley-on-the-Hill, Oakham, between 3 March and 27 July 1919.

Miss Edith Susannah **Parker** lived at 53 Gordon Street, Scarborough. Between 21 July 1917 and 7 April 1919 she worked at the Metropolitan Hospital, London.

Mr George Berthold **Parker** lived at 1 Lonsdale Road, Scarborough, having previously lived at 10 Cromwell Road in the town. He was employed as a motor launch engineer for the VAD in Mesopotamia between 6 September 1916 and 23 November 1918.

Mrs Louise **Parker** lived at 6 Westbourne Drive, Scarborough. Between 1914 and 1918 she worked as a part-time VAD nurse at the Cober Hill Officers' Hospital at Cloughton, Scarborough.

Mrs Edith **Paton** lived at 8 Granville Square, Scarborough. Between December 1914 and 3 May 1919, she worked as a part-time, voluntary probationary nurse at the 3rd Military Hospital, Westborough, the Weston House Red Cross Hospital, Scarborough and the Military Hospital, Burniston Road, Scarborough.

Miss Gwendolen Cecilia **Payton** lived at Stepney Court, Scarborough. Between 27 November 1916 and 6 July 1917 she worked as an X-ray assistant at Rugeley Military Hospital Camp in Staffordshire.

Mrs Katherine **Peirson** wasn't from Scarborough, but worked at the Military Hospital in Scarborough between October 1916 and 9 September 1917 as a part-time, voluntary probationary nurse.

Mrs Martha **Pill** lived at 20 Seamer Road, Scarborough. She worked as a nurse at the Weston House Hospital and the Military Hospital, both of which were in Scarborough. Between 1 January 1916 and 1 April 1916 she worked at the Scarborough General Hospital for no pay as she lived in. Later she worked at the 1st London General Hospital between 11 July 1916 and 11 August 1918.

Miss Bessie Colbert **Preston** lived at 14 Grosvenor Road, Scarborough and during the First World War worked as a VAD nurse between 24 July 1917 and 11 June 1919 in France. She was awarded one Scarlet Efficiency Stripe on 18 November 1918.

Miss Amy **Pritchards** had at some time lived at 44 Gladstone Road, Scarborough. She worked as a VAD nurse between 25 August 1915 and 25 September 1917 at the 2nd Western General Hospital in Manchester. On 3 August 1917 she was awarded two Scarlet Efficiency Stripes for her outstanding work.

Miss Muriel **Procter** lived at 20 Grosvenor Crescent, Scarborough and worked as a voluntary VAD nurse at the Military Hospital in Scarborough. It was relatively late on in the war when she began working at the hospital, starting on 22 April 1918 and she was still working there on 26 March 1919.

Mr Stanley Thornton **Pugh** lived at the Waverley Hotel Scarborough. During the First World War he enlisted with the Friends Ambulance Unit as an orderly between 18 February 1916 and 4 February 1919.

Miss Edith **Ramsden** lived at 'Ceara', Scalby Road, Scarborough. For two months between 11 April and June 1916, she worked at the Henham Hall Auxiliary Hospital in Suffolk as a nurse.

Miss Dorothy **Redfern** and Miss Marjory **Redfern** lived at 9 Holbeck Road, Scarborough. Their parents, Walter, a seed oil and cake merchant, and Edith Redfern, had two other children, sons Wilfred and John. Dorothy, the elder of the two daughters, began working as a voluntary section leader for the VAD on 17 August 1915 and was still working in that capacity as late as 26 March 1919. Her main work was at the Blind Soldiers and Sailors Hostel, St Dunstan's, Regents Park, London. She had been awarded three white Service Bars, which I believe were issued to denote the number of years a nurse had served for. Marjory worked as a VAD Nurse at the Auxiliary Naval Hospital at Hull between 31 May 1915 and 1 November 1916, initially on a voluntary basis, but paid £1 per month by the time she left.

Wilfred Redfern enlisted in the Army and became a private (STK/507) in the 10th Battalion, Royal Fusiliers. He went out to France, arriving there on 31 July 1915 and on 15 November the same year he was commissioned as a second lieutenant in the East Yorkshire Regiment. Further promotions followed, and by the end of the war he had reached the rank of acting captain. When his mother applied for his wartime service medals, which included the 1915 Star, she was living at The Red House, Hackness, Scarborough.

Miss Lillie **Riley** lived at 13 Market Street, Scarborough, with her parents Robert and Elizabeth Riley and her younger sister Lonie, whilst working as a voluntary, unpaid VAD Nurse at the Weston House Hospital in Scarborough. She began working there on 7 December 1914 and was still in post on 26 March 1919.

Mr William Unwin **Robinson** lived at 55 Gladstone Street, Scarborough, but during the First World War he worked as a motor boat engineer for the VAD, between 6 September 1916 and 1 March 1919, in Mesopotamia, which today is a combination of Iraq, Kuwait, parts of Syria and Turkey. He was Mentioned in Despatches for his continued hard work in April 1919.

Mr William E. **Robson** lived at 91 Gordon Street, Scarborough. During the First World War he worked for the Scarborough Ambulance Division of the St John Ambulance Brigade, which was part of the No.6 Northern Region of the organisation. He worked for most of the war, commencing on 2 February 1915 and continuing until May 1919.

Mr A. Claude **Rowntree** lived at Zealand Cottage, Carland Hill, Scarborough. He worked as an orderly for the Friends Ambulance Unit between 31 March and 1 May 1915.

Mr Harold **Rowntree** lived at Moss Dane, Manor Road, Scarborough. He was an orderly sergeant (F5638A) in the Scarborough Ambulance Division of the No.6 Northern District of the St John Ambulance Brigade. He worked full-time and was with the Friends Ambulance Unit, having first arrived in France on 27 January 1915. He was awarded the 1915 Star, the Victory Medal and the British Medal for his wartime service.

Mr Lawrence Edward **Rowntree** lived at Low Hall, Scalby, Scarborough. He worked as an orderly for the Friends Ambulance Unit between 31 October 1914 and 23 August 1916. Laurence was then commissioned as a second lieutenant and served with A Battery, 26th Brigade, Royal Field Artillery. He was killed in action on 25 November 1916 aged 22. He is buried at the New Military Cemetery, on the outskirts of the village of Vlamertinghe in the West-Vlaanderen region of Belgium.

Mr Sidney **Rowntree** lived at 89 Scalby Road, Scarborough. He worked as an orderly for the Friends Ambulance Unit between 18 April 1915 and 15 January 1919.

Miss Hilda **Saner** lived at 8 Ramshill Road, Scarborough and worked as a VAD nurse as part of the York's 22 section at the Sea Bathing Auxiliary Hospital, Scarborough. She had previously worked at The Barracks, Queen Margaret's and

Depot Works, Scarborough. In total she was a wartime nurse for the best part of five years from 1914 to 1919.

Mrs Hilda Mary **Scarisbrick** lived at 67 Tindall Street, Scarborough. From July 1918 until 14 July 1919 she worked for the VAD in a full-time clerical capacity and also in the stores department at the Croydon War Hospital in Surrey, as part of the Surrey Reserve British Red Cross Society.

Mr Arthur **Scott** lived at 110 Scarsbrook Road, Scarborough which was also a chemist shop. He worked for the VAD between January 1917 and June 1919 with his duties including convoys and air raids. He also worked at the Infirmary, St Luke's, Spring Hall.

Miss Olive **Sedman** was 24 years of age and living at Wrench Green, Hackness, Scarborough, when she began working for the VAD on 17 December 1917 as a general worker. She continued to work for them at the Auxiliary Hospital Brooklands, Weybridge, until after the war was over, finally leaving on 30 June 1919.

Mr Ethelburt **Sharpe** lived at Gordon Street, Scarborough. He was employed as a driver with the Scarborough Ambulance Division of No.6 Northern Division, St John Ambulance. His duties were on an ad hoc basis, he was called upon 'as and when needed'. He began working for them on 27 May 1916 and his service ended in the middle of 1919.

Miss Beatrice **Shield** lived at 'Cardigan', West Street, Scarborough. She enlisted with the VAD in December 1914 as an unpaid, voluntary nurse, working at the 3rd Military Hospital at Westborough, Scarborough and the Weston House, Red Cross Hospital, Scarborough. She later went on to work at the Military Hospital, Burniston Road, Scarborough where she was still working as late as 3 May 1919.

Mr Charles **Skilbeck** lived at 'Newlands', Cloughton, Scarborough. He worked as a night orderly and at Scarborough railway station, between 25 November 1914 and 10 August 1916, and at the Cober Hill Hospital, Cloughton, Scarborough.

Miss Muriel Jessie **Smith** lived at The Lodge, 7 Seamore Road, Scarborough. She began working for the VAD as a probationary nurse in December 1914 in a part-time, unpaid capacity until August 1915. She worked at three different locations, starting at the 3rd Military Hospital, Westborough, Scarborough, then the Weston House Red Cross Hospital Scarborough, ending up at the 2nd Northern General Hospital in Manchester, where she worked between 31 July 1917 and 19 March 1919, as a qualified nurse.

Miss Violet Maud **Sorby** lived at 'Thornbury', 79 Scalby Road, Scarborough, with her parents, Thomas, who was a tool manufacturer, and Annie Sorby. She worked as a full-time paid clerk between October 1918 and 3 May 1919, at the Military Hospital, Burniston Road, Scarborough.

Miss Hilda Crossley **Stabler** lived at Trafalgar Square, Scarborough. Her service card shows that she served with the VAD between 1912 and 1919, yet the detail only records that she worked as a voluntary trainee nurse, between September 1914 and September 1916, on the military ward of the Dean Road Hospital, Scarborough, where there is also a cemetery.

Hilda had a younger brother, George Frederick Stabler, who worked as an apprentice in the printing trade. At the beginning of the war he was still only 17 years of age. He eventually enlisted and according to the British Army's Medal Rolls Index Cards, he became a Private (2988) in the 5th Battalion, Yorkshire Regiment and first arrived in France on 18 April 1915. According to the Commonwealth War Graves Commission website, his service number was 240975 and he was killed in action on 17 September 1916. This is definitely the same man and the discrepancy over the service numbers is, I believe, down to one being his Territorial number and the other when he enlisted in the Army. He has no known grave, but his name is commemorated on the Thiepval Memorial in the Somme region of France. The UK Army Registers of Soldiers Effects for the period of the First World War states that his death was on or since 17 September 1916.

Miss Eleanor **Stephens** lived at 34 Royal Avenue, Scarborough. She began working for the VAD in December 1914 as a part-time, unpaid probationary nurse and quartermaster and was still working for them as late as 3 May 1919. During this time, she had served at the 3rd Military Hospital, Westborough, the Weston House Red Cross Hospital and the Military Hospital, Burniston Road, all in Scarborough.

Miss Adelaide **Stephenson** lived at Seamer in Scarborough, and worked at the Wykeham Abbey Hospital in Wykeham as a probationer nurse between May 1918 and 26 March 1919.

Mr John **Stevenson** lived at 64 Prospect Road, Scarborough, and worked for the Scarborough Ambulance Division of the St John Ambulance Brigade as a driver on an 'as and when needed' basis, between 17 August 1915 and 3 May 1919.

Mr William **Stevenson** was from Cloughton, Scarborough and worked at the Cloughton Hill Hospital between 1 August 1916 and 7 March 1919, as a part-time, volunteer night orderly and driver, when wounded soldiers needed collecting from, or delivering to, Scarborough railway station.

Miss Beatrice **Stewart** lived at the Dean Road Infirmary, Scarborough, where she worked part-time on the military ward as a nurse between September 1914 and September 1916.

Mr Sydney **Storm** lived at Aberdeen Walk, Scarborough, and during the war worked as part of the No.6 Northern District, local Ambulance Division of the St John Ambulance Brigade. He worked on a part-time, as and when needed basis, as a driver, picking up and dropping off wounded soldiers from the town's different military hospitals. The 1911 Census shows the Storm family, which consisted of Benjamin, who was a tailor, Martha Storm and their four children, Arthur, Evelyn, Sydney and Minnie, living at 46 Victoria Street, Scarborough

Mrs Maria Mary **Tatham**, who was born in Wales, lived at The Priory, Scarborough. She worked for the VAD on a part-time basis between 1915 and 1918 making dressings and a variety of hospital related garments, at the Hospital Supplied Depot at the Guildhall in Hull. She was married to George John Wilmer Tatham, who had been a Colonel in the Royal Army Medical Corps before returning to civilian life and becoming the Deputy Medical Officer of Health for Scarborough. They had one daughter, Murial Dorothy Tatham, and three servants to look after them. George Tatham had a long and distinguished military career, having been a surgeon captain as far back as 1892. He was still in the Army as late as 1916.

Mr Albert George **Taylor** lived at 1 Belvoir Terrace, Scarborough. He worked for the Scarborough Ambulance Division of the St John Ambulance Brigade, between 17 August 1915 and 1918, as a driver on an 'as and when needed' basis. After Albert left the employ of the St John Ambulance Brigade he joined the Royal Navy, enlisting on 26 August 1918 when he was already 45 years of age, and was put to work at Chatham Naval Hospital as a clerk (M33690). He was demobbed on 6 November 1919.

Mr Charles John **Taylor** lived at 11 Pavilion Square, Scarborough. He served with the VAD as an orderly between 27 September 1916 and 31 January 1919. His service card does not detail at which medical establishments he worked.

Miss Charlotte **Taylor**, who was 27 years of age, lived at Eastfield, Seamer, Scarborough. Her time working as a nurse for the VAD lasted for exactly one month, between 14 March and 14 April, 1917, and was at the 3rd London General Hospital at Wandsworth, London. Charlotte's father, Charles Taylor, was a local farmer who had made his business a true family affair, as Charlotte, her elder sister, Maggie, along with her two brothers, Charles and George, all worked on the farm. There were two other sisters, Sarah, who was a dressmaker, and Edith, who was still at school.

Miss Janet Everley **Taylor**, who was 25 years of age, lived at 34 Queen Street, Scarborough. She worked for the VAD in an unknown capacity, between 8 March 1917 and 22 July 1918, at the No.1 British Red Cross, Duchess of Westminster Hospital, in Le Touquet, France.

Miss Ada Bessie **Teetgen** was 36 years of age from Westgate-on-Sea on the Isle of Thanet. She worked at the Military Hospital in Scarborough as a dispenser between 16 February 1917 and 16 March 1918.

Miss Joan Mary **Thompsom** lived at 12 West Street, Scarborough. She worked for the VAD between October 1917 and January 1919 at the Roundhay Auxiliary Military Hospital,

The Casino de la Foret, now No. 1 British Red Cross (Duchess of Westminster Hospital), Le Touquet

Duchess of Westminster Hospital.

Leeds. She was a nursing member who worked on a full-time basis on the wards, in the kitchen pantry and undertook some of the cleaning and tidying.

Miss Augusta Shirley **Tindall** lived at 5 Royal Crescent, Scarborough. She worked for the VAD throughout the entire war, from August 1914 until April 1919. Officially she worked eight hours a day, but practically she quite possibly worked a lot longer. By the end of the war she had amassed 13,400 hours as the Commandant of the North Riding of Yorkshire Section. Her job involved organising the VADs and the different hospitals under her command.

Miss Dorothy **Verini** lived in Scalby, Scarborough and worked at Grove House VAD Hospital in Harrogate, Yorkshire, between 1916 and 1918, helping in the linen room once a week.

Miss Isabel **Waithman** lived at 9 Avenue Victoria, Scarborough. During the First World War she worked as a voluntary, part-time probationary nurse at Weston House Red Cross Hospital in Scarborough, between May 1915 and 3 May 1919. She also worked at the Military Hospital, Burniston Road, Scarborough.

Miss Hermione **Wake** was from Somerset, but during the First World War she worked for the VAD in different towns across the UK, including the Weston Hall Red Cross Hospital, Scarborough in May and June 1915. Between then and 1919 she also worked at Oulton Hall Officers' Hospital in Leeds, the Furness Auxiliary Hospital in Harrogate, the 3rd London General Hospital and the No.1 Eastern General Hospital in Cambridge, as a full-time nursing member. She was a member of the West Riding VAD Section.

Miss Ella Mary **Walker** was another who was not from Scarborough, but who worked in the town during the First World War. She worked at the Cober Hill Hospital, Cloughton, Scarborough, as a full-time assistant cook between 22 March 1918 and 15 March 1919, for which she was paid a £5 uniform allowance.

Mr Frank **Walker** lived at 147 Victoria Road, Scarborough and during the war he was a driver for the Scarborough Ambulance Division of the St John Ambulance Brigade No.6 Northern District. He worked on a part-time 'as and when required' basis between 17 August 1915 and May 1919. By way of employment, 31-year-old Frank was a local newsagent who lived with his elderly parents, Thomas and Elizabeth Walker, along with his brother George, who was a joiner, and sister Edith.

Mr Edward Arnold **Wallis** was born 22 April 1880 in Scarborough. He lived at 'Fairfield', Newby, Near Scarborough, and worked for the British Red Cross Society and Order of St John, Friends Ambulance Unit, working on both No.5 and No.16 Ambulance trains, between 18 November 1915 to 18 July 1918, as an orderly. He was awarded the Victory Medal, British War Medal and the 1915 Star, for his wartime service.

Mr Gerald Humphrey **Ward**, lived at 125 Scalby Road, Scarborough and worked for the VAD as an orderly between 31 October 1914 and 30 September 1915.

Miss Alice **Warwick** lived at 108 Victoria Road, Scarborough with her mother, Mary, and her two younger brothers, George and John. Because of the family butcher's shop that they ran, they had enough money to employ a servant. Alice worked as a voluntary VAD Nurse at Weston House, Scarborough, between 7 December 1915 and 29 August 1915. In her time at the hospital she worked for a total of 304 hours.

Mrs Florence **Whitaker** was 44 years of age and lived at 27 Manor Road, Scarborough. During the First World War she worked as an assistant cook for the VAD between 25 October 1917 and 5 June 1919. She initially worked at the No.13 Canadian Hospital in Hastings, from 25 October 1917. She then went on to work at the Purfleet Military Hospital in Essex between 24 April 1919 and 5 June 1919.

Miss Frances **Wiles** lived at 181 Dean Road, Scarborough and worked for the VAD as a nurse at the Stoke-on-Trent War Hospital between 9 June 1916 and December the same year. She later married and became Mrs Frances Wood.

Miss Jessica **Willan**, who was 42 years of age, lived at 39 Avenue Victoria, Scarborough. During the war she was an unpaid, voluntary probationary nurse at the Military Hospital, Burniston Road, Scarborough between July 1917 and 3 May 1919, where she worked a total of 3,804 hours.

Miss Ethel Maude **Williams** was from Aberystwyth in Wales, but between 22 March 1918 and 28 January 1919, she worked as a full-time dispenser at the Military Hospital in Scarborough. Between 8 December 1916 and 7 January 1918, she worked in the same capacity at the Herne Bay Military Hospital. Having left Scarborough, she went on to work at the Blackpool Military Hospital between 22 March 1919 and 18 July 1919.

Miss Catherine **Williamson** lived at 8 Royal Crescent, Scarborough but worked as a part-time voluntary nurse at the Belper Red Cross Hospital in Derbyshire between 10 December 1915 and 2 February 1916. She worked there for a total of 352 hours.

Catherine's sister, Miss Violette Vaughan **Williamson** who was 23 years of age, lived at the same address and worked as a nurse at the 1st Eastern General Military Hospital in Cambridge between 28 October 1916 and 30 May 1917. Violette also worked as a general service clerk at the Perth VAD Hospital, the Clipstone Military Hospital in Nottinghamshire and the Belper VAD Hospital in Derbyshire. She had begun working for the VAD as early as 1912, some two years before the beginning of the First World War, and worked her last day with them on 29 February 1919.

Miss Monica **Willoughby** was from Brompton in York, but during the First World War she worked as a full-time voluntary nurse at different locations around the country between 1916 and April 1919. These included the Grove House Auxiliary Hospital, Harrogate, the Brompton Auxiliary Hospital and the Scarborough Military Hospital.

Mrs Alice **Wilson** lived at 5 Langdale Road, Scarborough and between May 1917 and May 1919, she worked at the Military Hospital, Scarborough, as a part-time unpaid, voluntary probationary nurse.

Miss Dorothy **Winder** lived at 13 The Crescent, Scarborough. She started working for the VAD as a part-time, voluntary nurse between December 1914 and August 1915, at the 3rd Military Hospital, Westborough, Scarborough and the Weston House Red Cross Hospital. She then went to France, where she was a full-time paid nurse between August 1915 and 18 November 1919. On 3 June 1919 she was awarded the Royal Red Cross which is only for fully trained nurses from an officially recognised nursing service. The award was for showing exceptional devotion and competence in the performance of nursing duties over a continuous and long period of time, or for nurses who had performed an exceptional act of bravery and devotion at their post. She was also Mentioned in Despatches on 30 December 1919.

Mr John H. **Wingate** of North Street, Scarborough was a private (F5682A) in the Scarborough Ambulance Division of the St John Ambulance Brigade, which was part of the No.6 Northern District, between 11 August 1914 and 1916. He was engaged as a driver on an 'as and when required' basis.

Gertrude **Woods** lived at 10 Belvedere Road, Scarborough. She served as an unpaid part-time, probationary nurse at the Military Hospital, Burniston Road, Scarborough. She began working there in March 1917 and was still there as of 3 May 1919.

Miss Lilian Maude **Woodhouse** aged 36, who lived at 8 Grosvenor Crescent, Scarborough, served as a full-time staff nurse between 10 September 1917 and 12 April 1919 at the 17th Durham VAD Hospital, The Red House, Etherley, Bishop Auckland. She had previously worked at the Westwood Auxiliary Hospital in Scarborough.

Mrs Katherine **Wray** lived at 5 Crown Crescent, Scarborough and began working at the Military Hospital, Burniston Road, Scarborough in March 1917 as an unpaid part-time, probationary nurse. She was still serving in that capacity on 3 May 1919.

Miss Helen Mary **Wrigley** was 21 years of age and lived at Ganton Hall, Scarborough. She worked as an unpaid chauffeuse at the Étaples base in France between 6 March 1918 and 6 March 1919. Ganton Hall, a country house which was built in 1860, was home to Helen, her sister Mary, their parents, Harold and Mary Wrigley, as well as eleven servants. Harold Wrigley was recorded as being a man of 'private means'. Helen's brother, Edward Whittaker Wrigley, was born in 1893, and later attended the prestigious Harrow School. He served during the First World War as a second lieutenant in the Royal Flying Corps.

As can be seen from the numerous men and women who are mentioned in this chapter, they came from all walks of life and from many different elements of society, the affluent and the not so well off, the old and the young, parents and children, each one of them just simply wanting to work for the greater good. Many received no financial remuneration for their long and arduous hours of voluntary work. What did they get in return? The knowledge and contentment that when they were called upon to answer their country's call in its hour of need, they stepped forward and did their bit in which ever way they could.

CHAPTER 8

Those who Died After the Armistice

Here is a list of men from Scarborough, or those who had connections with the town, such as their parents lived there, who died of their wounds, an accident, illness or disease, in the years immediately after the end of the First World War, up to and including 1921.

Arthur **Wilson**, Canadian Infantry, died 4 August 1921. He and his wife Dorothy lived at 97 Murchison Street, Scarborough.

E. **Cavinder**, East Yorkshire Regiment, died 24 December 1920. He and his wife Agnes lived at 41 Wykeham Street, Scarborough.

J. **Copland**, Royal Field Artillery, died 20 September 1920. He lived with his wife Jane at 77 Trafalgar Street, Scarborough.

George Henry **Cappleman**, 1st Engineer, Mercantile Marine, died 4 September 1920 presumed drowned when the Scarborough steam trawler *Jack Johnson* hit a mine. He was born in the town and lived with his wife Emily, at 9 Lancaster Street, Scarborough.

Fred **Crosby**, Third Hand, Mercantile Marine, died 4 September 1920, also presumed drowned on the *Jack Johnson*. He was born in the town and lived with his wife Harriet, at 23 Durham Street, Scarborough.

Ernest **Eves**, Deck Hand, Mercantile Marine, died 4 September 1920, presumed drowned on the *Jack Johnson*.

He lived with his wife Norah, at 2 Westandgate, Scarborough. Ernest was born in the town in 1892.

Edmund Eves **Matson**, Deck Hand, Mercantile Marine. Died on 4 September 1920 presumed drowned on the *Jack Johnson*. His parents, Allan and Alice Matson, lived at 45 Quay Street, Scarborough.

John **Megginson**, Mate, Mercantile Marine, died 4 September 1920, presumed drowned on the *Jack Johnson*. He lived with his wife Jennie, at 41 Longwestgate, Scarborough. He was also born in Scarborough.

Albert **Nightingale,** Fireman, Mercantile Marine, died on 4 September 1920, presumed drowned on the *Jack Johnson*. He lived with his mother, Annie Nightingale, at 95a Longwestgate, Scarborough.

John William Claybourne **Pye**, Cook, Mercantile Marine, died on 4 September 1920, presumed drowned on the *Jack Johnson*. His father William Pye, lived at 39 St Sepulchre Street, Scarborough.

Isaac **Taylor**, Second Engineer, Mercantile Marine, died on 4 September 1920, presumed drowned on the *Jack Johnson*. He lived with his wife Lucy, at 17 Providence Place, Scarborough. He was also born in Scarborough.

Harry **Trotter**, Deck Hand, Mercantile Marine, died on 4 September 1920, presumed drowned on the *Jack Johnson*. He lived with his father at 5 Ebenezer Place, Scarborough.

William **Ipson**, Royal Garrison Artillery, died 15 August 1920 of heat stroke. He was born in Scarborough.

W.R. **Lawlor**. Indian Political Department, died on 5 June 1920. His mother lived at the Durham Hotel, North Marine Road, Scarborough.

William **Mollen**, Mercantile Marine, died 9 April 1920, was the only man killed when the Scarborough steam trawler *Taranaki* hit a mine, nine survivors were rescued. He lived with his parents, William and Agnes Mollen, at 98 Longwestgate, Scarborough.

George Evan **Smith**, East Yorkshire Regiment, died 4 April 1920. He lived with his wife Emma at 54 North Marine Road, Scarborough.

Tom **Temple**, Durham Light Infantry, died 3 March 1920 of phthisis, or pulmonary tuberculosis, which is a progressive wasting disease. He lived with his wife Elizabeth, at 3 Belmont Road, Scarborough.

Thomas **Atkin**, Mercantile Marine, died 23 February 1920 drowned after the fishing vessel *Strathord* struck a mine. He lived with his wife Ellen at 41 Quay Street, Sandside, Scarborough.

Edwin Coultas **Cappleman**, Mercantile Marine, also died on 23 February 1920 on the fishing vessel *Strathord*. He lived with his wife Elsie at 22 Clark Street, Scarborough.

George Andrew **Cowburn**, Second Hand, Mercantile Marine. Died on 23 February 1920, presumed drowned after the fishing vessel *Strathord*, he was working on, struck a mine. He lived with his wife Elizabeth at 32 Grange Avenue, Scarborough.

John **Flynn**, Mercantile Marine, also died on 23 February 1920 on the fishing vessel *Strathord*. He lived with his wife Elizabeth at 30 The Bolts, Scarborough. He was also born in the town.

Joseph **Hope**, Mercantile Marine, also died on 23 February 1920 when the fishing vessel *Strathord* struck a mine. He lived with his wife Isabella at 12 Aberdeen Terrace, Scarborough.

Alfred Hector **Littlewood**, Mercantile Marine, also died on 23 February 1920 when the fishing vessel *Strathord* struck a mine. He lived with his wife Gladys at 5 Long Greece Steps, Scarborough.

John **Warwick**, Mercantile Marine, also died on 23 February 1920 when the fishing vessel *Strathord* struck a mine. He lived with his wife Annie at 6 Clarkson's Buildings, Longwestgate, Scarborough. John was also born in Scarborough.

James Henry **Williamson**, Mercantile Marine, also died on 23 February 1920 when the fishing vessel *Strathord* struck a mine. His parents, Edward and Jane Williamson lived at 88 Longwestgate, Scarborough.

William **Ramm**, 10th Battalion, Northumberland Fusiliers, died 20 December 1919 after having been medically discharged from the army suffering from bronchitis and tuberculosis. He was the brother of Mrs A. Roe of 6 Raleigh Street, Scarborough.

Charles **Lummas**, Royal Army Medical Corps, died 20 November 1919. He was born at Scalby in Scarborough.

E. **Armstrong**, Royal Army Medical Corps, died 21 September 1919. His parents lived in Scarborough.

Edward William **Ruddock**, Royal Field Artillery, died 19 September 1919. His father, Charles Ruddock, lived at Newby, Scarborough.

Augustine **Wells**, Royal Garrison Artillery, died 27 August 1919. He was born in Scarborough.

Fred **Hick**, The Queen's Lancers, died 21 August 1919. He was born in Scarborough.

Anthony George **Mead**, Royal Engineers, died 26 May 1919. He lived with his wife Maud, at the Red House, Scarborough.

Charles Alfred **Parker**, Mercantile Marine, died on 13 March 1919 presumed drowned when the steam trawler *Scotland* hit a mine. He was born in Scarborough.

William Sydney **Urwin**, Sherwood Foresters, died 16 March 1919. His father lived in Scarborough.

W. **Smith**, Yorkshire Regiment, died 11 March 1919. He lived with his wife Mary at 8 Cross Street, Scarborough.

James Avison **Teale**, King's Hussars, died 9 March 1919. His parents lived in Scarborough.

H.W. **Fletcher**, Royal Engineers, died 27 February 1919. He lived with his wife Annie, at Woodlands Cottages, Scalby Road, Scarborough. His parents, George and Mary Fletcher, also lived in the town.

Alexander Schalom **Liggi**, London Regiment, died 26 February 1919. His father lived at Marine Parade, Scarborough.

Charles Thomas **Bevis**, Royal Engineers, died 18 February 1919. He lived with his wife Enid at 18 Crown Terrace, Scarborough.

William Melton **Patrick**, Royal Army Ordnance Corps, died 6 February 1919 of phthisis. His parents, Stephen and Esther Patrick, lived in Scarborough.

Arthur **Bullamore**, Royal Naval Reserve, died 2 February 1919 by accidental drowning. He lived with his mother at 9 Whitehead Hill, Scarborough.

L.W. **Moss**, Northumberland Fusiliers, died 2 February 1919 of pneumonia. He lived with his parents at 30 Garfield Road, Scarborough.

Peter **Mack**, Canadian Infantry, died 31 January 1919 by drowning. His wife Ada lived at 21 Dean Road, Scarborough.

William **Thornton**, London Regiment, died 31 January 1919. His father Richard Thornton lived at 53 Rothbury Street, Scarborough.

George Douglas **Patrick**, Machine Gun Corps Infantry, died on 7 January 1919. His parents, Robert and Margaret Patrick, lived at 12 Manor Road, Scarborough.

Robert **Swift**, Royal Garrison Artillery, died 3 January 1919. He lived with his wife Lilian, at 92 North Maine Road, Scarborough. His parents also lived in the town.

Francis William **Collier**, South African Field Artillery, died 26 December 1918. His mother Ann Collier lived at 30 Durham Street, Scarborough. Francis was also born in the town.

Cyril Vernon **Larkin**, Royal Army Medical Corps, died 17 December 1918 of malaria. His parents, Vernon and Florence Larkin, lived at 2 Aberdeen Terrace, Scarborough.

Frank **Tindall**, Mercantile Marine, died 15 December 1918 presumed drowned with six other crewmen when the steam trawler *Grecian Prince* was sunk by a mine caught in her trawl net. He was born in Scarborough.

William Allan **Pirnie**, Royal Engineers, died 6 December 1918. His father, Duncan Pirnie, lived at 2 Alga Terrace, Scarborough.

Thomas William **Dobinson**, Royal Engineers, died 1 December 1918 of pneumonia. He lived with his wife Mary at 23 Albermarie Crescent, Scarborough.

Arthur Temple **Wray**, Mercantile Marine, died 1 December 1918. He was presumed drowned when the steam trawler *Ethelwulf* was blown up by a mine. He was born in Scarborough.

Christopher **Archer**, Royal Field Artillery, died 30 November 1918 of dropsy. He lived with his wife Margaret at 13 Hibernia Street, Scarborough. His parents also lived in the town.

Henry **Ireland**, Canadian Infantry, died 30 November 1918 of unspecified sickness. His mother, Annie Ireland, lived at 11 Elder Street, Scarborough.

G. **Taylor**, Yorkshire Regiment, died 27 November 1918. His parents lived in Scarborough.

David **Bailey**, East Yorkshire Regiment, died 25 November 1918. He lived with his wife Eliza at 17 Albion Street, Scarborough, and his parents, James and Hannah Bailey, also lived in the town.

Albert Victor **Brackenbury**, Royal Naval Reserve, died on 25 November 1918 of pneumonia. He lived with his wife at 8 Friars Entry, Scarborough.

R.E. **Coulson**, Durham Light Infantry, died 19 November 1918. His father lived at 83 Candler Street, Scarborough.

J. **Marchant**, Royal Field Artillery, died 14 November 1918. He lived with his mother at 82 Hampton Road, Scarborough.

Robert Allan **Medd**, Lincolnshire Regiment, died on 14 November 1918 of his wounds incurred in action. His parents, Robert and Christiana Medd, lived at 1 Franklin Street, Scarborough.

Daniel **Sheehan**, Royal Field Artillery, died 13 November 1918 of pneumonia. He was born in Scarborough.

Francis Baden **Woolfe**, Life Guards, died 13 November 1918. He lived with his mother at 59 Gladstone Road, Scarborough.

Robert Arthur **Nendick**, West Yorkshire Regiment, died, according to the Commonwealth War Graves Commission, on 11 November 1918, but on the British Army's Register of Soldiers effects for the period of the First World War, Robert is shown as having died on 12 November 1918. The War Diaries for the 1st/5th Battalion West Yorkshire Regiment show that on 11 and 12 November 1918, they were in trenches at Evin and an entry for each day specifically states that there were no casualties on either day. His parents, Matthew and Mary Nendick, lived at 16 Cambridge Street, Scarborough.

I would never claim that this is in any way a complete list, but it is as detailed as I have been able to make it and it emphasises the fact that the First World War did not end on

11 November 1918, just because the killing had stopped. Men were still serving in the military and undertaking war related work, or as with those from the Mercantile Marine, they were still losing their lives because of the war. No longer did they have to worry about the threat of being sunk by an unseen German submarine, but the threat hadn't disappeared, it simply changed to the possibility of striking a mine, left over from the war, which could have either been laid by the British or the Germans.

In some respects losing a loved one after the fighting had stopped and the war was finally over, must have been even more painful for the families of these men, because most of them had already told themselves that their husbands, sons, brothers, uncles and nephews, were safe. They were expecting them to return home, but sadly for some, that would never be.

CHAPTER 9

Scarborough War Memorial – Oliver's Mount

The Scarborough War Memorial sits resplendently on top of Oliver's Mount in Jackson's Lane. Its setting is the serenity of a large grassed area which is adorned with trees and wooden benches, allowing visitors to the site to sit and enjoy the scenic views out to sea, perhaps whilst contemplating the memory of a loved one long since passed.

As with most such war memorials, the one at Oliver's Mount has an inscription:

> *They shall grow not old, as we that are left grow old,*
> *age shall not weary them, nor the years condemn,*
> *at the going down of the sun and in the morning we will remember them.*

This is taken from the fourth paragraph of the 'Ode of Remembrance', written by Laurence Binyon and part of his poem 'For the Fallen', which was first published in *The Times* newspaper in September 1914.

The British Expeditionary Force suffered many casualties in the opening months of the war due to their participation in both the Battle of Mons and the Battle of the Marne. It was for these men that 'For the Fallen' was written.

Despite being too old for military service, Binyon twice volunteered to work as an orderly in a British hospital for

Scarborough War Memorial.

wounded French soldiers, first in 1915 before returning in 1916. The hospital in question was the Hôpital Temporaire d'Arc-en-Barrois situated in the Haute-Marne region of France.

Below are the names of the men, women and children from Scarborough, who lost their lives as a result of the First World War.

ACKSON, A
ADAMS, G E
ADAMSON, W B
ADDY, J C
ALCOCK, J R
ALLAN, H
ALLAN, W
ALLANBY, J H
ALLEN, F
ALLISON, C
ALLISON, H
ANDERSON,
ANDERSON, E S
ANDERSON, G
ANDERSON, G W
ANDERSON, H W
ANNADALE, W
APPLEBY, A
APPLEBY, A T
APPLEBY, G
APPLEBY, J R
APPLETON, H
ARCHER, C
ARCHER, J E
ARCHER, L M
ARMITAGE, T E
ARMSTRONG, C S
ASHWELL, E
ATKINSON, F A
ATKINSON, R
ATKINSON, R C
ATKINSON, W P
ATKINSON, W S
BAKER, A E
BARKER, G
BARKER, G O
BARKER, J T
BARKER, T C
BARKLEY, E
BARRACLOUGH, A
BARTLYFFE, C E
BAYES, C
BAYES, G
BAYES, J J
BEAN, E W
BEAN, W H
BEANLAND, G M
BEDFORD, K S
BENNETT, A F
BENNETT, C C
BENNETT, J V
BENTON, B J
BERRY, C V C
BETTS, G
BETTS, H
BIELBY, T C
BILLHAM, H
BIRD, G B
BIRDSHALL, G
BLAND, A

BLAND, C W
BLAND, J
BLOOME, A
BLYTHE, W
BOGG, G H
BOOTE, W E
BORROWS, W
BOURNE, J T
BOWES, G A
BOYES, A E
BOYES, F
BRADLEY, A G H
BRADLEY, S
BRIGGS, A D
BRIGLIN, A M
BROADBENT, W H
BROWN, D E
BROWN, F M
BROWN, H C
BROWN, J
BROWN, T W
BROWN, W E
BROWN, W T
BRYCE, F
BULLIMORE, A
BURNETT, A G
BURNETT, A W
BURNETT, G W
BUSHFIELD, H C
CADMAN, W
CALVERT, F
CALVERT, W
CAMMISH, W H
CANDLER, F G
CAPPLEMAN, H
CARR, W H
CARTWRIGHT, F

CARTWRIGHT, R C
CATTLE, J
CAWINDER, E
CHAMPNEY, H D
CHAPMAN, F
CHARTERRS, H
CLARK, J C
CLARK, J H
CLARK, S
CLARK, T
CLARKE, A
CLARKE, J P
CLARKE, J W
CLARKE, W
CLARKSON, W H
CLOUGH, P R
COATES, F H
COBE, R J P
COCKERILL, T G
COCKERILL, W
COLLEY, G E
COLLIER, F
COLLINSON, A R
COOPER, E
COPLAND, J
CORDUKES, G W
CORREY, S E G
COSTELLO, A
COSTELLO, J W
COULSON, J W
COULSON, R E
COVERLEY, T C
COWARD, W
COWLING, F W
COWTON, E
COWTON, J S
COX, S H

COYNE, G P
CRAVEN, R E
CRAVEN, T
CRAVEN, W
CROMACK, A G
CROMACK, J W
CULLEN, W
DALE, S W
DALEY, A R
DARLING, C
DARLING, J E
DAVIS, C W
DAVIS, C W
DAVIS, J
DAVIS, J
DAVISON, A
DAVISON, C H
DAWS, E
DAWSON, W B
DEAN, R C
DEIGHTON, R W
DENT, C G
DENTON, J D
DEVLIN, J H
DIXON, G H
DODGSON, C H
DOLBEN, J A
DOODY, W S
DOVE, F W
DRAKE, G W
DREWER, A W
DRUMMER, H H
DRYDALE, S
DUCK, W G
DUGGLEBY, G E
DUNCAN, T A
DUTCHMAN, J

DYER, H
DYER, R
EAMON, L
EDWARDS, W H
ELLERSHAW, S
ELLIOT, A
ELLIOT, H E
ELLIOT, W A
ELLISON, F S
ESCREET, F
ETCHES, A J
ETCHES, T S
EVANS, W A
FAIRLY, H
FAULDER, A
FEATHERSTONE, C E
FELL, M H
FENWICK, R W
FERGUSON, H
FERGUSON, J L
FERNANDES, D L D
FIDLER, J
FINN, J
FINN, T
FIRTH, J H A
FITZPATRICK, R M
FLEMMING, C
FLETCHER, W B
FOSTER, W E
FOUND, E
FOWLER, H
FOWLER, V
FOWLER, W L
FOX, W
FRATER, F R
FRITH, E H
GARBUTT, T

GARBUTT, W S
GARWOOD, W G
GIBSON, J R
GILBERT, S
GILL, H
GODDARD, W G
GOLDER, J
GOOD, W B
GOODRICK, W H
GOODWILL, F
GOODWILL, G W
GOODWIN, T N
GOOSWILL, S
GOSPEL, C W
GOWAN, J W
GRAHAM, A
GRAHAM, H
GRAHAM, H C
GRAY, E
GRAY, H
GRAY, J W
GREEN, F
GREEN, J
GREEN, R
GREY, J
GRIMMER, B
GROGAN, J F
GROVES, R M
HALDER, A M
HALDER, A W
HALL, F G
HANSOM, A
HARDISTY, A E
HARLAND, A E
HARLAND, H
HARLAND, H
HARLAND, P

HARLAND, R
HARMAN, C A
HARRIS, W H
HARTLEY, A G
HARTLEY, J P C
HARTLEY, W
HARWOOD, J W
HASTINGS, W
HAWXWELL, F
HAYLES, A L
HAYTON, T
HEBBRON, C E
HEBDON, E
HEBDON, E S
HEBDON, R S
HEPWORTH, S
HICK, A C
HILL, C A
HILL, F
HILL, G
HILL, G A
HIND, H H W
HINSLEY, J W
HIRD, G W
HODDEN, C
HODDEN, J
HODGSON, F
HODGSON, H C
HOGG, G
HOLDERNESS, F
HOLLINGSWORTH, A J
HOLLINGSWORTH, R
HOMPSON, H
HOODS, W A
HOPKINS, A H
HORNBY, A
HORNER, F

HORSLEY, E
HORSLEY, J S
HORSMAN, S B J
HORTON, D
HOUSTON, A
HUMFRAYS, R
HUNT, J
HUNTER, A N
HUNTER, B
HUNTER, F
HUNTER, F L
HURD, J
HUTCHINSON, G R
INCHBALD, J W
INGLE, F
INSALL, J R
IRELAND, F
IRELAND, M B
IRELAND, M B
IRELAND, R
JACKSON, E
JACKSON, E H
JACKSON, J
JACKSON, T
JAQUES, H P
JEFFERSON, J A
JEFFERSON, W
JOBLING, L A
JOHNSON, C
JOHNSON, G H
JOHNSON, W
JOHNSTON, L
JORDAN, A
JOWSEY, W G
JUDD, R J
JUDD, R W
KAY, J D

KELLY, J A
KELLY, T
KENDALL, J S
KIDD, J
KING, F
KING, G S
KING, H
KING, R F
KITCHEN, W W
KNOWLES, F H
KNOX, F M
LAKE, W F
LAMB, C
LAMBOURNE, G A
LAMBPLUGH, J H
LANCASTER, C
LANCASTER, G H
LANCASTER, H J
LANCASTER, J E
LANCASTER, J W
LANCASTER, W
LANGTOFT, F
LARKIN, C V
LAWRENCE, H
LAWTY, P
LAZEMBY, G A
LAZENBY, J B
LEA, E H
LEADBEATER, A
LEADBEATER, C
LEADLEY, F
LEAFE, J R
LEE, J N
LEMPRIERE, H A
LENTON, C
LEPPINGTON, R
LIGGI, R

LIGHTFOOT, C
LIGHTFOOT, J
LIGHTFOOT, W
LINSKILL, M
LIVINGSTON, R W
LOFTUS, A
LONG, W H
LONGMAN, T
LORD, J
LOUTH, J
LOUTH, J
LOWSON, W R
LOWSON, W R
LYON, G H
LYTH, C W P
MAGSON, FRANK
MAGSON, FRED
MAINPRIZE, T J
MAJOR, A E
MANN, J E
MANSFIELD, W
MANSON, S
MARCHANT, W
MARR, A W
MARSAY, J H
MARSHALL, A H
MARTIN, H
MASON, H P
MASON, R T
MATSON, G
MAWMAN, H
MAWMAN, W
MCBEAN, H
MCBEAN, J R
MCCOURT, P
MCCRICKARD, J
MCINNES, P N L
MCNAUGHT, A G
MCNULTY, C
MCREYNOLDS, J B
MEADS, T E
MEDD, C N
MEDD, G J
MEDD, R A
MEEK, C S
MEGGINSON, H
MEGGINSON, J
MEGGINSON, W A
MERHOR, A W
MERRYWEATHER, W A
METCALFE, D
MIDGLEY, F
MILLER, T
MILNER, A
MILNER, J W
MILNER, W H
MILNES, J W
MITCHELL, A R
MOFFAT, R H R
MONKMAN, H
MONKMAN, J E
MOORE, C W
MOORE, E R
MOORE, P
MOORE, R
MOORING, L
MORELY, W H
MORGAN, T W
MORLEY, H
MORRIS, I
MORRIS, J W
MORRISON, J S
MOSS, L W
MYERS, A

NALTON, E S E
NASH, A H
NELSON, T C
NENDICK, A F
NENDICK, R A
NEWBY, E W
NEWBY, H
NEWHAM, C H
NEWLOVE, F
NEWMAN, W
NEWSOME, G E
NEWSOME, L
NEWTON, F
NICHOLSON, C R
NICHOLSON, H H
NICHOLSON, J W
NIGHTINGALE, C
NORMANDALE, R W
NORMANTON, L R
NUNDY, H W
OLDRIDGE, A
OLDROYD, H
OVERTON, C
OVERTON, L
OWEN, C
OWSTON, C
OWSTON, H
OWSTON, H T
OWSTON, J
OXLEY, F J
PALMER, E
PALMER, J W
PALMER, W
PARK, C E
PARKER, H
PARKINSON, A
PARKINSON, J R

PARKINSON, W
PATRICK, G D
PATRICK, J W
PATTRICK, A V
PAYNE, H P
PEACOCK, T
PEARSON, F F
PEARSON, W H
PEGG, J R
PENNOCK, C
PERRYMAN, A H
PETCH, E
PETCH, E S
PETCH, J
PETCH, S
PEXTON, F
PHILP, F G
PICKERING, A
PICKERING, F
PICKERSGILL, H
PICKUP, E H
PICKUP, W P
PIERCY, G
PIPES, T W
PLUMMER, L
POPPLEWELL, B
POSTHILL, J W
POTTAGE, T
POTTS, G W
PRESTON, D
PRESTON, L
PRIEST, B
PRIESTLEY, R
PROST, H
PUGMIRE, H
PURNELL, E
RAINE, C

RAINE, J
RAINE, J L
RAINE, R A
RAMM, H H
RAPER, J W G
RAWLING, W D
RAYNER, A
REDMAN, S C
REDSHAW, W
REED, A J
REED, E R
REED, T W
RENWICK, T H
RENWICK, W
RINES, E T
ROBINSON, A
ROBINSON, C R
ROBINSON, E D
ROBINSON, G
ROBINSON, J E
ROBINSON, S W
RODGERS, E
ROLLINSON, G R P
ROUSE, W E
ROWBOTTOM, J W
ROWLEY, C E
ROWLEY, J E
ROWLEY, S
ROYLE, F L
ROYTT, L G
RUDEFORTH, H
RUTELEDGE, G W
SADLER, J
SAILS, J H
SALTER, G C T
SALTER, J E R
SANDERSON, A

SANDERSON, E
SANDERSON, L
SATURLEY, G E
SAVILLE, G S
SAYER, F V
SCOTT, A
SCOTT, J W
SCOTT, T S
SHAW, J F
SHEADER, G T
SHEADER, N
SHEPHERD, A
SHEPHERD, G E
SHORT, H
SIMPSON, G W
SIMPSON, H
SIMPSON, J W
SIMPSON, S
SINCLAIR, H
SLIEGHTHOM, E
SMALLEY, E S
SMITH, A
SMITH, C F
SMITH, G
SMITH, GEORGE
SMITH, J
SMITH, T R
SMITH, W
SMITH, WHITTAKER
SMITH, WILLIAM
SMITHSON, C
SMITHSON, R
SNOWDEN, C
SOWERBY, W L
SPOFFORTH, E R
STABLER, F
STANDING, C E

STEAD, J E
STEPHENSON, A
STEPHENSON, H
STEPHENSON, H C
STEPHENSON, J R
STEPHENSON, R
STEVENSON, A
STEWART, J F
STEWART, W T
STONEHOUSE, H
STONEHOUSE, S D
STORRY, G W
SUNLEY, G E
SWALWELL, H
SWALWELL, W
SWAN, H
SWIFT, R
TADMAN, W
TASKER, F
TASKER, W
TATE, J
TAYLOR, G
TAYLOR, M G
TAYLOR, W
TAYLOR, W O
TEMPLE, P
THOMAS, W C
THOMPSON, W
THORNTON, F
THORNTON, W
THORP, R O U
THORPE, G T
TISSIMAN, J
TOSE, H
TOSE, W E
TOWELL, J
TRANMER, W H
TRAVIS, W
TROTTER, E
TROTTER, W
TROTTER, WILLIAM
TROUSDALE, J
TUCKER, S
TUCKER, S W
TUGWELL, G A
TURNBULL, H
TURNBULL, W A
TURNER, E
TURNER, S
URWIN, W S
V LEECH, N A
VASEY, E
VASEY, F
VOLLUM, H J
W H BAKER, J A
WAKE, J L
WALKER, W W
WALLER, A J
WALLER, E
WALTERS, A J
WALTERS, A V
WALTERS, J G
WARD, C W
WARD, R W
WARDMAN, H
WARLEY, G
WARWICK, J W
WATERSON, J E
WATERWORTH, F E
WATKINSON, J T
WATSON, A
WATSON, A E
WATSON, E
WATSON, F

WATSON, G W
WATSON, T E
WEBB, P C
WEBSTER, A
WEBSTER, H
WELBOURN, J F
WELBOURN, J T
WHARTON, H
WHEATER, S
WHITE, A W
WHITE, W
WHITE, WILLIAM
WHITEHEAD, H
WHITELEY, C
WHITELEY, W W
WHITTAKER, A B
WHITTAKER, J D
WHITTINGHAM, H
WHITWORTH, J
WHITWORTH, J
WIFFEN, W T
WILKINSON, A
WILLIAMSON, A
WILSON, A
WILSON, A G
WILSON, A W

WILSON, C
WILSON, E F
WILSON, G
WILSON, H
WILSON, H W
WILSON, HARRY
WILSON, L
WILSON, S
WILSON, T
WILSON, W
WINSNIP, W
WISEMAN, J P
WOOD, A E
WOOD, E J
WOOD, H
WOOD, J
WOOD, T
WOODALL, W
WRIGHT, H
WRIGHT, J
WYNNE, G W
WYNSPEAR, J W
YAXLEY, I
YOUNG, J
YOUNG, J E

CIVILIANS BOMBARDMENTS 1914 AND 1917

Adults

BEAL, A
BENNET, A F
BENNETT, J
CROSBY, E E
CROW, A
DUFFIELD, A
ELLIS, L
FRITE, L
H MCINTYRE, B
HALL, J
HARLAND, H
MERRYWEATHER, E L
PAINTER, A
PECKUP, T
T PRUE, M
TAYLOR, G P

Children

BARNES, G J
RYALLS, J S
WARD, J C H

Those Lost at Sea

APPLEBY, R J
ATKIN, T
BARKER, J C
CAPPLEMAN, E C
COWBURN, G A
CROSBY, F
EVES, E
FLYNN, J
HOPE, J

JOWSEY, R
KIPLING, H
LITTLEWOOD, A H
MANSFIELD, J C
MATSON, E E
MEGGINSON, J
MOLLOW, W
MORLEY, W
NIGHTINGALE, A
NOMANDALE, S W
PERCY, W
PYE, J W C
SMITH, R J
TAYLOR, I
TINDALE, F
TROTTER, H
WALKER, J
WARWICK, J
WILLIAMS, J H
WILLIAMSON, J H

VADS

APPLEBY, J H
APPLEBY, F
ASH, A
BAYES, A
BAYES, T W
BETTS, R W
BLAKEY, J
BOLTON, G R
BOREMAN, R
BRANSON, W G
BROWN, G T
CAMMISH, R

CAPPLEVAN, G H
CASEY, J
CAVE, A
CHATWIN, F S
COULTAS, S W
COULTAS, T
COXWORTH, F
CRISS, A E
DELL, C S
DONKIN, T
DOVE, E W
EARDLEY, D
ECCLES, H A
FEATHER, J R
FENBY, H P
FLEMING, R F
FOX, C J
GLAISBY, E
HARDING, H
HARRY, T
HEPTON, T
HERITAGE, R
HOLIDAY, Y P J
JARVIS, W E
KAY, J H
KEYMER, E G H
LEEFE, H
LORD, J W E
MCLAUGHLIN, E W
MCLAUGHLIN, M M
MILLNER, A
MUDDIMAN, G A
NEWLAND, A

NICHOLSON, H
NIGHTINGALE, M
NOLAN, W C
PARK, L
PERCY, A
PICKERING, J W
POTTER, F H
POWELL, E B
PURNELL, H W
REYNOLDS, T
ROBSON, W
RUDD, F O
RUSSELL, H
SELLORS, E P
SOMERS, W
SPENCER, C
STRICKLAND, A
STRICKLAND, H
SWIFT, G K
TAYLOR, E E
TAYLOR, J H
TEALE, J
THOMPSON, G
TINDALL, E V
TINDALL, R F
TREEFITT, J W
WALKER, E W
WATSON, H
WILDING, C
WILLIAMS, J
WILSON, I
WRIGHT, A H

CHAPTER 10

Aftermath

With the war over after four and half years of bloody and barbaric fighting, those men from the town who had gone off to war and survived gradually started returning home to their families.

There were also those who had gone off to fight earlier in the war, who had survived, but who had been badly wounded; many had lost limbs or been gassed. For them, life would never quite be the same again, because not only did they have to deal with their debilitating injuries, but also with the emotional scars which came with what they had experienced. The memories of those years would stay with them for the rest of their days. For many, the only way to deal with what they had seen and done was never to talk about it again. Sometimes memories were far worse than any physical injury, and unlike the latter, they could never be seen with the human eye.

There were those who had suffered with a new wartime phenomenon, shell shock. For these men, their nervous system had simply imploded as they struggled to deal with being on the receiving end of prolonged German artillery bombardments. It wasn't just the deadening noise of the exploding shells, it was seeing their friends and colleagues dying all around them and also the not knowing, the constant fear of wondering, if they would be alive or dead once the bombardment was over.

Those returning home had to start their relationships all over again. Some soldiers hadn't seen their wives and children for months or years. Many of them had changed as a result of the war and were no longer the same person they were when they had left. It was a difficult time for everybody. Many of the cheerful and carefree young men – some no more than boys – who had gone off to war to give the 'Hun' a bloody nose and be back home in time for Christmas, returned a lot older than their real age. They had seen at first hand how horrible and brutal life could be, where life had little or no value. Their innocence had been snatched from them and it caused many to question their religion and faith, the very bedrock on which their lives had been formed.

The other issue was a social one; people now wanted and expected more out of life. For many, if the war was to truly be a victory then there had to be social change on a massive scale, it was the only way that they could reconcile the war years having had any real value and purpose, otherwise, what was the point of it all. The war had touched nearly every family throughout the length and breadth of the nation and it was the working men who had paid the highest and heftiest price of all. Now they wanted something tangible in return, a better tomorrow for them and their families.

To keep the country ticking over on the home front, and everyday life as normal as it could possibly be in a time of war, women had to take up a lot of the slack. Literally, overnight they had to cast off the restraints of a life which society had placed upon them before the war, and take on all of the roles which had previously been the sole domain of their men folk. They did it and they did it with aplomb; they became the bus drivers, the taxi drivers, the mechanics, the secretaries, they delivered the post, they worked in the fields, on the farms and in the extremely dangerous environment of the munitions factories. Many of them became nurses, some joined the Police, many joined wartime voluntary services such as the Women's Auxiliary Army Corps and the Women's Volunteer Reserve.

Women now had a wide choice of jobs that they could choose from. This brought them freedom and money, a lot more than they could ever otherwise hope to earn, but it was still not the same as what a man would be paid to do the same work.

The problem was that when the war ended, some elements of society had just assumed that life in all aspects would simply revert back to what it had once been. This caused something of an impasse because women wanted to keep the jobs they had been given and the money which they had earned, whilst the men who had returned from the war naturally expected their old jobs back.

As a community, Scarborough pre-war had been one of the premier holiday destinations in the UK. The war had not been good for business and the town's bombardment by ships of the German Imperial Navy on 16 December 1914, certainly didn't help. The hotels and restaurants in particular, had never really struggled to fill their rooms and tables, as people flocked to the seaside destination for leisure, relaxation and the opportunity to overdose on a constant supply of clean, smog free, fresh air. But sadly, the war began to change all that, as visitors, whether out of guilt or fear, had started to become more and more noticeable by their absence.

The ink on the Armistice had still not dried by the time of the first post-war general election in the UK on 14 December 1914. What had been a pre-war Liberal government had become a post-war Conservative one, although the turnout at the ballot boxes was, at 57.2 per cent, surprisingly low.

The new parliamentary seat of Scarborough and Whitby went the same way, with the Conservative politician, Major Gervase Beckett, winning the seat with a near 4,000 majority over his nearest rival, the Liberal candidate, Captain, later Sir, Osbert Sitwell. Many Liberals were understandably disappointed with the result, although realising from the outset that their candidate faced an uphill struggle to have a realistic chance of winning the seat.

Gervase Beckett, MP, speaking at the Constitutional Club after the announcement of the result, said that they should now have confidence in their party's leaders, whilst exercising patience whilst they carried out their wishes. He also made the somewhat unusual and unclear comment that he regarded his victory as a non-party one. Later that evening he travelled to

Whitby, where he was met by large crowds and gave an address from the balcony of the Royal Hotel, thanking those present most heartily for their support and the faith that they had shown in him. From there he travelled on to Pickering and onwards to his home at Nawton Towers.

Captain Sitwell, who spoke at the Liberal Club on the evening of Saturday, 28 December 1918 told his audience that with an end to the war had come a wave of reaction that had swept across the country and what they had to do was to see that this was turned round at once.

The end of the war left many with mixed emotions, happy in the knowledge that it was over at last, but sad at having to deal with the loss of loved ones. For one man it was a particularly difficult time. Walter Kershard, as he was referred to in the newspapers – although I could not find any reference to him in the 1911 Census – was a member of the crew of the fishing vessel *Loch Ryan,* that was captured by the German submarine *U-64* on 28 September 1916. All the crew were taken on board the submarine, whilst a party of German sailors went on board the trawler, and both vessel and crew were taken back to Germany. The crew spent the following two years as prisoners of war in Germany. The *Loch Ryan* was the only one of the fifty victims of *U-64* which had been captured as a prize. The other forty-nine vessels were either sunk or damaged. The *U-64* wasn't so fortunate, she was sunk by depth charges dropped by HMS *Lychnis* on 17 June 1918, resulting in the deaths of thirty-eight of her crew. Only five survived.

On Sunday, 1 December 1918, Walter returned to his home at 10 Quay Street, Scarborough looking forward to being reunited with his wife and two sons. Sadly, she had been suffering with influenza, which had then turned to pneumonia, from which she died, just two days after Walter had returned home, on Tuesday, 3 December 1918. His younger son Alfred died of the same ailment the next day, whilst his eldest son was in hospital recovering from the effects of influenza.

On Saturday, 21 December 1918, 49-year-old Arthur Edward Edwards, a gentleman of independent means, was found dead in the bathroom of his home at 46 Royal Avenue, Scarborough. Although a married man, he and his wife had lived apart since September of the same year, when she had gone to live with her sister in London. Mr Edwards had previously had a breakdown and had been described as having an artistic temperament as well as being prone to mood swings. His wife returned to the matrimonial home on the Saturday of his death, but it is not clear whether she was the one who found him dead, or whether she returned after his body had already been discovered.

An inquest on Monday, 23 December held by the Scarborough Borough Coroner, Mr G.E. Royle, heard that Mr Edwards was found dead on the bathroom floor of his home. The gas tap was turned full on, and a rug was nailed over the top of the door, a folded blanket at the bottom and the windows were locked shut. Having heard all the evidence, the coroner recorded a verdict of suicide whilst of unsound mind. The reason why Mr Edwards determined it necessary to end his life was unknown. Yet another moment of deep sadness during a period of rejoicing, which had been in place since the signing of the Armistice.

July 1919, a time set aside for nationwide post-war peace celebrations, had been disrupted by a miners' strike in the north of England after the Miners' Federation had refused a government pay rise of 6 shillings, which coincided with a strike on the North Eastern Railways.

Saturday, 19 July 1919 saw queues at Scarborough railway station as uncertainty over train timetables became apparent. But it wasn't just train passengers who relied on the trains to get to work who were affected, it was holiday makers and day trippers trying to get to Scarborough who were also suffering. Some of the local traders struggled to replenish their dwindling stocks as they relied heavily on the railways for their transportation

With the war now officially over, Saturday, 19 July 1919 was the chosen day for nationwide peace celebrations and the people of Scarborough were no different from those in other towns, they certainly knew how to celebrate. The harbour looked resplendent, adorned with flags and streamers as if they were expecting a boat full of dignitaries to arrive. The weather had played its part, the clear blue skies were as tranquil as the sea was calm. Smiling and cheering, people made their way through the streets, growing in numbers, quickly becoming crowds as they made their way like a fast flowing tide towards the harbour and the sands.

Everybody took part in the celebrations from the smartly dressed young children, some even too young to realise what all the fuss was actually about, to the very old who sadly, had seen it all before. The town's old age pensioners had been encouraged to attend the Town Hall to receive what had been advertised as a gift. Many of those who did turn up were very old and struggled to climb the steps of the Town Hall, something which apparently hadn't been considered. One old man was heard to say, 'It isn't worth coming for,' but perhaps even more strangely was the lack of any official to meet them on their arrival.

There was an organised gathering of representatives from all the military forces for entertainment at one of the popular pleasure houses, followed by a meat dinner. There were serving officers and men of all ranks, demobilized men and those who had been medically discharged having been wounded during their service. The invitation had been to all HM Forces who had served during the war no matter what part they had played.

One of the highlights of the day was the moving of the First World War tank to its final resting place in the town. It must have been a somewhat confusing sight, watching this grey and battered tank slowly meandering along the streets, bellowing out dark grey smoke, as it was being led by a troop of Boy Scouts, waving flags and handkerchiefs as they went. Following behind were line upon line of school children, immaculately turned out in white. A guard of honour from the Boys Cadet Corps acted as outriders along each side of this huge chunk of mobile metal. The procession finally came to a halt at the harbour, where many of the local children had gathered to burst into song as the tank slowly trundled into its final vantage place.

Photographers were snapping away, although possibly not fully appreciating the longevity and importance of the events that they were recording. Some things were so intimate and spontaneous they could not be recorded by the cameras of the day: the beaming smiles, the glint of an eye, the pride in how they felt about themselves and what others had done on their behalf during the war. What a contrast the day was in comparison to the previous four years the people of Scarborough had witnessed and endured. But this one was different, it was the beginning of a whole new era where people now had expectations of a brighter and better tomorrow.

By September 1919 the National Union of Railwaymen (NUR) and the Associated Society of Locomotive Engineers and Firemen (ASLEF) had called a national railway strike, which had greatly affected many towns and cities up and down the country, Scarborough being one of them. The strike, which lasted for nine days, proved successful and prevented a proposed government wage reduction for railway workers and also guaranteed them a working day of only eight hours. The government argued that the rates of pay for railway staff were simply being lowered back to the rate which they had been at prior to being raised during the exceptional circumstances of the First World War.

CHAPTER 11

Some who Returned

Here is a list of some of the men from Scarborough who enlisted and served their country in the Army during the First World War and managed to survive it. I do not suggest for one moment that this is a complete list, but more a random representation of all of the men from the town who did their bit when they were called upon to do so, even if in some cases it was only for a very short period of time.

Private (43678) James Alfred **Acklam** enlisted with the 80th Training Reserve of the Northumberland Fusiliers on 26 June 1917. He lived at 51 Trafalgar Street West, Scarborough, and prior to that he had lived at 6 Fish Yard, St Thomas Street, Scarborough. Before the war he had been an errand boy.

He was the oldest of five sons born to Alfred and Annie Acklam. Alfred was a blacksmith striker. James was discharged on 30 August 1917 at York when he was 22 years of age, for no longer being physically fit enough for wartime military service. He only served for sixty-six days, but he should never have been allowed to enlist in the first place as he had a major, and what would have been an extremely obvious problem with his left foot that was so severe it was painful when he attempted to walk in Army boots. In essence, and as recorded on the man's Army Pension Record, he had a club foot.

Only two of James's brothers were old enough to have served in the war, William and Percy, both of whom had chosen to serve in the Royal Navy. William enlisted as a Boy 2nd Class (J31034) on 2 May 1914 when he was 17 years of age. He survived the war and after having served his twelve years, he was discharged having completed his contract of service on 15 October 1926.

Percy enlisted on 7 August 1915 when he was only 15 years of age, like William as a Boy 2nd Class (J43088). He survived the war and his last day of service was 12 November 1928, after he had also served for twelve years.

Private (9251) John **Adams** had been a stone mason before the war, but when he enlisted in the Army, he joined the 2nd (Garrison) Battalion, Yorkshire Regiment. He lived at 9 Providence Place, North Street, Scarborough when he was discharged from the Army on 28 February 1917 at York. By this time, he had served in the Army for two years and 124 days.

The records show that he had a tattoo on his right forearm, of clasped hands with the names Sarah and Jack. When he was discharged as no longer physically fit for wartime military service, he was 48 years of age. His Army Pension Record shows that the reason for his discharge was because of a malignant epithelioma of the tongue. The report of the Medical Board in John's case dated 7 February 1917, included the following:

> *Originated in 1910, Scarborough. Man states in 1910 a small ulcer appeared on the point of his tongue. This healed up but 5 or 6 months after, another ulcer appeared on the right side of the tongue. Seven months ago owing to its size, the growth became painful, mastication being difficult and painful, also a good deal of cachexia. Not a result of nor aggravated by service.* <u>Permanent – Total incapacity</u>.

Sapper (112, 455) James Robinson **Allan** joined the Royal Engineers. He lived at 65 Norwood Street, Scarborough and had originally enlisted on 17 August 1915 at Scarborough. At the time he was nearly 36 years of age, a married man with three young children and a plumber by trade. He had previously served with the 5th Battalion, Yorkshire Regiment, a Territorial unit.

He served with the Egyptian Expeditionary Force, between 21 January and 28 December 1916, where he was attached to the 13th Base Park Company in Alexandria. His medical problems seem to have begun when he was admitted to the 15th General Hospital with an unspecified sickness on 3 October 1916. Between then and 21 November 1916, he was transferred to two other hospitals before being invalided back to England on board HM Hospital Ship *Panama* from Alexandria on 11 December 1916.

He spent the remainder of his military service in England, before being medically discharged from the Army on 22 September 1917. His brother, Richard Allan, was a Police Constable during the war.

Bandsman (43697) Bertrand **Allanson** was a in the 80th Training Reserve Battalion, when he was medically discharged from the Army on 28 November 1917 at York, for no longer being physically fit enough for wartime military service. He had enlisted on 1 October 1916, but wasn't called up for service until 25 June 1917, only five months earlier. His wartime military career was over in just 157 days, which begs the question of how he passed his initial Army medical assessment, as he was medically discharged because of disease of the heart, something he had been aware of since about 1912. It turned out to be nothing too serious as he went on to live to be 72 years of age, before passing away in March 1965. He was 25 when he enlisted and lived at 'The Lilacs', Cloughton, Scarborough.

Private (2306) John **Appleby** had served with the Yorkshire Hussars (Alexandra Princess of Wales's Own) between 1908 and 1913. When the war broke out, he re-enlisted in the regiment on his twenty-fifth birthday, on 1 September 1914 at Malton. On 25 November 1914 he was promoted to the rank of lance corporal, possibly because of his previous military experience.

He served in France with the British Expeditionary Force between 29 February 1915 and 3 March 1916, and was medically discharged on 1 May 1916. There was no detailed explanation as to why it had been necessary to discharge him, but he died in September 1916, aged 27. He lived at Bleak Trowse, Burninston Road, Scarborough.

Private (227179) Frederick **Archer** was in the 298th Reserve Company, Labour Corps. He was medically discharged on 17 October 1917 at Nottingham, having served for a total of 129 days after enlisting on 14 June 1916. He was deemed to be physically unfit due to having a bad physique, an affliction he had since infancy. He was also only just a fraction of an inch over 5ft tall. Once again it is strange how this was not picked up at the medical examination at his enlistment. Maybe an example of how much pressure the enlistment officers were under to recruit as many men as possible.

A medical report attached to his pension records included the following:

> He says he was delicate as a child. He states he has had a cough all of his life. During the bombardment of Scarborough, he says a shell burst near him, and he has been nervous ever since. He is very undersized and his chest is poorly formed. There are no physical signs of tuberculosis in his chest but he is a weakling, both physically and mentally.

It would be interesting to see what type of jargon would be used today to describe the same symptoms. It also strikes me as to what a brave individual this man was. It would appear that he had an obvious ailment, which understandably prevented him from continuing his military service, yet he went along to enlist, conscripted or otherwise, without making any attempt to use his condition to avoid military service. Before he enlisted he was a wood chopper and lived at Ebenezer Place, Long Westgate, Scarborough.

Gunner Albert **Atkinson** (134259) was 30 years of age and serving in the Royal Field Artillery. He enlisted on 1 March 1916 at Scarborough but was not mobilized until 31 March 1916. On 11 April 1916 he was posted to No.6 Reserve Battery, before being discharged from the Army on 19 June 1916 under King's Regulations para 392 (iii) (c), which meant that the recruit was unlikely to become an efficient soldier. He served for just 110 days. Better that such a problem was recognised during his basic training, rather than when he had been posted to the front. Although there appears to be a detailed explanation of why Atkinson was unlikely to have made an efficient soldier, included in his pension records, it is not completely legible. The best I can make it out to be is: *'Soldier states he has had a weak chest from childhood.'* The initials TB are apparent as well, which suggests that his ailment was possibly connected to tuberculosis.

He lived at East Ayton, Scarborough, with his parents, brother and sister. Before enlisting, Albert had been a farm labourer, an extremely physical occupation, suggesting he would have had to have been reasonably fit. Maybe it was a case of the Army simply not wanting to take a chance with his condition becoming worse whilst he was serving at the front, having to operate as part of a gun team.

Private (25594) Robert **Banks** enlisted in the Army Service Corps (railway labourer) on 2 December 1915 at Whitehall in London. He was 29 years of age. After being in the Army for only nineteen days he was sent to France with the British Expeditionary Force on 21 December 1915, but only remained there until 24 February 1916, when he returned to England. On 1 April 1916 he was medically discharged from the Army after serving for only 122 days.

Robert's case is truly remarkable by any stretch of the imagination, as it turns out that he had been deaf since he was a young child, but despite this he not only wanted to enlist, but he managed to fool the recruiting system and actually get himself out to France, before his disability was discovered. A medical report attached to his Pension Records includes the words, 'completely deaf'. He lived at 55 Oak Road, Scarborough.

Private (11066) Tom **Barker** was 47 years of age when he enlisted in the Army Veterinary Corps on 22 July 1915 in Scarborough. Prior to enlisting he had been a groom and lived at 4 Greenfield Road, Southcliffe, Scarborough, with his wife Elizabeth and their five children. On 11 March 1916, after having been in the Army for 234 days, he was discharged. His

Army pension record shows that he was no longer physically fit for war service. This entry has been crossed out and underneath it the following has been entered, *'Found to be permanently unfit for General Service. Authority of Army Council instruction 232 of January 1916.'*

Private (072688) William **Barrowcliff** was a married man with six children when he enlisted on 26 March 1915 in Scarborough. He was 31 years of age and joined the Army Service Corps. Before the war he had worked as a canteen manager. After just 37 days he was discharged from the Army as unlikely to become an efficient soldier. In William's case, this was because he suffered from chronic bronchitis, once again begging the question of why this wasn't recognised at the time of his enlistment, part of which would have been a medical examination. He lived at 47 Mayville Avenue, Scarborough, with his family.

Private (8709) Paul **Batty** was 37 years of age when he enlisted on 31 July 1915 in Scarborough, and joined the Army Cyclists Corps. There was no mention on his pension record as to why, when or if he was medically discharged, or whether he was simply demobbed at the end of the war, but the entry for Paul in the First World War Medal Rolls index cards, records that he was medically discharged due to an unspecified sickness on 10 August 1916. He was a married man who lived with his wife Mary at 51 Langdale Road, Scarborough.

Private (5981) Frederick **Benson** was 38 years of age when he enlisted on 6 November 1916 and joined the $2^{nd}/6^{th}$ Highland Light Infantry, at which time he was living with his wife Mary at 1 Esplanade Road, Scarborough. He was discharged on 2 March 1917, although I could find no explanation on his British Army pension record as to why.

Gunner (5406) William **Berry**, a general labourer, enlisted on 28 November 1914 at Scarborough when he was already 49 years of age. He joined the Royal Garrison Artillery, a regiment with which he had previously served in 1897. Because of his previous service he was almost immediately promoted to the rank of lance corporal, a promotion that was extremely short lived as just eleven days later, on 8 December 1914, he was discharged for having defective vision. He lived at 89 Hampton Road, Scarborough with his wife Lillian and their six children, Lillian, William, Albert, Marjorie, Elsie and Dorothy. William was unusual in so far as he was nearly 6ft tall at a time when most men were a lot smaller.

Private (24100) Albert Edward **Bland** was 27 years of age when he enlisted on 1 February 1917 in the 41st Labour Company, Labour Corps, although he was not actually mobilized until 30 March 1916. He was discharged on medical grounds on 22 July 1918 at Nottingham, by which time he had been in the Army for one year and 148 days. He had been diagnosed with having epilepsy and deafness, although it would appear that he had been so disposed for many years. It can only be assumed that he did not mention the ailment at the time of his enlistment. He had previously served in France with the British Expeditionary Force between 13 March 1917 and 24 April 1918. He had first been taken ill less than a week after arriving in France, when he was admitted to the 56th Casualty Clearing Station with what has been recorded as 'mental deficiency'. He was evacuated to England the next day on 23 April. He lived at 107 Lower William Street, Scarborough.

Private (39915) Charles William **Bourn** was 34 years of age and a clerk living at 84 Highfield, Scarborough. He enlisted in the Army on 22 February 1916, although he wasn't mobilized until 29 March 1916, when he joined the Prince of Wales's Own (West Yorkshire Regiment). At the time of his enlistment he was part of the Army Reserve. On 28 April 1917 he was transferred to the Depot Company and on 1 May 1917 he was declared surplus to military requirements and, having enrolled as a national service volunteer, was transferred to Class W of the Army Reserve. This was introduced in June 1916 by Army Order 203/16. In essence this was used when it was deemed that a man was more valuable to his country working in civil employment rather than military employment, even though in Charles's case, he was a clerk.

On 1 December 1917 he was discharged on medical grounds, although under the requirements of the Military Services

Act 1917, he was required to present himself for a medical re-examination on 1 December 1918, to see if there had been any change in his condition which would render him liable once again to be called up.

Gunner (3105, 761390) George Frederick **Broadrick** was 31 years of age and lived at 185 Falsgrave Road, Scarborough, with his mother, sister and two younger brothers. He enlisted in the 2nd Northumbrian Brigade, Royal Field Artillery on 7 February 1916, the same regiment he had previously served with for a period of six years. The same day that he enlisted saw him promoted to the rank of sergeant and on 2 July 1916 he arrived in France as part of the British Expeditionary Force with the 316th Brigade, Royal Field Artillery and on 30 August 1916, he was transferred to the 317th Brigade.

On 31 August 1918 he was medically discharged from the Army after receiving gun shot wounds to his left thigh and hip. He was issued with a Silver War Badge, which was worn in civilian life to indicate to others that he had been wounded whilst serving his country. He had served for two years and 206 days.

Private (16139) Michael **Brogan** was 37 years of age and married to Mary Flinn. They lived at 5 Goodline's Yard, Cross Street, Scarborough. Their marriage on 8 May 1900 in Scarborough had not resulted in any children. He enlisted in the Yorkshire Regiment, on 16 November 1914 at Scarborough. On 25 November 1914 he was posted to the regiment's 11th Battalion. The next entry on his Army Pension Record, says that he was discharged on 20 July 1916 as no longer physically fit for wartime military service. There is also a separate report from the Army Medical's Board enquiry into his case. It states:

> *This man was found to be unable to carry out ordinary military duties during last 7 months and has only done light fatigue duties. Complains of shortness of breath and rheumatic pain. Looks as stated and has no teeth. Visibly unable to perform duties of a soldier. Not the result of, or aggravated by military service.*

Private (204366) James **Brogan** was 27 years of age and a married man who lived at 5 Globe Street, Scarborough. He originally enlisted in the 5th (Reserve) Battalion, Durham Light Infantry on 19 June 1917. Just over a month later, on 22 July 1917 he was admitted to hospital at Lichfield in Staffordshire, where he was treated for syphilis and placed on the syphilis register. After being a patient for thirty days, he was released on 30 August 1917. He was transferred to the Labour Corps at Ripon on 22 February 1918 as a non-combatant soldier and became a private (520671).

He was discharged from the Army on 23 March 1918 at Nottingham on medical grounds. A medical report which formed part of his Army Pension Record, shows that as a 9-year-old boy he had suffered with rheumatic fever. Prior to his medical discharge he had suffered with pain all over the area of his upper chest and had never been fit for heavy work. He also complained of frequent attacks of bronchitis and suffered from deafness in his right ear. All of these ailments were not exactly conducive to serving in the Labour Corps.

Private (19374) Hugh **Campbell** was 38 years of age and lived at 5 Globe Street, Scarborough. He enlisted in the 15th (Service) Battalion, Cheshire Regiment (1st Birkenhead) on 30 November 1914 at Scarborough. On a soldier's enlistment papers is a section for the name and address of their next of kin. On Hugh Campbell's papers, the following has been written, 'No next of kin'.

After enlistment he was sent to Birkenhead to commence his basic military training. The first entry on his service record reads as follows, *'He is not likely to become an efficient soldier. Medically unfit.'* Yet again, a situation when a man is passed as being medically fit when he had enlisted at his local recruitment office, but by the time he commences his military training, he is declared to be medically unfit for wartime service. Hugh Campbell was officially discharged from the Army on 26 February 1914.

Private Frederick (2355) **Cardwell** lived at Carlton House, Belle Vue Parade, Scarborough. He had previous military service with the 4th Battalion, King's Regiment (Liverpool) from 1899 – 1905, and the Duke of Lancaster's Yeomanry from 1905 – 1907. On 2 September 1914 at Malton, he once again enlisted, this time in the Yorkshire Hussars (Alexandra, Princess of Wales's Own), but on 11 November 1914 after only seventy-one days of service, he was discharged from the Army for what has been classed as unsatisfactory behaviour. This involved being drunk, absent without leave and causing a nuisance in his billet. He went before his commanding officer to explain himself, but it was deemed that his combined actions merited his discharge from the Army. The section in the record which allows for comment on a man's character, has the word 'Bad' written in it.

Private (15123) Ernest **Charnock** lived at 1 Pextons Yard, Church Stair Street, Scarborough. With the outbreak of the war he enlisted in the Army on 29 September 1914 at Scarborough in the Yorkshire Regiment, but on 16 October 1917 he transferred to the Labour Corps, becoming private (395195) before he was medically discharged on 6 February 1918 at Nottingham by an Army Medical Board. He had been wounded in action when he was shot in the head and left forearm. The wounds he sustained subsequently left him physically unfit for further military service.

Prior to the wounds which led to his medical discharge, he had previously been wounded on at least two other occasions. On 5 July 1916 he received a bayonet wound to his left hand, resulting in bone fractures and the amputation of his middle finger. He was sent back to England and spent thirty-nine days in the 2nd Western General Hospital in Manchester, finally being discharged on 15 August 1916. The following year, having returned to France, he once again received a bayonet wound, this time to the upper forearm. Again he was sent back to England and this time he spent sixty-seven days in the 1st Southern General Hospital, in Dudley Road, Birmingham, between 19 April and 25 June 1917.

He had served for three years 139 days. During this time he had twice served in France with the British Expeditionary Force. The first time was between 26 August 1915 and 7 July 1916 and the second, 20 January and 18 April 1917.

Private (3270) Wilfred **Clayton** lived at 57 West Bank, Scarborough, with his wife, Emily. He enlisted on 5 May 1915 in his home town just a month shy of his forty-third birthday, and was sent to the 5th Battalion (2nd Line), Yorkshire Regiment, a Territorial Unit. Prior to the outbreak of the First World War, he had previously served in the 1st Battalion, Prince of Wales's Own (West Yorkshire) Regiment, retiring as a sergeant.

He was promoted to the rank of corporal on 23 August 1915 and then further promoted to second sergeant on 22 September 1915. Having then served for a period of one year and five days, he was medically discharged from the Army on 9 May 1916, because of neurasthenia. This we would today know as nervous exhaustion.

Gunner (8173) James **Crake** lived at 4 Brunswick Terrace, Scarborough. On 3 August 1915, aged supposedly 19, he enlisted in the Army at Scarborough and joined the Royal Field Artillery. Just twenty days later he was discharged from the Army under King's Regulations para 392 (vi)(a), which meant that James in his eagerness to enlist, had lied about his age, and that he was actually under 17 years of age on the date of his discharge.

Private (26469) William Solva **Davies** lived at Glen Ord, Vansen Street, Scarborough, with his parents David and Miriam Davies and his two younger sisters, Millie and Gladys. He enlisted in the Yorkshire Regiment when he was 22 years of age on 11 December 1915, although he wasn't mobilized until 31 January 1916. Before enlisting he was a theological student.

On 1 May 1916 he was transferred to the 2nd Battalion, Highland Light Infantry, and on 10 January 1917, he was medically discharged from the Army having served for 345 days. A medical report on his pension record showed that he had been diagnosed with dilation of the myocardium, which is a heart related ailment. Despite this he went on to live to 95 years of age, passing away in January 1989.

Private (7613) Robert Beal **Davison** lived at 37 Rothbury Street, Scarborough and before the war he had been employed as a clerk. He enlisted on 9 July 1915 at York in the Army Pay

Corps, when he was 22 years of age. He served throughout the war, finally being demobilized on 6 September 1919, after a total of four years and sixty days. He was then transferred to Class Z of the Army Reserve, before being finally discharged on 31 March 1920. He was one man who had survived the war in one piece.

Company Sergeant Major (4282) Henry **Dell** was 30 years of age and lived at 29 Westborough, Scarborough. Before the war he was an optician. He served in the 11th and 13th battalions, Royal Fusiliers. He was medically discharged on 1 September 1917 as a result of a gun shot wound to his left leg, whilst serving in France with the British Expeditionary Force between 28 July 1915 to 27 November 1916. The actual wound occurred on 14 November 1916 during fighting at Beaucourt during the Battle of the Ancre (13-18 November 1916). Beaucourt was captured by the 63rd Royal Naval Division on 14 November, the day Henry Dell was wounded. This was to be the final full-scale British attack of the Battle of the Somme.

On his return to England he was admitted to the York Military Hospital on 16 February 1917 and remained there until 9 July 1917. The doctor's notes on his hospital admissions sheet, read as follows:

> *Shrapnel bullet wound. Wound is healed. Patient walks fairly well. Slight oedema of leg. Both leg and thigh swell after walking. Bullet is embedded in the upper end of the tibia.*

His Army service record included the following comments about his military character:

> *Record most satisfactory. Has proved himself a most efficient man and was awarded the DCM Medal. States he was 4 years Optician with F J Hunt, 29 Westborough, Scarborough.*

The award of the Distinguished Conduct Medal provided Henry with an extra 6d per day in his army pension.

Private (15) Alfred William **Dobson** lived at 25 Castle Road, Scarborough with his parents, Thomas and Mary Dobson, his three sisters, Ada, Alice and Annie and his brother John. He enlisted in the 3rd Battalion, Northumberland Fusiliers on 15 November 1915. He was discharged from the Army on medical grounds on 2 August 1917 in York when he was 22 years of age. Having arrived in France on 19 May 1916 he suffered a gunshot wound to his left foot on 1 July 1916, the first day of the Battle of the Somme. A medical report on his Army Pension Record describes how the wound occurred:

> *He states that in the advance he was hit in the left foot by 5 pieces of shell. One passing through his left foot. One hitting his foot, and three embedded within his foot. After being attended to on the spot, he was moved to the base hospital and then home to the 3rd Northern General Hospital, in Sheffield, where he remained for six months.*

As a result of the injury Dobson found difficulty walking long distances, due to the pain which it caused him. Most military pensions awarded as a result of involvement in the First World War, usually only lasted for a year in the first instance and then the men had to apply to have them continued.

Private (21626) Francis **Doran** lived at 28 Lyle Street, Scarborough. When he enlisted in the Army on 19 January 1915, in Barry, he was 38 years of age and joined the 12th Battalion, Welsh Regiment. He had previously served in the 3rd Battalion, York Garrison Artillery (Militia). But just a week after enlisting, he was deemed to be physically unfit for wartime military service.

Driver (2340) (761326) John Harrison **Eddon** lived at Woodlea, Newly, near Scarborough. He enlisted in the North Riding Battery, Royal Field Artillery on 15 May 1915 at Scarborough. On 2 July 1916 he went to France with C Battery of the 316th Brigade, Royal Field Artillery. On 30 August 1916, he was transferred to the 317th Brigade, Royal Field Artillery.

The medical officer who examined John when he enlisted, commented about the state of his bad and defective teeth as well as the varicose veins in both legs. Despite these entries, he still passed him as being fit enough for the British Army. He served in France between 3 July and 28 December 1916.

On 5 January 1917 he was admitted to the Military Hospital in York for treatment to wounds he had received on both hands. These included a fracture and ulcers. He remained a patient until 5 February 1917.

On 16 March 1917 he was transferred to Class W of the Army Reserve. John Eddon had written on his Army Reservist form that he had a ruptured tendon. A septic poisoned system of the ankles, legs and hands, as well as valvular heart disease. He also had written on the same form that he believed that his ailments were either caused or aggravated by his military service. His ruptured tendon occurred as a result of opening 'bully beef' tins with a knife which slipped whilst he was serving at Beaumont Hamel on the Somme, cutting his hand which then became septic. He further stated that it was due to having been worn out and run down that the septic poison spread all over his body and his heart problems had occurred.

On 10 July 1917 it was recommended that John Eddon should be transferred to Class P or PT of the Army Reserve. On 19 July 1917 he was discharged from the Army for being physically unfit for wartime military service. His condition was such that he was permanently excluded from having to have his case reviewed on an annual basis, as part of the Military Services (Review of Exceptions) Act 1917. His disability was an injury to one of his fingers and his pension was set at £27 10s.

Part of a report from the Army Medical Board, which met on 10 July 1917 to review this particular case, stated: *'This is a doubtful case both as to causation and real extent of injury – 1% permanent or less. 10.8.17.'*

Private (18245) Michael **Fitzpatrick** was 36 years of age and lived at 17 William Street, Scarborough with his wife Mary and their two children, Alice and Richard. Before the war he was a general labourer. He enlisted on 7 December 1914 at Scarborough, joining the 3rd Battalion, Yorkshire Regiment. He was discharged from the Army on 1 April 1915, because it was felt that he was not going to become an efficient soldier. This was due to an accident he had before joining the Army, which left him with a limp, which in turn affected the way he walked and his ability to march in a disciplined and cohesive manner.

Private (32/657) Charles Percival **Freeman** was 27 years of age and lived with his wife, Patience, at 3 Barry's Cottages, Scarborough. He initially enlisted on 15 May 1915 at Scarborough and was attached to the 32nd Battalion, Northumberland Fusiliers on 28 April 1916, although he had originally attested on 15 November 1915 and was then placed on the Army Reserve. On 10 September 1916 he was transferred to the 1st/5th Battalion, York and Lancashire Regiment and became private 242272.

He was discharged from the Army on 29 August 1918 at York, due to a gun shot wound to his head which he had sustained on 19 April 1918. He had served in France from 29 August 1916 until 19 April 1918. Despite his head wound he went on to live until he was 80 years of age, passing away at the end of March 1971.

Private (238090) William Henry **Gibson** was 25 years of age and lived at 117 Hoxtol Road, Scarborough. Prior to the war he worked as a shop assistant at a local retailers. He attested on 7 February 1915 at Leeds, but wasn't mobilized until 2 October 1916 when he joined the Army Service Corps (Mechanical Transport). On 5 May 1917 William was transferred to the Army Reserve Class W. He was discharged from the Army on 14 December 1918 on the grounds that he was surplus to military requirements.

Private (2843) Thomas **Gibson** was 20 years of age and lived at 76 Trafalgar Place, Scarborough when he enlisted on 28 November 1914 at Scarborough in the Yorkshire Hussars. He was then transferred to the 4th Battalion, East Yorkshire Regiment as a private (203117) on 9 December 1916, the day he arrived in France where he remained until 3 May 1917. He was medically discharged on 21 December 1917 after sustaining a gun shot wound to his left shoulder whilst on active service. In total he served for a total of three years and twenty-four days.

Driver (19709) Thomas **Godwin** was 35 years of age and lived at 43 Hoxton Road, Scarborough. He enlisted in the Army on 10 May 1915 at Scarborough and served in C Battery, 161st (Yorkshire) Brigade, Royal Field Artillery. On 19 January 1916 he was posted to the 7th Reserve Battery and on 13 March 1916 he was medically discharged from the Army. In the years prior to the war, he had served with the Prince of Wales's Own (Regiment).

He had been diagnosed with having tubercle of the lung. A report by the Army Medical Board in relation to Thomas's case included the following explanation for his discharge:

States that ever since boyhood has suffered from indigestion and pain in the stomach. Underwent an operation in April 1910 for repair of perforated ulcer of stomach. Enlisted at Scarborough, worked quite well until he contracted a cold by getting wet through during a field inspection.

This led to problems with both his lungs and was made worst by the discovery of a gastric ulcer. The reports on soldiers' pension records generally make for interesting reading, as a large part of what is often written on many of them is the justification, both for and against, depending on the individual case, as to the amount and period of time that any pension should be paid for. Most reports are finished off with a specific wording about whether or not the man's medical condition was aggravated by their wartime service. This is an important aspect, because this will ultimately dictate the amount paid on the pension and for how long. Here's how it was worded in Thomas's case:

This man was not subjected to any exceptional hardship, strain or exposure other than usual. Exceptionally inclement weather was experienced during the whole of the time the Battalion was in training at Forant. During the period of training referred to, the men were in hutments which were leaky and draughty and far from satisfactory in view of the heavy weather experienced. Proper clothing was issued. This man's present condition may be regarded, for pension purposes, as aggravated by service since the declaration of war.

Private (9594) Robert **Gordon** was 28 years of age and lived at 19 Hewish Street, Scarborough. Before the war he had been employed as a miner. He enlisted in the Army at Norwood on 17 June 1915, when he joined the 11th Battalion, East Surrey Regiment, but on 14 July 1915, he was medically discharged. The Medical Officer wrote his reasons as to why he felt Robert Gordon was unfit for service: '*Recruit is weak both in mind and body and absolutely unfit for any service.*'

There was certainly no sugar coating of comments by most of the medical officers. They said it exactly how they saw it, whether that was good or bad. I am not so sure such direct observations would be allowed or encouraged, in today's world, especially with civil litigation in mind. Tangible evidence to support such comments would most definitely be required to stave off any legal challenges.

Private (35910) John **Gospel** was 18 years of age and lived at 44 William Street, Scarborough. He enlisted on 26 June 1917 at Richmond in Yorkshire into the 9th Training Reserve. He was discharged from the Army on 28 August 1917. The reason behind why John was discharged, wasn't because he had been wounded in action, or because he was suffering from some debilitating disease or illness, it was because his arms were deformed and therefore he would never be fit enough to serve in any of the military services. What is strange about this case was that he had actually managed to get past the initial enlistment stage, but he did and then it was a further two months before he was medically discharged. The fact that he did get through the initial process, suggests that despite his obvious disability, he still wanted to enlist and do his bit, regardless. What character John Gospel must have had.

It is interesting to note that on his Army Pension Record, it had the obligatory phrase, 'no longer physically fit for war service'. Quite clearly he never was going to be fit enough; he had a malfunction of both of his elbow joints. It's incredible that he passed his enlistment medical.

The following paragraph had been entered on to his pension record by an un-named second lieutenant: *'Liable to be sent a statutory order on 28 August 1918, requiring him to present himself for medical re-examination under the military service (Review of Exceptions) Act 1917.'*

Yet again, somewhat of a strange paragraph, as having malfunctioning arms was not something that was going to clear up overnight.

Private (12839) Walter James **Gray** lived at 106 Nelson Street, Scarborough. He enlisted in the Army Pay Corps on 10 April 1917, carrying out the duties of a clerk. Initially he had been allocated as a private (48446) in the West Yorkshire Regiment. His enlistment medical shows that he had an osteoma of the tibia, which is another word for a benign tumour, but this was deemed not to be sufficient to warrant his rejection as a recruit. He was appointed to the rank of acting lance corporal, but in an unpaid capacity, on 18 October 1917 and promoted to the substantive rank of corporal on 16 April 1918.

On 6 July 1918 he was admitted to the Military Hospital, York, where he was treated for chronic bronchitis, where he remained until 16 August 1918. During his time under medical observation, it was noticed that his heartbeat could be seen as a visible pulsation, which placed Walter's health at even more risk than his bronchitis, and meant that he was no longer physically fit for military service. After he was discharged from the hospital, he still required further treatment, but which he received as an out patient for a further three months. He was discharged from the Army on 6 September 1918 at York, having served for a total of 1 year 150 days. The pension he was awarded expired on 1 April 1919.

Private (26222) Frank **Gregory** was 33 years of age and lived at 64 Terrington Avenue, Scarborough with his wife Florence and their son Stanley. Before the war he had held the position of theatre manager. With the war now into its second year, he attested on 10 December 1915 and was placed on the Army

Reserve. He was eventually mobilized on 1 June 1916, and joined the 3rd Battalion, West Yorkshire Regiment. On 7 April 1917 he was transferred to the Works Battalion of the Durham Light Infantry as a private (70208). On 25 April he was then placed on the Army Reserve, Class W, and on 7 January 1918, he was medically discharged as no longer being physically fit for wartime military service, although he was liable to be sent a statutory order to undergo a review of his medical condition on 7 January 1919, exactly a year to the day that he was medically discharged. He had served for a total of two years and twenty-nine days.

Private (22104) Thomas **Hardington** lived with his wife Margaret and their three children, Dorothy, George and John, at 13 Milton Road, Scarborough. He enlisted at Scarborough on 9 August 1915, initially in the West Yorkshire Regiment, but then he was transferred to the 2nd (Garrison) Battalion, King's Own Yeomanry, Light Infantry as a private (30479) on 22 June 1916. He was 44 years of age.

He had previously served with the 3rd Battalion, Yorkshire Regiment, after enlisting on 3 September 1889 aged 18. He served for twelve years, seven with the colours and five in the reserve, and was discharged on 11 August 1902. Thomas's Army pension record shows that he was not discharged from the Army, but simply demobilized at the end of the war, which in his case was 14 January 1919 whilst he was on leave in the UK.

Private (6194) Thomas George **Harrison** was 38 years of age and lived at 40 Sepulchre Street, Scarborough. He was in the King's Own Yorkshire Regiment and was discharged on medical grounds on 16 September 1916 at York. The obligatory phrase of being no longer physically fit for wartime military service, adorns his Army Pension Record, but on closer examination we see that is because he was shot in the face and lost the sight of one of his eyes. At the time of his discharge this particular old soldier had been in the army for nearly sixteen years, having previously served in South Africa during the Second Boer War. He held the Queen's South African Medal and clasps for Cape Colony and

Orange Free State as well as the King's South African Medal and clasps for 1901 and 1902, Transvaal and South Africa.

Private (289395) Herbert Cyril **Hodgson** lived at 46 Westborough, Scarborough with his parents James and Olivia and his five brothers and sisters. His father was a hairdresser and earned enough money from his business to be able to afford to employ two servants. Before the war Herbert had been an electrician by trade. He enlisted in the Army, as soon as he was able to, on 1 November 1916, but he wasn't mobilized until 13 February 1917 when he joined the Army Service Corps. Still not quite 19 years of age, he was discharged from the Army on 25 September 1917 at Woolwich Dockyard, on medical grounds as he was suffering with tuberculosis of the lung. Sadly, Herbert's condition worsened and he died on 18 November 1918 having not even reached his twentieth birthday.

Private (9436) Benjamin **Hunter** was 38 years of age and lived at 24 The Bolts, Landside, Scarborough. He enlisted in the Army on 22 December 1914 and joined the 2nd Garrison Battalion, Yorkshire Regiment. As a younger man he had previously served with the 3rd Battalion, Yorkshire Regiment. Three months after enlisting, Benjamin arrived in France on 25 March 1915 and remained there until 30 November later that same year. On 17 April 1917 he was transferred to the regiment's 18th Battalion and on 8 November 1917 he was medically discharged due to rheumatism which was aggravated by his time in the army.

Private (3221) Alfred **Inchbald** lived at 105 Candler Street, Scarborough. He enlisted on 15 February 1915 at Scarborough and became of part of the 5th (Reserve) Battalion Yorkshire Regiment, a Territorial unit. The Attestation document showed that this was for a period of four years service within the United Kingdom. He had previously served with the 2nd (Volunteer) Battalion, Yorkshire Regiment, for six years. On 9 March 1916, Alfred was, for some obscure reason, transferred to the regiment's 24th Battalion, where he became a drummer, but just six months later on 5 September 1916 he was discharged from the Army at York, as he was deemed to be no longer physically fit enough for wartime military service. There was no detailed information included in his Army pension record, as to the specifics of why he was discharged.

Private (96051) John William **Ingham** was nearly 41 years of age and lived at 3 Filey Road, Scarborough with his father, brother and sister. He enlisted in the Army on 28 October 1916 at Ripon. The personal description form of his Army pension record, showed his 'trade or occupation' to be that of a 'gentleman'. Initially he was allocated to the Royal Army Medical Corps but on 25 June 1917, he was transferred to the Leicestershire Regiment as Private 39391. He went on to serve with their $2^{nd}/5^{th}$, 6th and 4th battalions.

He received gunshot wounds to his abdomen and his left arm whilst serving in France on 29 April 1918. He was sent back to England for treatment and ended up at the Wharncliffe War Hospital in Sheffield, arriving there on 4 May 1918, where he remained for the following five months whilst his wounds were being treated, before finally being released on 3 October 1918. It was because of his wounds that he was subsequently discharged. Ironically, his discharge date was 11 November 1918. His pension expired on 11 November 1919, just one year later.

Guardsman (29872) Thomas Henry **Jackson** was 23 years of age and a chartered accountant who lived at Osgodby, Cayton, Scarborough, with his mother, grandmother, three brothers and sisters, as well as nine servants. He joined the Grenadier Guards from the Army Reserve, Class B, on 16 April 1917, although he was deemed to have enlisted as of 1 October 1916.

Whilst serving in France with 3 Company, 4th Battalion, Grenadier Guards, he was reported as missing in action on 13 April 1918, before being confirmed as having been taken as a prisoner of war on 11 May 1918. He returned to England on 8 December 1918, just in time for the Christmas festivities. He was eventually discharged on demobilization on 8 March 1920.

Rifleman (12813) Alexander **James** was 38 years of age and lived at 17 Princes Royal Terrace, Scarborough. He enlisted in the Army on 10 December 1915 at Scarborough and joined the 21st Battalion, King's Royal Rifles. Prior to enlisting he had been a chemist. He was sent out to France as part of the British Expeditionary Force on 5 May 1916, before returning to England on 3 July 1916, and being discharged for being no longer physically fit for wartime service, just 25 days later, on 28 July 1916. It would appear from his Army Pension Record that he was suffering from shell shock.

Third Class Air Mechanic (83514) John Sunley **Jarvis** was 28 years of age and lived at 39 Cross Street, Scarborough, with his wife Mary and their two children, Rhoda and George. He enlisted in the Royal Flying Corps on 24 June 1916, but was not called up for service until 4 June 1917, although he had previously served with the 5th Battalion, Yorkshire Regiment and the Army Service Corps, Mechanical Transport section.

He had to forfeit eleven days pay for being absent without leave for eleven days between 8 and 18 June 1917, fortunately at the time he was still in England and had only been with the Royal Flying Corps for two days. If he had done the same whilst serving in France, there is every chance he would have faced the death penalty and been shot by firing squad.

On 7 December 1917 he was discharged for no longer being fit for wartime military service, although he had to present himself for a statutory medical re-examination on 6 December 1918 under the conditions of the Military Service (Review of Exceptions) Act 1917.

Charles **Johnson** was a 25-year-old builder's labourer and a married man, who lived with his wife Mary, at 6 Dyson's Yard, William Street, Scarborough. He enlisted on 16 November 1914 at Scarborough as Private (16280) in the 1st Battalion, Yorkshire Regiment. On 1 February 1915 he was tried, convicted and sentenced by a District Court-Martial, to 35 days detention, for drunkenness and conduct to the prejudice of good order and military conduct. Just nine days later he was discharged form the Army for not being likely to become an efficient soldier as 'mentally defective'. This was carried out by the General Officer Commanding the 89th Infantry Brigade, Lieutenant Colonel R.L. Aspinall.

Private (94287) Walter **King** was 21 years of age and lived at 41 Harcourt Avenue, Scarborough. At 6ft 2ins he was exceptionally tall. He enlisted in the Royal Army Medical Corps and was trained in both first aid and ambulance duties. He was medically discharged on 31 December 1917 at Woking, as no longer physically fit for wartime military service due to having ametropia, astigmatism, and corneal opacities; both eyes were affected.

Private (31817) William **Lauchlan** was 35 years of age and married man who lived at 1 Vosey Road, St Sepulchre Street, Scarborough with his wife Mary and their four children. He joined from the Army Reserve, Class B on 3 November 1916 at Richmond in Yorkshire, joining the 4th Battalion, South Staffordshire Regiment. As part of the British Expeditionary Force, he arrived in France on 10 February 1917, and was posted to the regiment's 2nd Battalion. He returned to the UK on 18 May 1917 and during the following six months, he would also serve with the 3rd and 4th battalions.

He was discharged from the Army on 13 November 1917 for no longer being physically fit for wartime military service, but there were no specific details on his Army Pension Record as to the precise details of the reasons for his discharge.

Private (43685) William Henry **Lee** was 25 years of age and lived at Prospect Cottages, Burnette, Scarborough. Before enlisting in the Training Reserve on 25 June 1917, he worked as a tailor. He was discharged from the Army just over three months later on 5 October 1917, for no longer being physically fit for wartime military service. There was no detailed information on his Army Service Record to indicate the specific reason for his discharge.

Driver (036916) Thomas **Luntley** was 37 years of age and a married man who lived at 1 Chapel Yard, Batty Place, Scarborough with his wife and young son. Prior to becoming a soldier, he had worked both as a labourer and a groom. He enlisted in the Army on 31 December 1914 at Scarborough and joined the Army Service Corps. His has to go down as one of the shortest military careers on record, as just three days later, on 2 January 1915, he was discharged for being likely not to make an efficient soldier. It would appear this decision was based on Thomas's very poor physique.

Private (5197) Thomas **Mackinstosh** was 44 years of age, a married man who lived at 56 Castle Road, Scarborough with his wife and two children. He enlisted as in the Army Pay Corps on 6 January 1916 at York. After carrying out acting roles on many occasions, he was finally promoted to the substantive rank of corporal on 15 March 1920, before being discharged on demobilization, less than a month later on 11 April 1920. He had served for five years and 97 days, all of which was within the UK.

Driver (761360) Charles Edward **Malton** lived at 55 Commercial Street, Scarborough. He enlisted on 27 May 1915 at Scarborough in the 2nd North Battalion, Brigade, Royal Field Artillery. On 2 July 1916 he was transferred to the 316th Brigade and on 30 August 1916, he was further transferred to the 317th Brigade, Royal Field Artillery.

He was eventually discharged on medical grounds on 29 March 1918, due to gun shot wounds to his fingers, left knee and right forearm, received on 1 December 1917 whilst on active service. He was issued with a Silver War Badge.

Private (3636) Patrick Joseph **Martin** was 48 years of age and lived at 10 Castle Spring Gardens, Scarborough. He enlisted in the 2nd/5th Battalion, Yorkshire Regiment on 9 April 1915. On 25 November 1915 he transferred to the 2nd/9th Battalion, Durham Light Infantry, before ending up in the Royal Defence Corps, when he transferred to the 156th Protection Company on 29 April 1916 and then finally to the 157th Protection Company on 23 September 1916. He remained with them for the rest of his service until 28 January 1917, when he was discharged from the Army for being no longer physically fit for wartime military service. This is another case of no detailed information included on the man's Army Pension Record that can shed any light on why he was no longer fit for war service.

Private (16123) John **McLaren** was 35 years of age and lived in Scarborough. He enlisted in the Army on 14 December 1914

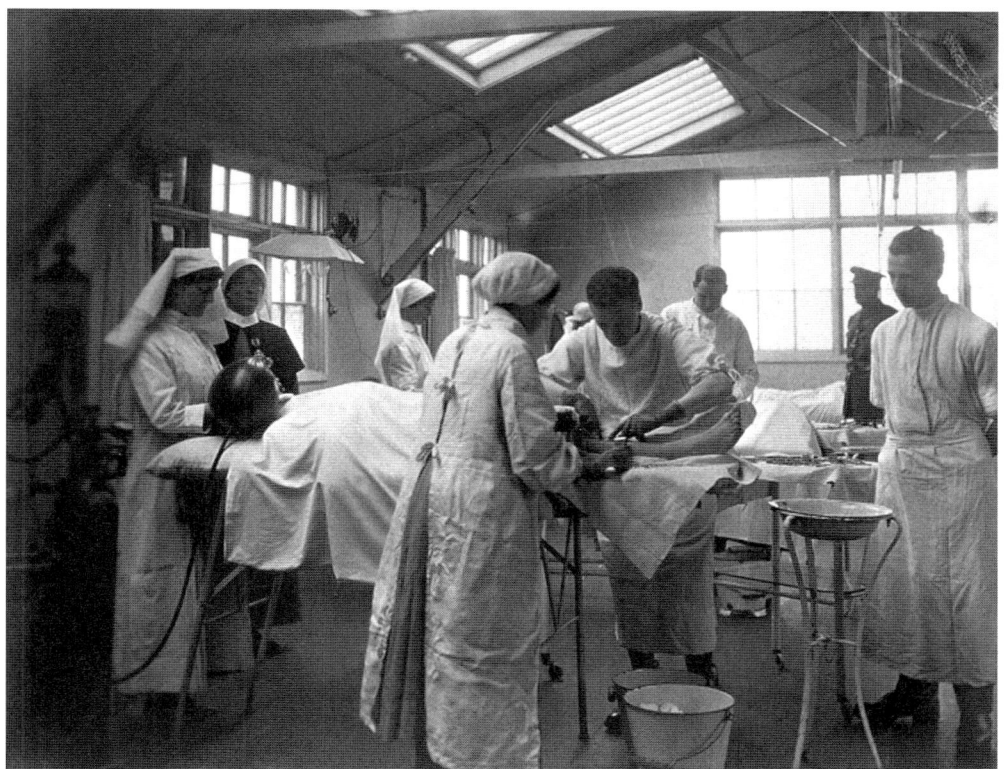

Wimereux Hospital.

at Bridlington but wasn't mobilized until 30 December 1914, when he joined the 3rd Battalion, East Yorkshire Regiment. On 9 April 1915 he was discharged from the Army on the grounds that he would not make an efficient soldier, due to the fact that he had flat feet, flatness and deformity in his left foot and a weak ankle on his right foot.

Private (4181) James **McMurtrie** was 35 years of age and lived at 6a Castle Road, Scarborough. Before the war he had worked as a tailor, but on 24 February 1916 he enlisted in the Yorkshire Regiment at Scarborough. On the personal details sheet of his Army Pension Record, in the section marked, next of kin, two words have been written, 'No Friends.'

James appears to have been quite a character. He served with the British Expeditionary Force on two occasions. The first time was between 12 July 1916 and 9 April 1917 when he was wounded in action, a gunshot wound to his right shoulder, leg and ankle on 2 April 1917. He returned home on 9 April on board the Hospital Ship *Stad Antwerpen*. His second time in France was between 29 July and 2 October 1917. On 10 April 1917 he was admitted to the War Hospital in Halifax. During his second time in France, he was admitted to the 51st General Hospital at Étaples on 1 August 1917 and released on 7 September 1917. Later the same month, on 26 September, he was treated at the 63rd Casualty Clearing Station, for what appears to be a sprained ankle, and two days later he was admitted to the 14th Stationary Hospital at Wimereux near Boulogne, after which he was returned to England for further treatment.

On his return to England in October 1917 he was admitted to the Lancashire Military Hospital in Blackpool. He was also awarded the Military Medal, the award of which was mentioned in the *London Gazette* on 22 January 1917.

James was medically discharged on 6 May 1918, and such were his injuries, which included a previously unknown fracture of his left fibula, that he was exempt under the Military Service (Review of Exemption) Act 1917 from the need to undergo any future medical examinations.

Private (026646) Stephen **Meggison** was 27 years of age and lived at 42 Sandringham Street, Scarborough. He enlisted on 26 November 1914 at Scarborough in the Army Service Corps. Before signing up for his military service he had worked as a farm labourer. He was deemed to be unfit for further wartime military service on 6 May 1915 because of his flat feet, which he'd had since birth and a squint as a result of rheumatic fever which had left him with a cast in his right eye.

After the bombardment of Scarborough on 16 December 1914, he had enlisted at Scarborough Town Hall and had passed the medical, although since he had been in the Army he had not done one day's duty because of his medical conditions.

Wounded Blues.

Rifleman (21020) Joseph Valentine **Miller** was 19 years of age and lived at 158 Castle Road, Scarborough. He enlisted in the in the King's Royal Rifles on 21 February 1916 at Scarborough and subsequently served with the 24th, 16th and 6th battalions. He was with the latter when he was medically discharged on 17 May 1917, for no longer being physically fit enough to serve.

He first arrived in France on 10 July 1916 with his battalion, and quickly became involved in the fighting. He was wounded in action on 24 August 1916, which was only of a minor nature and resulted in him being treated at No.19 Field Ambulance. Less than a week later on 30 August he was treated by No.21 Casualty Clearing Station on the Somme for the effects of shell shock. He was transferred to No.11 Stationary Hospital on 3 September 1916 and sent back to England by hospital ship later the same day. His condition never recovered for him to be fit enough to continue his military service.

Private (266016) Cecil William **Moses** was 31 years of age and lived at 28 Falsgrave Road, Scarborough. He enlisted in the Army Service Corps serving in France between 30 August 1917 and 13 January 1918. His Army Pension Record does not include any specific details about injuries, illnesses or diseases which he incurred that resulted in his discharge. On 14 March 1918 at Woolwich Dockyard he was deemed to be no longer physically fit enough for wartime military service.

Private (22102) Joseph Edward **Mulvana** was 43 years of age, a married man who lived at 55a Dumple Street, Scarborough with his wife Mary and their three children. By the outbreak of war, he had already been married for some twenty years. He enlisted in the Prince of Wales's Own (West Yorkshire) Regiment on 23 July 1915 at Scarborough. He went on to serve with the regiment's 10th, 13th, 16th and depot battalions.

Whilst in France, (17 March 1916 to 3 November 1917) he was wounded in action at La Bassée, when he received a gunshot wound to his right hand, which resulted in two of his fingers, the fore and middle fingers, having to be amputated at the first joint. This resulted in his return to England and was the cause of his subsequent discharge from the Army, his discharge taking effect on 11 January 1918. As a younger man he had also seen service with the 3rd Battalion, East Lancashire Regiment.

Gunner (99903) Charles **Newham** was 29 years of age and a married man who lived with his wife Mary and their three children, at 22a Hope Street, Scarborough. At the time of the 1911 Census, Charles and Mary were living at 2 Black Union Street, Scarborough and Charles earned his living as a slaughterman.

Charles enlisted in the Army on 10 December 1915 at Scarborough. The next day he was placed on the Army Reserve and was eventually mobilized on 24 June 1916 when he joined No.4 Depot Battalion, Royal Garrison Artillery.

He was discharged from the Army on 31 October 1918, suffering with gastritis, an inflammation of the stomach. This resulted in him finding it uncomfortable to eat and he could only drink milk. His condition had been aggravated by his military service. By the time of his discharge, his family were still living in the town, but had moved to 65 Castle Road.

Gunner 90587 John **Newlove** was 44 years of age, a married man who lived with his wife Mary and their four children, at 33 Prospect Road, Scarborough. John and Mary had married on 12 May 1894 at Driffield. He enlisted in Army Service Corps on 11 November 1914 at Scarborough as a private (4421). He was transferred to the Royal Field Artillery on 21 December 1914.

John had joined from the Army Reserve and was by now an older man. He went before an Army Medical Board on 16 March 1918, where he stated that he could no longer carry out a hard day's work as he could when he first enlisted, mainly because of his age. He stated that overall he felt well, but struggled and felt tired when it came to any kind of prolonged work. John's condition was accepted by the medical board, and he was discharged from the Army with effect from 12 April 1918.

Rifleman (302523) Arthur Herbert **Nicholson** was 33 years of age and lived at 4 Mayvilles Avenue, Scarborough, when he was discharged from the Army on 19 September 1918 due to 'Trench Foot'. He had enlisted as with the 5th (City of London) Battalion, The London Regiment, London Rifle Brigade, on 11 November 1915, but had not been mobilized until 28 February 1916. He subsequently served with the British Expeditionary Force in France between 10 July 1916 and 26 April 1917, initially being attached to No.2 Entrenching Battalion.

He was treated at No.20 Casualty Clearing Station where he spent three days, 14 and 16 April 1917, and then on 18 April he was admitted to No.20 General Hospital, before being sent back home to England, in relation to his continuing foot problems. The phrase 'Trench Foot' is synonymous with the First World War and was caused by prolonged exposure to wet and cold conditions. The symptoms included swelling, discolouration and an unpleasant odour. Once diagnosed it had to be treated quickly or else gangrene could set in, which led to amputation in extreme cases.

Private (3578) Frank **Ogden** was a married man who lived with his wife Louise at 32 Westbourne Park, Scarborough. He enlisted as in the 5th Battalion, Yorkshire Regiment, which was a Territorial unit, on 17 September 1915 at Scarborough. He had previously served with the 1st Volunteer Battalion, King's Own Yorkshire Light Infantry. He was discharged from the Army on 2 March 1916, after 168 days on medical grounds as he was suffering from asthma and chronic bronchitis.

Private (23570) Cecil **Owen** was 35 years of age and lived at 79 St John's Road, Scarborough. He enlisted on 14 September 1915 at Scarborough in the 13th (Service) Battalion, Yorkshire Regiment. He served in France with the British Expeditionary Force between 5 June 1916 and 5 January 1917, and was subsequently discharged on 29 June 1917, having reached the rank of lance sergeant on medical grounds as he was suffering with pulmonary tuberculosis.

Trooper (30391) Ernest **Parratt** was 22 years of age and lived at 40 Gladstone Street, Scarborough. He was an ex soldier recalled for service with the Grenadier Guards on 6 December 1916 at Scarborough. He served in France between 22 April and 16 October 1917, which would turn out to be an interesting experience for him in more ways than one. On 10 September 1917 he was charged with being in contravention of battalion order No.5 d of 7 September 1917, 'stealing fruit the property of a French civilian resident.' He was found guilty, the sentence for his crime was three days of No.2 Field Punishment. This consisted of being shackled in irons for a period of up to two hours a day.

As if that wasn't bad enough, he was then wounded in action on 12 October when he suffered a gunshot wound to the face. Initially he was treated at No.12 Casualty Clearing Station before being transferred to No.83 General Hospital in Boulogne and sent back home on board the HMHS *Jan Breydel,* a Belgian steam ship. This was the same ship that had been used to take the Belgian Government and Royal Family to Britain. It could accommodate six officers, as well as thirty-six cots and 116 berths for men of the other ranks. On his return to England on 16 October 1917, he was admitted to the Military Hospital, Hampstead, to have his wounds treated. He spent sixteen days there before being discharged to the Convalescent Hospital in Eastbourne, where he remained for a further thirty days before he was discharged on 1 December 1917. Whilst back in England for treatment he was placed on the Reserve list, 'to retain Household Cavalry rate of pay'.

His wounds cannot have been as bad as they sounded as Ernest returned to France for a second time on 1 April 1918, but was back home in England after less than two months on 25 May 1918, after receiving an undisclosed wound. On 4 June 1918, he was admitted to the 1st Northern General Hospital at Newcastle-upon-Tyne, which was a requisitioned building with the capacity to treat 104 officers and 1,420 men from the other ranks at any one time. He remained a patient there for forty-four days, finally being discharged on 18 July 1918.

If I have interpreted his Army Pension correctly, he then appears to have been kept on the Reserve in Class Z, until he was discharged on demobilization on 8 March 1920. That is certainly what you call a case of looking after your own.

1st Northern General Hospital.

Private (28593) William **Pashby** was 32 years of age and a married man who lived with his wife Sarah and their daughter May, at 4 Barry's Passage, St Mary's Street, Scarborough when he enlisted in the Army on 23 January 1915. He had previously served with the 4th Battalion, Yorkshire Regiment, in which he enlisted on 23 May 1900, when he was 19 years of age. During his service with the Yorkshire Regiment Private (4818) Pashby, received a gun shot wound on 27 October 1902, which resulted in him being discharged from the Army.

On 13 October 1915, with the war still less than a year old, and having served for just 264 days, William was discharged from the Army as his services were no longer required. At the time he was serving at the No.3 (Northern) Hussars Cavalry Depot at Scarborough. William Pashby passed away on 13 August 1954 at 12 West Place, Scarborough aged 74.

Private (25134) James **Pearson** was a married man who lived at 39 Candler Street, Scarborough with his wife Kate and their son Henry. When he enlisted on 11 December 1915, he was 40 years of age, but he was not mobilized until 16 June 1916. He joined the 11th Garrison Battalion, Northumberland Fusiliers, although initially he had been allocated to the Yorkshire Regiment as Private 30554.

He served overseas in Malta between 18 November 1916 to 6 May 1917, after which he returned to England and he was discharged on 3 July 1917. The writing on his Army Pension Record isn't totally legible, but it appears that he was suffering from some kind of intermittent paralysis of his legs, which had also affected his bladder and rectum. This started on 22 February 1917 for no apparent reason when he was in barracks on Malta. He was also diagnosed as suffering from myelitis (inflammation of the spinal cord). The medical board that heard his case declared his condition was permanent, was a total incapacitation and intriguingly enough, had been aggravated by 'misconduct', but did not elaborate as to what that actually meant. He subsequently required an operation and after-care treatment.

Private (19390) Frederick Francis **Pearson** was 19 years of age and lived at 41 Auboro Street Long, Westgate, Scarborough. Prior to the war he earned his living as a labourer. He enlisted in the 15th (Service) Battalion, Cheshire Regiment at Scarborough on 30 November 1914. He was discharged from the Army on 15 February 1915 after having served for just seventy-eight days, for being unlikely to become an efficient soldier, although there was no explanation as to why this was the case. Frederick Francis Pearson passed away on 1 November 1918 in hospital in Plymouth of broncho-pneumonia. He was 23 years of age.

Private (584369) George **Percy** lived in Snainton, Scarborough. He enlisted in the Army on 3 December 1915 at Scarborough and served in the Labour Corps in both 428 and 363 companies. His Army Pension Record doesn't include much detail, but he survived the war and was discharged from the Army Reserve on 28 July 1919, having served for three years eighty days. He then re-enlisted the next day in the Suffolk Regiment as Private (747), and was finally discharged on 22 November 1920. He had previously served as Private (70736) in the 1st Battalion, Suffolk Regiment and as Private (T/364798) in the Army Service Corps.

Ultimately his problems appear to have stemmed from being on a training course at Thetford in Norfolk when he was sleeping in damp blankets, which resulted in contracting rheumatism, and it also appears to have affected his nerves. He was treated at Cannock Chase Hospital for the rheumatism.

Corporal (36009) Frederick George **Pitt** was 44 years of age and lived at 21 Sandringham Street, Scarborough. He enlisted on 29 September 1914 in the Royal Field Artillery. He was discharged whilst serving with No.1 Battery Royal Field Artillery on 30 October 1914 at Newcastle-upon-Tyne for not being likely to become an efficient soldier, after having served for only thirty-one days. It would appear that this was because he was suffering with a lack of strength and power in his upper body due to an old fracture in his left humerus bone. At his initial medical examination when he enlisted, the old compound fracture of the bone in his upper left arm was noted, but it was deemed not to be a sufficient problem to prevent him from enlisting.

Driver (349867) Harry **Plaxton** was 20 years of age and lived at 24 Caledonian Street, Scarborough with his parents. He enlisted in the Army on 2 March 1916, but wasn't called up for service in the Royal Engineers, until 3 May 1918 at York. Three months into his initial training, on 27 August 1918, he was discharged for no longer being physically fit for wartime military service, but his Army Pension Record does not include the reasons why.

Private (2017) Arthur **Race** lived at 34 Moorland Road, Scarborough. He enlisted on 3 September 1914 in the 5th Battalion, Yorkshire Regiment, which was a Territorial unit. He was declared to be medically unfit for further military wartime service, as per King's Regulations, Paragraph 392 (xvi), on 26 February 1916.

On 16 February 1915 he was playing football in Darlington when he fell down and struck his right knee on the ground. So badly had he damaged his knee that he was taken to Darlington Hospital, where he remained for eight to nine weeks having it treated. After being discharged he was then unable to walk without the aid of a stick. His knee never fully improved or recovered and he was unable to march or carry out basic drill. The pain was emanating from within the knee joint and varied in degree depending on the weather. The colder and wetter it was, so the level of pain and discomfort increased. Officially, Arthur was medically discharged because of a sprained left knee joint.

Private (2051) Richard **Race** was Arthur's brother who also lived at 34 Moorland Road, Scarborough, although at the time of the 1911 Census the family lived at 9 Howard Street, Scarborough. Arthur, who was the oldest of the five children born to Andrew and Mary Race, was a house painter by trade, whilst Richard was a tailor. Elsie, Mabel and Wilfred, made up the family.

Richard enlisted in the 5th Battalion, Yorkshire Regiment, two days after his brother Arthur, on 5 September 1914 at Scarborough, and even though the Territorial units did not have to serve overseas, he volunteered to do so, until the end of the war. At the time of his enlistment it was noted by the doctor who examined him that he suffered with varicose veins but they were not considered a serious enough issue to prevent him enlisting.

He served in France from 18 April 1915. On 19 May he was admitted to a Dressing Station at Ypres due to a loose cartilage in his right knee. The following day he was transferred to the 1st Canadian Stationary Hospital at Wimereux, and on 21 May 1915 Richard Race and his by now swelling right knee, were sent back to England on board HM Hospital Ship *St Patrick*.

His Army Pension Record became slightly confusing as it shows that Richard only served in France between 18 April and 21 May 1915, yet there is also reference to his having injured his right shoulder and right knee during the Battle of Hooge on 20 July 1915, by a shrapnel shell burst, as well as being buried by sand bags. With his injuries having been accepted as being attributable to his wartime service, he was subsequently discharged from the Army on 16 August 1916 at York.

Private (5866) Walter Barfield **Reeder** was 24 years of age and lived at The Holt Villa, Scotby, Scarborough with his parents William and Elizabeth Reeder, and younger siblings, Ethel and Harold, whilst working as a grocer's assistant. On 26 October 1916 he enlisted in the 2nd/5th Battalion, Highland Light Infantry, at Richmond in Yorkshire.

Just three months later on 21 January 1917 he was discharged from the Army on medical grounds. He was diagnosed with having aortic stenosis, which in laymen's terms means he had an abnormal narrowing of the aorta in the heart. This can occur as a result of having such illnesses as rheumatic fever. The history of his heart problems appear to stem from a couple of years earlier when he overstrained his heart whilst cycling, which resulted in him being laid up for a while.

Private (124730) Fred **Reynolds** was 43 years of age and lived at 111 Prospect Road, Scarborough. He enlisted in the Labour Corps on 26 June 1916. He was discharged on 15 December 1917 for no longer being physically fit enough for wartime military service, at Nottingham. Unfortunately, his Army Pension Record does not include any detailed information about the ailment which caused him to be discharged. All his military service was in the UK.

Gunner (756017) George **Reynolds** was 40 years of age and a married man who lived at 18a Castlegate, Scarborough with his wife Eliza and their three children, Charles, Eliza and Frederick. Before the war he had earned his living as a fisherman. With the outbreak of war, he enlisted in the North Riding Battery, 2nd Northumbrian Brigade, 2nd Line, Royal Field Artillery on 22 May 1915 at Scarborough.

His discipline record wasn't exactly exemplary. On 13 October 1915 at Newcastle-upon-Tyne, he was charged with two counts of being absent without leave, one of which lasted for three days, and for being drunk and disorderly. For these breaches of military discipline, he was sentenced to seven days' detention. On 25 October 1915, 25 November 1915, 10 April 1916, and 17 July 1917, he was charged with four further counts of being absent without leave. The first two of these charges saw him fined a total of two days' pay, and the latter two saw him being confined to barracks for five days for each offence. On 4 August 1917 he was charged with refusing to obey an order and for using abusive language to a non-commissioned officer, for which he received Field Punishment No.2.

He was discharged from the Army as no longer physically fit for wartime military service, on 6 September 1918 after having served for three years and 109 days, although his Army Pension Record did not include any detailed information as to why.

Gunner (19666) William **Richardson** was 22 years of age and lived at 98 Tennyson Avenue, Scarborough. He enlisted in the 161st Yorkshire Brigade, Royal Field Artillery on 25 May 1915. On 1 July 1915 he was transferred to the 175th Yorkshire Brigade, but by 20 September 1915 his military career was over, when he was discharged for not likely to become an efficient soldier, due to misconduct issues, although his Army Pension Record did not include the specifics of these matters.

Private (209538) Tom **Robinson** earned his living as a blacksmith, he was 42 years of age and lived at 180 Auborough Street, Scarborough. Having previously served in the Army with the Royal Engineers as a younger man, he once again enlisted, this time at Scarborough on 12 September 1916 when he joined the Army Service Corps.

His Army Pension Record shows that he had a son, William Brown who was born in 1912, but that his next of kin was shown as being his sister, Mrs Mary Ann Armitage.

He appeared before an Army Medical Board on 24 August 1917, as a result of which he was placed on the Army Reserve, Class 3. On 8 October 1917, he was discharged from the Army as no longer physically fit for wartime military service. The fact that he was subsequently excluded from the liability to have to undergo a yearly medical review of his case, under the Military Service (Review of Exceptions) Act 1917, suggests that his was a permanent disability.

Driver (209881) George Lance **Roper** was 19 years of age and a motor mechanic, living at 99 North Marine Road, Scarborough. He enlisted on 26 September 1916 in the Army Service Corps, specifically in the Mechanical Transport section. On 10 January 1917 he was transferred to the 105th Training Reserve Battalion, in Edinburgh, and ten weeks later on 21 March 1917, he was discharged for being no longer physically fit for wartime military service.

On 16 February 1917 George Roper was transferred from the 2nd Scottish Reserve Hospital, in Edinburgh to the Murthly War Hospital in Perthshire, Scotland. During the First World

War it was used as a Military Psychiatric Hospital and could cater for 350 men at any one time.

The same day George was discharged from the Army, his father, Robert Roper, wrote a memorandum to the Infantry Records Office, which was situated in Hounslow. It said:

> *Sir,*
>
> *On behalf of my 'son' (George Roper) above description, who is at present detained at the East Riding Lunatic Asylum, Beverley, Yorkshire. I beg to acknowledge receipt of Army Forms, W.3464 and B.2067. Was B.2079 sent, as I cannot find the same.*
>
> *I am yours sincerely*
>
> *Robert Roper*
>
> *73 North Marine Road,*
>
> *Scarborough.*

By the fact that George was incarcerated in a lunatic asylum, I can only assume that he was suffering from an extreme case of shell shock. However, his state of mind must have improved somewhat, as he returned to Scarborough after the war and died there in September 1961 when he was 64 years of age.

Driver (027055) William **Rouhan** was 35 years of age and lived at Nixon's Yard, William Street, Scarborough. He enlisted on 7 December 1914 at Scarborough in the Army Service Corps, but just four days later he was discharged for being unlikely to make an efficient soldier

Private (064229) Edward **Ruddock** was 19 years of age and employed as a groom whilst living at The Bungalow, Newby, near Scarborough. He enlisted in the Army Service Corps on 14 April 1915 at Lathom Park. On 14 March 1917 he was transferred to the Reserve Brigade of the Royal Field Artillery becoming Driver (215624), before being posted to the 426th Battery the following month on 10 April.

Due to being deemed unfit for further wartime military service, Edward, was discharged from the Army on 16 April 1918. He had served for a total of three years and three days, but his Army Pension Record, did not elaborate as to the specific details of why he had been discharged. Edward died at Scarborough in September 1919 at just 21 years of age.

Private (30589) Walter **Sands** was 32 years old and lived at 67 Dean Road, Scarborough. Before the war he had been employed as a chief cashier in a local bank. With the outbreak of the war he enlisted at Scarborough on 10 December 1915, but was immediately placed on the Army Reserve, and not mobilized until 16 June 1916, when he joined the Yorkshire Regiment. On 13 October 1916 he was posted to the No.37 Supply Base Depot, the same day that he began serving with the British Expeditionary Force in France, where he remained until 9 March 1917.

On his return to England he was attached to the No.6 Officers' Cadet Battalion at Oxford and on 1 April 1917, he was posted to the 3rd Battalion, Yorkshire Regiment. It would appear that he didn't pass his officers training course, because when he was discharged from the Army on medical grounds on 16 August 1917 at York, he is recorded as being a private.

He suffered from ulcerations of the stomach, a condition which was aggravated by being gassed whilst on active service, but despite this it was still marked up that he was to be sent a statutory reminder for a medical re-examination on 16 August 1918 under the conditions of the Military Services (Review of Exemptions) Act 1917.

The aptly named Private (225547) Thomas Henry **Scarborough** was 37 years of age and lived at 43 Cross Street, Scarborough. He was called up for service on 13 June 1916, as a private in the Northumberland Fusiliers, but was transferred to the 5th (Cyclist) Battalion, East Yorkshire Regiment on 9 August 1916.

He was discharged from the Army on 1 February 1918, after having served for one year and 234 days, as no longer being physically fit enough to undertake wartime military service.

His Army Pension Record stating that the disability for which he was invalided and therefore, discharged, was because he couldn't read or write, was nervous and mentally deficient, and that during the time that he had been in the Army, all he had been able to do was light fatigues.

Amazingly, despite the comments on his Army Pension Record concerning his health, he was liable to be sent for a statutory re-examination a year after he was discharged, under the terms of the Military Service (Review of Exemptions) Act 1917.

Private (027880) Harry **Sedman** was 38 years old and lived at 8 Tollergate, Longnostgate, Scarborough with his wife Christiana and their five children, when he enlisted on 13 November 1914 at Scarborough in the Army Service Corps. As a younger man he had served with the Prince of Wales's Own (Yorkshire Regiment). He was discharged from the Army on 4 March 1915 as not being likely to become an efficient soldier, because of his extremely poor eyesight, which wasn't improved by wearing glasses.

Guardsman (19225) James Thompson **Sellers** was 25 years of age and lived at 95 Tennyson Avenue, Scarborough, when he enlisted at Scarborough on 7 December 1915. He was immediately placed on the Army Reserve, before being mobilized on 26 September 1916, in the Coldstream Guards. Before enlisting he had worked locally as a fish packer. He served for the rest of the war and was discharged when he was demobbed, on 25 May 1919, and placed in Class 'Z' of the Army Reserve.

Acting Sergeant (TF/5/36017) William **Shepherd** lived at 1 Parnell's Yard, Cross Street, Scarborough with his wife and five children. He enlisted at Scarborough on 29 December 1914, originally as Private (9470) in the Yorkshire Regiment, but was promoted in the 261st Infantry Battalion by the time he was discharged at York on 27 September 1917. He was 44 years of age when he was deemed to be no longer physically fit for wartime military service, because of curvature of the spine, having been in the Army for two years and 273 days.

It would appear that he had previously been discharged from the Army on 19 May 1897 when he was 35 years of age. On this occasion it was due to a hernia which he had suffered whilst serving in Malta and was invalided home and admitted to the Herbert Military Hospital at Woolwich; after treatment he was discharged in April 1897. The writing on his Army Pension Record isn't totally legible but it appears that the hernia and spinal ailments were connected by an accident where he was run over by a cart whilst serving in Malta. It is definitely the same man as both were born in Gainsborough, Lincolnshire, although there is a discrepancy over his age, if he was 35 years of age on 19 May 1897, that would mean he would have been 52 years of age when he re-enlisted in 1914.

Driver (026901) William **Small** was 34 years of age and lived at 3 Lower William, St Nixon's Yard, Scarborough, when he enlisted in the Army Service Corps on 3 December 1914 at Scarborough. But just two months later on 10 February 1915 he was discharged from the Army, with his Army Pension Record showing that he was 'medically unfit for service' and 'unlikely to make an efficient soldier,' having served for just seventy days.

His record shows that 'he is quite unfit in the duties he has to do' and that he 'looks at least 10 years older than the age given.' He was also twice sent to hospital by his commanding officer because he was unable to do his work.

William Small's case is an example of the lengths men would go to, to enlist in the Army so that they could do their bit for King and country.

Driver (T/3/026789) John William **Smith** was 33 years of age and a married man who lived at 13 Howard Street, Scarborough, with his wife Sarah and their three daughters. He enlisted in the Army Service Corps at Scarborough on 30 November 1914. He was discharged from the Army on 12 March 1915 as not being likely to become an efficient soldier. According to a medical report written, he was believed to be suffering from a gastric ulcer which was causing him to have vomiting fits. It appears that his medical condition was a long-standing one which he knew required an operation to resolve, but for whatever reason wouldn't have the required medical procedure carried out.

Private (11584) Richard Henry **Smith** was a married man who lived at Throxenby, near Scarborough with his wife Hilda and their son Malcolm. He joined the Army Pay Corps from the Army Reserve, attesting on 8 December 1915 at Scarborough, then was returned to the Army Reserve before being mobilized on 31 May 1916. He was promoted to the rank of corporal on 22 February 1918, and was discharged from the Army on 21 March 1919 to take up the appointment of civilian acting pay master, having served in the Army for three years and 104 days.

Gunner (338194) George Henry **Smith** was 37 years old and a married man who lived at 13 Howard Street, Scarborough with his wife Amy and their four children. He worked as a butcher. When he was called up for military service on 12 September 1916, George, who was an Army Reservist, stated that he would like to serve in the Army Service Corps, but he ended up in the Royal Garrison Artillery in the 139th Siege Battery, having previously served with the 357th unit.

Whilst serving in France on 26 September 1917, George was hit by a shell, badly injuring his left femur and invalided back home to England. He was eventually discharged from the Army as a result of the wound to his left thigh, with effect from 26 November 1918, by which time his family had moved to 39 Stepney Avenue, Scarborough.

I found the following letter amongst his Army Pension Record. It is written by George's wife Amy to the Royal Garrison Artillery records department which was located in Dover.

> *Dear Sir,*
>
> *I beg to inform you that I have removed from 7 Mill Yard, Seamer Road, to the above address (39 Stepney Avenue, Sealley Road, Scarborough). I should be glad to know if I could be granted a free pass to visit my husband as I hear he has had his leg amputated and is now at Netley Hospital, Southampton.*
>
> *Trusting you will give this your immediate attention.*

Netley Hospital.

The letter is shown as having been received by the Records Office on 12 October 1917, some thirteen months before George was discharged from the Army.

After leaving the Netley Hospital in January 1918, he was admitted to the Queen Mary Convalescent Auxiliary Hospital at Roehampton House, London, to be fitted with an artificial limb.

Gunner (111661) Enoch **Smithson** was 19 years of age and lived at 29 Royal Avenue, Scarborough. He had enlisted in the Royal Field Artillery at Scarborough on 26 October 1915. He was discharged from the Army on 13 February 1918 whilst serving with the 5th Reserve Brigade as no longer physically fit enough for wartime military service, having served for two years and 111 days. His Army Pension Record did not include the specific reasons as to why he was discharged.

Private (19970) Percy **Standidge** was 46 years old, a labourer and a married man who lived at 49 Hoxton Road, Scarborough with his wife Florence and their four children. He had previous military experience dating back to 1892 with the Yorkshire Volunteer Reserve. He enlisted in the Army Service Corps at Whitehall in London on 14 October 1915. He had an operation for haemorrhoids in 1906, but despite this they were still a problem. He also had varicose veins, defective teeth and, whilst serving in France between 7 November 1915 and 29 February 1916, he was wounded. He was medically discharged from the Army on 22 April 1916 at Aldershot having served for a total of 192 days.

Somewhat surprisingly, when he was 50 years of age, he re-enlisted in the 3rd Labour Company, Labour Corps as Private (700636) on 3 June 1919 in Leeds, but on 30 August 1919, he was once again discharged as no longer physically fit. During this time he served in France for just one day, 12 August 1919.

The medical officer in his case stated that although Standidge 'is' 50, he looks 60. Maybe another case of a man lying about his age so as to be able to join the Army to do his bit for the war effort, or maybe he just looked older than he was.

Battery Sergeant Major (756018) William **Stephenson** was 41 years of age and lived at 1 Avenue Cottage, Lordsborough, Scarborough when he was discharged from the Army on 12 June 1918 as no longer being fit enough for wartime military service. He was serving with the 396th Battery Royal Field Artillery at the time. He had originally enlisted on 11 June 1908. The reason for his discharge was down to the state of varicose veins in his left leg, which although he had them at the time of his original enlistment, had become progressively worse over the course of time.

Gunner (176449) George William **Stockdale** was 27 years old and lived at 64 Westborough, Scarborough. Prior to enlisting he had worked as an insurance agent. He enlisted on 1 March 1916, although he wasn't mobilized until 28 August 1917, when he joined No.4 Depot, Royal Garrison Artillery.

Although his medical board had taken place at the Military Hospital at Ripon on 22 October 1917, he wasn't finally discharged from the Army until 28 December 1917 at Dover, due to suffering with neurasthenia, a word which is no longer in technical use, but is nervous debility and exhaustion, or nervous exhaustion. This was a condition George first had in about 1910, after a bout of jaundice, which in turn was followed by a nervous breakdown. He had served for a total of one year and 303 days.

Guardsman (22002) William **Stockdale** was 22 years of age and a married man who lived at 3 Mill Yard, Seamer Road, Scarborough with his wife Mary and their daughter Frances. He enlisted on 27 May 1916 at Scarborough and was placed on the Army Reserve, but wasn't mobilized until 13 March 1917, when he joined the Coldstream Guards. He was admitted to The Holborn Military Hospital, at Western Road, Mitcham, Surrey on 29 January 1918 suffering with impetigo. So bad was his condition that he spent nearly five months in hospital receiving treatment. He was finally discharged on 17 June, but just nine days later he was re-admitted to the same hospital suffering with the same complaint, which resulted in him being hospitalised for a further twenty-five days. He survived the war and was finally discharged on demobilization on 8 November 1919.

Private (5/50127) John William **Stork** was 24 years old and lived at The Priory, Valley Road, Scarborough. After enlistment he joined the 82nd Training Reserve Battalion. He was discharged from the Army on 26 October 1917 because of being diagnosed with suffering from periostitis, inflamation of the membrane enveloping a bone, after having served for 135 days.

It was determined by an Army Medical Board that his condition was neither attributable nor aggravated by his military service during the First World War. He appealed this decision, his appeal being put before a Pensions Appeal Tribunal, which sat on 7 June 1920 in Leeds, who after having given the appeal due consideration, which included having visited John Stork at Scarborough Military Hospital on 5 June 1920, the board disallowed it, even though he claimed the problem had only begun after the time of his enlistment, although its origins dated back to 1907.

Private (083201) John Richard **Storry** was 33 years of age and a married man who lived at 14 Potters Yard, Potter Lane,

Scarborough with his wife Isabella and their three children, when he enlisted in the Army on 5 April 1915. He joined No.1 Company, Army Service Corps and served with the Mediterranean Expeditionary Force between 29 May 1915 and 12 July 1916, during which time he was admitted to hospital in both Salonica and Malta, suffering with bronchitis, from which he had suffered since 1905. He was medically discharged from the Army on 1 September 1916.

Private (16122) Valentine **Thornton**, aged 29, lived at Patts Brompton Sawton, Scarborough when he enlisted in the East Yorkshire Regiment on 21 December 1914 at Bridlington. He was discharged on 9 April 1915 as not likely to become an efficient soldier, mainly because of his poor eyesight. In particular he had problems with the optic nerve in his right eye for which nothing could be done.

Private (22766) Leonard **Thornton** was 25 years of age and lived at 23 St John's Walk, Scarborough, when he enlisted in the 4th (Reserve) Battalion, Yorkshire Regiment on 27 February 1917. He had previously served as Private (19179) in the 11th Battalion, Yorkshire Regiment, enlisting on 10 December 1915, but he was discharged on that occasion on 8 May 1916, yet less than a year later he was enlisting again.

He was discharged from the Army just three months later on 29 May 1917, for being no longer physically fit for wartime military service, because he was 'mentally deficient'. This sounds more like a case of where the individual was unlikely to make an efficient soldier, than for medical reasons.

Private (32576) Leonard **Thornton** was 23 years old and lived at 16 St Thomas Walk, Scarborough, when he enlisted in the Yorkshire Regiment on 19 July 1916. Just eight days later he was discharged from the Army for being not likely to become an efficient soldier, but there are no specific reasons recorded as to why he was discharged.

Guardsman (29605) Henry **Tidd** was just 18 years of age and lived at Burniston, Scarborough. Before enlisting in the Army he had worked both as a gardener and a postman. On 16 June 1916 at Scarborough he attested but was then immediately placed on the Army Reserve, before being mobilized on 7 March 1917 when he joined the Grenadier Guards. Whilst serving with the British Expeditionary Force on the Western Front in France on 26 January 1918 he was gassed. He was initially treated by the Canadian 19th Casualty Clearing Station. From there he was moved to the 3rd Australian General Hospital in Abbeville.

He had served in France between 30 November 1917 and 11 March 1918. He remained in the Army and was discharged on demobilization on 31 March 1920. Having arrived back in England on 11 March 1918 he was admitted to the 3rd Western General Hospital at Newport for the treatment of the gas inhalation, where he remained until 26 April 1918 when he was transferred to the St John Auxiliary Military Hospital in Porthcawl, where he stayed until 10 August 1918, while he recovered his health.

Private (327912) Frank **Tindall**, aged 22, lived at 4 Clarence Place, Scarborough, when he joined up from the Army Reserve to the Army Service Corps on 4 May 1917 at Scarborough, although he was deemed to have enlisted on 1 October 1916. He was discharged from the Army on 2 November 1917 as he was suffering from tuberculosis. His Army Pension Record included the facts that the tuberculosis was not the result of, nor aggravated by ordinary military service, and had been a disability that Private Tindall had prior to his enlistment.

Private (3641) (241335) Charles Edward **Turner** was 30 years of age and a married man who lived at 2 Henrietta Court, St Thomas Street, Scarborough with his wife Elizabeth. He enlisted in the 3rd/5th Battalion, Yorkshire Regiment on 1 November 1915 at Scarborough. He served in France between 30 March 1916 and 20 February 1917 and was discharged to the Army Reserve, Class T on 10 July 1917. The reason for this was due to his being deaf in his left ear, an ailment which he already had before he enlisted, but which had been compounded by wartime military service.

Private (24741) Albert Edward **Upton** was 32 years old and lived at 31a Dumple Street, Scarborough. He enlisted at York on 28 October 1915 and joined the 13th Battalion, Yorkshire

Regiment. He was discharged on 20 March 1916, but I could not find it recorded on his Army Pension Record, what for, although there were elements of his record that were illegible.

Private (20260) Charles **Walker** was 36 years of age and a married man who lived at 18 Brooke Street, Scarborough with his wife, when he enlisted in the 11th Battalion, Yorkshire Regiment, on 30 January 1915. He was discharged from the Army on 5 June 1916 for being no longer physically fit for wartime military service, due to being diagnosed with ametropia, which is faulty refraction of light rays by the eye. More commonly known today as astigmatism or myopia.

Battery Quartermaster Sergeant (756029) Arthur **Ward**, aged 38, was a married man who lived at 25 Tindall Street, Scarborough, when he enlisted in the Royal Field Artillery on 5 June 1908 in Scarborough. At the outbreak of the First World War he was serving with the 2nd North Riding Brigade, although he would go on to serve with five other units during his years of service.

On 31 December 1917 his case was heard by an Invaliding Board which decided that he was permanently unfit, so he was accordingly discharged from the Army on 21 January 1918 after having served for nine years 231 days.

In January 1916 Arthur Ward stated that he was depressed and suffering with gout and that if he attempted to exert himself, that he very quickly became short of breath and was suffering with a systolic murmur of the heart.

Private (19387) Jonathon William **Waterson** was 19 years old and lived at 3 Rosebery Avenue, Seamer Road, Scarborough when he enlisted on 30 November 1914 at Scarborough in 15th Service Battalion, Cheshire Regiment (1st Birkenhead). He was discharged on 26 February 1915 as not being likely to become an efficient soldier, due to being unfit, having served for just eighty-nine days.

Private (173526) Joseph **Webster** was 23 years of age and a married man who lived at 26 James Street, Scarborough, and earned his living as a baker before the war. He enlisted in the Army Service Corps on 5 April 1916 at Scarborough.

He was admitted to the Central War Hospital at Lichfield suffering with gonorrhoea on 9 October 1917 and remained there until 7 December 1917. On 21 January 1918 he was admitted to The Military Hospital at Cannock Chase, with a swollen testicle. He remained there for a month before being discharged from the hospital on 25 February 1918. By 1 April he had sufficiently recovered to re-join his unit and be sent out to serve in France. He was discharged on demobilization on 6 October 1919.

Private (12167) James Francis **Wellburn** was 26 years of age, a married man who lived at 21 Clark Street, Scarborough with his wife Florence and their daughter Ethel. He enlisted in C Battery, 161st Brigade, the Royal Field Artillery on 3 April 1915 at Scarborough. He had previously served with the 3rd North Riding Battery, Royal Field Artillery, which was a Territorial unit and at the time of his enlistment he was a serving Police Constable.

He was discharged on 8 September 1915, having served for just 127 days. Unfortunately, I could not find the specific details or reason as to why James Wellburn was discharged.

There exists another record of a man with the name James Francis Willburn who lived at 11 Spring Bank, Scarborough. He was recalled to the Colours from the Army Reserve, and had previously served in the Royal Field Artillery. When he re-enlisted on 23 November 1916 at Ripon, his age was shown as 28 years and 3 months. His trade however, was shown as a labourer and not that of a Police Constable, but his wife's name was Florence and they had a daughter, with the dates of the wedding and the birth of the child, both being the same as in the previous entry for James Francis Wellburn. Gunner 284438 Willburn of the 241st Siege Battery, Royal Garrison Artillery is shown as having being killed in action on 20 March 1918 whilst serving in France.

Private (M/322311) Herbert Arthur **Whitaker** was 37 years of age, a married man who lived at Park Dene, Scarborough with his wife Evelyn, when he enlisted in the Mechanical Transport Section of the Army Service Corps, on 7 June 1916 at Scarborough and was placed on the Army Reserve. It was a further eleven months before he was eventually mobilized on 11 May 1917.

He was medically discharged from the Army on 3 April 1918 as he was diagnosed with chronic nephritis, an inflammation of the kidneys. In about 1908 he had an attack of rheumatic fever. After that he continually suffered with pains in his back and legs and swelling in his feet and legs. He was unable to stand for long periods of time and suffered with depression, dyspepsia and haemorrhoids. Yet another case of wonderment at how this man managed to pass his initial Army medical and then deteriorate so quickly in just eleven months, or why he even wanted to enlist in the first place.

Private (6/17957)Thomas **Wilson** was 35 years old and a married man who lived at 62 Raleigh Street, Scarborough with his wife Edith and their son Tom, when he attested on 12 December 1915 at Scarborough. He was then placed on the Army Reserve before being mobilized on 13 November 1916 and joining the Army Service Corps.

He was discharged on 25 May 1917 at Lichfield as no longer fit enough for further military service. His record states that he had a pallid appearance and the slightest exertion left him breathless, he had a rapid pulse rate of 160 beats per minute and heart related issues. He slept badly and had a poor appetite and had previously suffered with rheumatic fever on several occasions; in about 1903 he had to give up any type of job which involved lifting and take office work, none of which was ever going to permit him to become an efficient and effective soldier. He was diagnosed as suffering with dilation of the myocardium, which is the muscular substance of the heart.

Private (35574) Thomas **Woodall**, aged 36, lived at Seamer, Scarborough with his wife Annie and their three children. He joined up from the Army Reserve on 23 July 1916 at York in the 5th Reserve Cavalry Battalion, West Yorkshire Regiment. Five months later he was transferred to the 25th Battalion, Durham Light Infantry on 16 December 1916. He was on the move again just two months later when he was posted to the Durham Light

Infantry's Labour Company on 19 February 1917, and just nine days after that he was sent to France. But that wasn't the end of his travels.

On 14 May 1917, whilst still in France, he was transferred to the 36th Labour Company of the Labour Corps as Private (21441), before returning home to England on 25 August 1917. On 16 December 1917 he was transferred yet again, this time to what his Army Pension Record shows as the NCLC, the Non-Combatant Labour Corps.

On 22 December 1917 he appeared before No.3 Standing Invaliding Board in Ripon where he was found to be permanently unfit. He was then officially discharged from the Army on 8 February 1918, having served for one year and 225 days. The official diagnosis of his condition was that he was suffering with myalgia which in layman's terms is muscular rheumatism.

As can be see from all the men mentioned, there were numerous reasons why they were discharged from the Army, but whilst writing about them it struck me the number of them who had enlisted knowing full well that they were far from being 100 per cent fit, but still they turned up at the recruiting office to enlist. There were men who had clearly been less than truthful about their age, many of them being in the higher age bracket. There were others who clearly should have never passed their initial medical when they went along to enlist, but somehow they did. Was this because the recruiting officer was paid for every man he enlisted and simply turned a blind eye to ensure that he received his payment.

The overriding thought I was left with was the bravery of each one of them. When called upon to do their bit for their country they did so without question. Most of them not only left their jobs behind, but their wives and children too to fight for the common good, and in doing so to safeguard not only their family's future, but those of the generations that would follow. From me personally, a massive thank you.

Index

Adamthwaite, Tom, 56–7
Appleby, Robert, 34, 38, 62
Armistice Dead, 173
Audacious, HMS, 9

Barrowcliff, Mr William, 65–6
Beckett, Gervase, 196
Bedford Street, 28
Belvoir Terrace, 21–2
Bennett, Christopher Candler, 104
Benson, Walter, 88
Bestwick, Mrs Annie, 110
Boston, HM Trawler, 33
Brockwell, Maj A.B., 40
Buckle, Emily Jane, 105

Castle Hill Barracks, 18
Chief Constable, 76
Commercial Street, 24
Crampton, James, 96–8, 101

Dean Road Cemetery, 74
Dell Family, 78–9
Derfflinger, SMS, 6, 31
Donkin, Tome, 62

East Yorkshire Regiment, 5

Fernandes, 2nd Lt Dudley Luis de Tavora, 5
Formidable, HMS, 35

Fowler, Alderman V., 59
Fowler, Lt Col Williams Hasting, 68–9

Garma, HM Trawler, 32
Graham, Christopher Colbourne, 13, 15, 30, 76, 107, 112–13
Graham, Lt Hugh Colbourne, 112
Grand Hotel, The, 19

Harland, Mr Richard, 127
Hartley, Mr John Davis, 126
Hawkswell, Emily Louisa, 105–106
Heritage, Robert, 61–2
Heugh Battery, 41
Highgate, Thomas James, 100
Hornby, Mrs Annie, 90–1
Hume, Robert, 108
Hutchinson, Lt George Russell, 115–16

Kennedy, Francis Ernest, 104
Kidd, Pte Tom, 130–2, 134
King, Herbert, 112
King's Royal Rifle Corps, 60
Kolberg, SMS, 9

Lister, Claud Lindsay, 82–3
Londesborough Road, 28

Lusitania, RMS, 36, 54, 84

Marchant, John, 83
McReynolds, John Bernard, 89
Mercantile Marine, 63
Mellor, 2nd Lt Arthur William, 5
Meritorious Service Medal, 69
Merryweather, Harold, 85–6
Merryweather, Mr G.H., 22–3, 86
Merryweather, William Alfred, 86
Moore, Lt Percy, 107
Morgan, H. Lee, 45

North Riding Battery, 57

Passing, HM Trawler, 31–2
Pickup, Thomas Temple, 110
Poperinghe New Military Cemetery, 96
Powell, Lt Gen Sir Robert Baden, 76, 82
Probation of Offenders Act, 78
Prospect Road, 29

Rowntree, Lt Laurence Edward, 114
Royal Hotel, The, 20
Royal, Mr G.E., 198
Royal Warwickshire Regiment, 63
Rumford, Alice, 105–106

Sails, Joseph Henry, 103
Salta, HMHS, 121
Salter, 2nd Lt John Henry Raymond, 116
Scarborough Sea Scouts School, 76
Scarborough War Memorial, 180
Scott, Elizabeth, 111
Some Who Returned, 201

Taylor, Edith Elizabeth, 107–108
Taylor, George, 109
Thompson, Lt A.F., 122
Thorpe, Pte George Thomas, 48

VAD Nurses, 136
Vincent's Pier, 15
Von Der Tann, SMS, 6, 31
Von Donop, Col Pelham George, 44

Westbourne Park, 29
White, F.A., 81
Wilkinson, J.R., 90
Witting, Stanley Newson, 124
Wright, George William, 64
Wykeham Street, 25–7
Wordsworth, Capt John Lionel, 6
Wounded Blues, 227

Yorkshire Regiment, 58, 63, 69–70, 74, 96